Thinking about Language T[e]
Selected articles 1982–2011

OXFORD
UNIVERSITY PRESS

Great Clarendon Street, Oxford, OX2 6DP, United Kingdom

Oxford University Press is a department of the University of Oxford.
It furthers the University's objective of excellence in research, scholarship,
and education by publishing worldwide. Oxford is a registered trade
mark of Oxford University Press in the UK and in certain other countries

© Oxford University Press 2012

The moral rights of the author have been asserted

First published in 2012

2015 2015 2014 2013 2012
10 9 8 7 6 5 4 3 2 1

No unauthorized photocopying

All rights reserved. No part of this publication may be reproduced, stored
in a retrieval system, or transmitted, in any form or by any means, without
the prior permission in writing of Oxford University Press, or as expressly
permitted by law, by licence or under terms agreed with the appropriate
reprographics rights organization. Enquiries concerning reproduction
outside the scope of the above should be sent to the ELT Rights Department,
Oxford University Press, at the address above

You must not circulate this work in any other form and you must impose
this same condition on any acquirer

Links to third party websites are provided by Oxford in good faith and for
information only. Oxford disclaims any responsibility for the materials
contained in any third party website referenced in this work

ISBN: 978 0 19 442481 3

Printed in Great Britain by Clays Ltd, St Ives plc

This book is printed on paper from certified and well-managed sources

Thinking about Language Teaching

Selected articles
1982–2011

MICHAEL SWAN

OXFORD
UNIVERSITY PRESS

OXFORD UNIVERSITY PRESS has great pleasure in publishing this collection of articles by Michael Swan, in recognition of the importance of his contribution to English language teaching in general and to OUP's ELT Division publications in applied linguistics, grammar, and English language studies in particular. His many articles in professional journals have, over the last three decades, sparked lively debate which has enriched and stimulated teacher development worldwide.

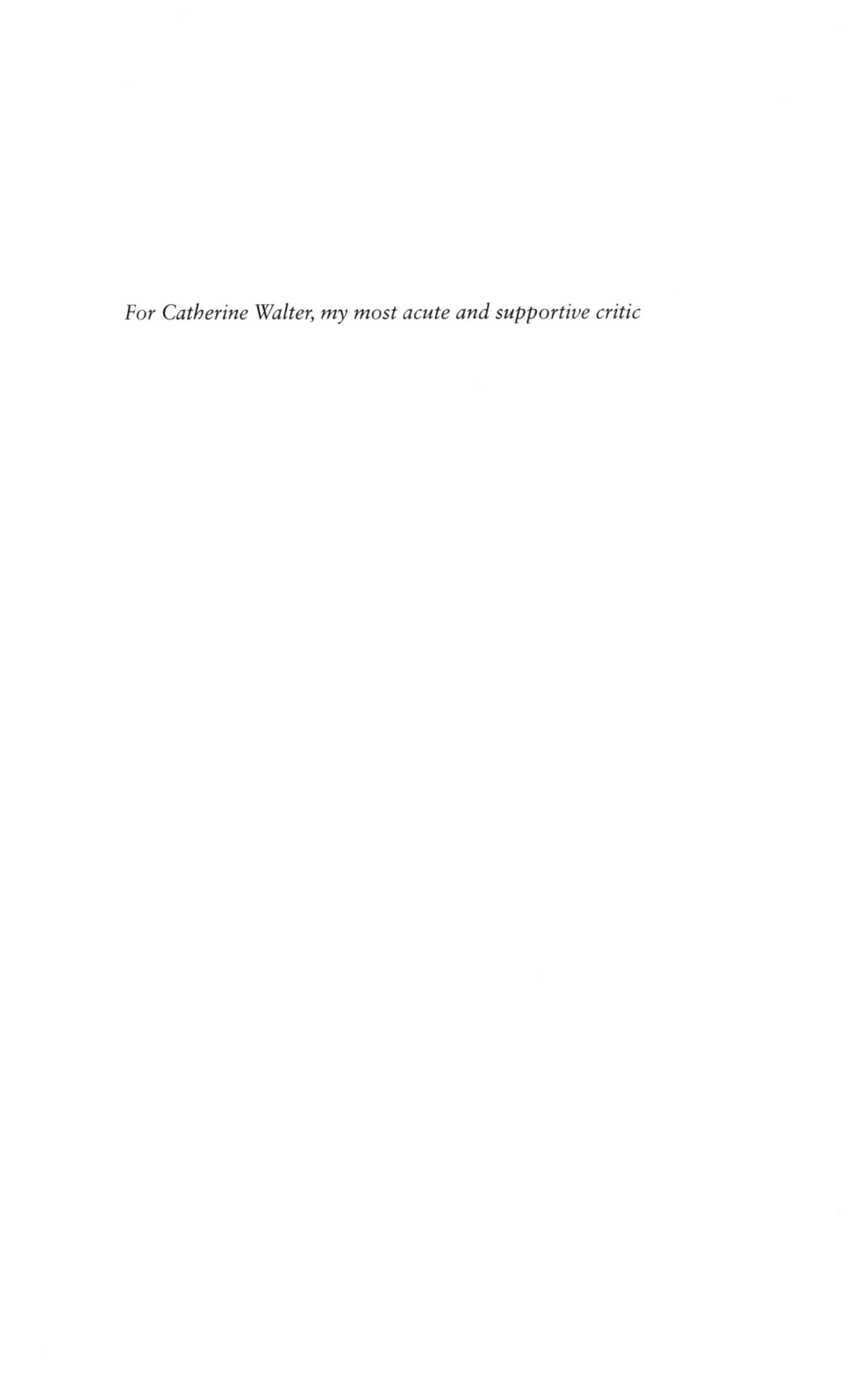

For Catherine Walter, my most acute and supportive critic

Acknowledgements

The authors and publisher are grateful to those who have given permission to reproduce the following extracts and adaptations of copyright material:

p. 1 'A critical look at the Communicative Approach (1)' by Michael Swan, from *ELT Journal*, Volume 39, Issue 1, 1985. Reproduced by permission of Oxford University Press.

p. 14 'A critical look at the Communicative Approach (2)' by Michael Swan, from *ELT Journal*, Volume 39, Issue 2, 1985. Reproduced by permission of Oxford University Press.

p. 28 'Against dogma' by Henry Widdowson, from *ELT Journal*, Volume 39, Issue 3, 1985. Reproduced by permission of Oxford University Press.

p. 32 'Correspondence' by Michael Swan, from *ELT Journal*, Volume 39, Issue 4, 1985. Reproduced by permission of Oxford University Press.

p. 36 Michael Swan, 'Where is the language going?' (1985), from *English Today*, Volume 3, 1985. pp. 6-10. © Cambridge University Press.

p. 41 'The textbook: bridge or wall?' by Michael Swan, from *Applied Linguistics and Language Teaching*, Volume 2, Issue 1, 1992.

p. 45 Published in *Grammar and the Language Teacher*, eds. Bygate, Tonkyn and Williams, © 1994 Prentice Hall/Pearson Educational Ltd.

p. 68 Michael Swan, 'The influence of the mother tongue on second language vocabulary acquisition and use', pp. 156-80 in Schmitt N. and M. McCarthy (eds.): *Vocabulary: Description, Acquisition and Pedagogy* 1997 © Cambridge University Press

p. 90 'Legislation by hypothesis: the case of task-based instruction' by Michael Swan, from *Applied Linguistics*, Volume 36, Issue 3, 2005. Reproduced by permission of Oxford University Press.

p. 114 'Chunks in the classroom: let's not go overboard' by Michael Swan, from *The Teacher Trainer*, Volume 20, Issue 3, 2006. Reprinted by kind permssion.

p. 119 'Forty years of language teaching', remembered by Michael Swan, from *Language Teaching* 40 (1): pp. 3-4 (2006). © Cambridge University Press

p. 122 'Teaching grammar--does grammar teaching work?' by Michael Swan. This article was first published in *Modern English Teacher*, Volume 15, Issue 2, April 2006. Reprinted with kind permission.

p. 134 *Two Out of Three Ain't Bad*. Words and music by Jim Steinman © 1977, Edward B Marks Music Company. All Rights Reserved. Lyric reproduced by kind permission of Carlin Music Corp London NW1 8BD.

p. 138 'History is not what happened: the case of contrastive analysis' by Michael Swan, from *International Journal of Applied Linguistics*, Volume 17, Issue 3, 2007. © Wiley Blackwell.

p. 143 'Grammar, meaning and pragmatics: sorting out the muddle' by Michael Swan, published on line in *TESL-EJ*, Volume 11, Issue 2, September 2007. © Michael Swan.

p. 152 'Talking sense about learning strategies' by Michael Swan, from *RELC Journal*, Volume 39, Issue 2, 2008. © 2008, Sage Publications.

p. 157 *Sisyphus* by Robert Garioch. Reproduced by kind permission of The Saltire Society.

p. 162 'We do need methods' by Michael Swan, from *RELC Journal*, Volume 39, Issue 2, 2008. © 2008, Sage Publications.

p. 186 'Grammar' by Michael Swan, from *The Routledge Handbook of Applied Linguistics*, Simpson, J. (ed.), 2011. Reproduced by kind permission of Routledge, Taylor & Francis.

p. 203 'The use of sensory deprivation in foreign language teaching' by Michael Swan and Catherine Walter, from *ELT Journal*, Volume 36, Issue 3, 1982. Reproduced by permission of Oxford University Press.

Contents

Introduction – *ix*

PART ONE **Pedagogic and academic articles**

1. A critical look at the Communicative Approach (1) – *1*
2. A critical look at the Communicative Approach (2) – *14*
3. Where is the language going? – *36*
4. The textbook: bridge or wall? – *41*
5. Design criteria for pedagogic language rules – *45*
6. Language teaching is teaching language – *57*
7. The influence of the mother tongue on second language vocabulary acquisition and use – *68*
8. Legislation by hypothesis: the case of task-based instruction – *90*
9. Chunks in the classroom: let's not go overboard – *114*
10. English teaching in the nineteen-sixties and seventies – *119*
11. Teaching grammar—does grammar teaching work? – *122*
12. Two out of three ain't enough: the essential ingredients of a language course – *131*
13. History is not what happened: the case of contrastive analysis A follow-up to Claire Kramsch's review of Linguistics across Cultures – *138*
14. Grammar, meaning and pragmatics: sorting out the muddle – *143*
15. Talking sense about learning strategies – *203*
16. We do need methods – *162*
17. Using texts constructively – *180*
18. Grammar – *186*

PART TWO **Satirical pieces**

19   The use of sensory deprivation in foreign language teaching – 203
20   Brief abstracts – 207
21   Module 2: Critical text study. Paper 1: Cross-examining the text – 209
22   Notes from the broom cupboard – 210
23   Trajectories of identity construction – 212
24   PIGTESOL – 215
25   Learning the piano in Fantasia – 217

Bibliography – 221

Introduction

Half a century ago I started working as an untrained teacher in an English language school. Over the following years, as I did my best to educate myself in my chosen profession, I spent a good deal of time trying to come to terms with the findings of applied linguists and the views of influential practitioners, to relate these to my own experience as a teacher and materials writer, and to understand why they often seemed to offer incompatible or contradictory guidance. This led me to publish one or two articles in professional journals in an attempt to clarify matters for myself and others involved in language teaching, and to arrive at a realistic and coherent conceptual framework within which we might better understand one aspect or another of our work. Further articles followed in the course of time; a selection is collected here.

Some of the articles have a relatively theoretical slant; these are occasionally polemic. In thinking, writing, and speaking about language teaching and learning, I have sometimes found myself swimming upstream against the prevailing intellectual current, addressing conceptual confusions which, in my view, act as obstacles to a clear understanding of our professional concerns. It can be difficult to take issue with ideas without at the same time appearing to criticize those who hold them, and I am conscious that I have not always expressed my disagreements in the tactfully veiled terms that are conventional in the academic world. This may sometimes have led to hurt feelings: *reductio ad absurdum* is a classic and effective technique in intellectual debate, but it is not a good way of making friends. I must stress that the people whose views I have contested are generally scholars whom I like and respect, and for whose work, regardless of disagreements, I have considerable admiration.

Looking over these articles, I am struck by the extent to which certain themes recur throughout: the confusions inherent in the so-called 'communicative approach', the drawbacks of 'one size fits all' solutions, the value of limited goals and informed prioritizing, the dangers of perfectionism, the importance of teaching at least some grammar, and the need for various kinds of balance: between form and function, knowledge and skills, teacher-directed and student-directed learning, product and process.

These repetitions may suggest that I feel English language teaching, and the theory and research that support it, have progressed little over the quarter-century spanned by the collection. This is certainly not the case: there has of course been very considerable progress. Methods and materials have improved enormously, and our conceptualization of language itself, along with our understanding of instructed language acquisition, have developed out of all recognition. I feel, however, that we are still a long way from establishing a coherent view of what we are about. Languages are vast, complex, and notoriously hard to learn. While the theorizing and research that have taken place over the period have certainly contributed greatly to our knowledge, they have perhaps raised almost as many questions as they have answered.

Language teaching practitioners need some kind of comprehensible overview of the enterprise in which they are engaged. In a praiseworthy attempt to make their task more manageable, teachers and trainers may adopt uncritically the latest theoretical insight (or the last insight but one, or the last but two). Such insights, however, sometimes promoted with more assurance than is justified, can offer misleadingly simple routes through the complicated language teaching landscape: 'It's all a matter of habit formation/comprehensible input/communicative tasks/lexis/———' (fill in the blank). Generalizations can be dangerous in our business. Languages contain elements of very different kinds which are not all learnable in the same way; learners themselves and their priorities and purposes vary enormously, as do the contexts of language learning. These contexts are also changing rapidly, as technological developments transform and enrich the ways in which we can enable learners to engage with language. However much these changes benefit language learning and teaching, they are unlikely to make it any more straightforward.

When I was first teaching, there was often a considerable gulf between academic researchers and language-teaching practitioners. This may have narrowed, but it has certainly not disappeared. Unfortunately, some teachers still know little about current theory and research, while the work of some theorists and researchers is not well informed by real teaching experience. This can lead to negative attitudes on both sides, with teachers mocking ivory-tower academics who would not recognize an ordinary classroom if they found themselves in one, and scholars criticizing language teachers for their failure to abandon 'discredited traditional methods'.

Clearly, contributions from both communities are essential. Applied linguistic research and theory-building have helped a great deal to systematize and deepen our understanding of how languages are learnt and can be taught, and to define and clarify the many questions that remain to be answered. At the same time, as in other areas of human enquiry, the accumulated experience and reflection of generations of practitioners have provided us with an impressive body of knowledge, wisdom, and professional expertise. Both of these complementary sources of enlightenment need to be valued, attended to, and drawn on as appropriate by those involved in language teaching, teacher training, course design, and materials writing. We must also accept, however, that both have their shortcomings, and neither should be expected to provide clearer or more reliable answers to our questions than they are able to.

I hope that these articles, the product of much hard thinking about my own work as a teacher and writer, may have some value to those who are interested in bridging the gap between theory and practice. They are in chronological order, apart from a small group of satirical pieces at the end of the collection. I have made a few abridgements to reduce repetition, but they are otherwise in their original form. All of them owe a good deal to discussion with colleagues and friends. My thanks to those; my thanks also to the various journal and book editors who originally published the articles, for the hospitality of their pages.

PART ONE
Pedagogic and academic articles

1

A critical look at the Communicative Approach (1)

(Originally published in *ELT Journal* 39/1, January 1985.)

This and the following article addressed three main concerns:

1 *The danger that the new 'communicative' focus on functions, notions and skills, valuable though it was, risked replacing rather than complementing a focus on language forms and how to teach them.*
2 *The possibility that the theoretical underpinnings of the new ideas (e.g. the alleged need to teach 'rules of use' and to replicate the processes of 'real-life' language acquisition in the classroom) were not well-founded.*
3 *The dogmatic nature, as I saw it, of the prescriptions and proscriptions that were being handed down to language teaching practitioners by the academic wing of the profession.*

The articles had a certain impact, perhaps justifiably. I still hold to pretty much the same views, and I think the fears mentioned above have largely been borne out. However, I would not express myself in the same way today. The articles were written when I was not long out of the classroom, after twenty years at the chalk-face. At the time I was (perhaps unfairly) somewhat disenchanted with the extent to which the relatively new discipline of applied linguistics had made a real difference to teachers' and learners' ability to achieve their aims. (In 1969 Peter Strevens, himself a prominent applied linguist, questioned the payoff of applied linguistics research in an unpublished paper entitled 'Where has all the money gone? The need for cost-effectiveness studies in the teaching of foreign languages.') So while I did not at that time actually use 'applied linguist' as a term of abuse, I sometimes came close. The tone of the articles was consequently excessively polemic, anti-academic, and at times downright rude. I now offer my belated apologies to the several distinguished scholars for whom I showed less respect than they certainly deserved.

One of these, Henry Widdowson, published a riposte ('Against dogma: a reply to Michael Swan') in the following issue of ELT Journal. In the next issue I published a rather waspish letter in response to his reply. Twenty-five years later, with the hatchet long since buried, Henry has generously agreed to round off the exchange with a retrospective note. The whole exchange is printed here on page 28 after the two articles.

Introduction

There is nothing so creative as a good dogma. During the last few years, under the influence of the 'Communicative Approach', language teaching seems to have made great progress. Syllabus design has become a good deal more sophisticated, and we are able to give our students a better and more complete picture than before of how language is used. In methodology, the change has been dramatic. The boring and mechanical exercise types which were so common ten or fifteen years ago have virtually disappeared, to be replaced by a splendid variety of exciting and engaging practice activities. All this is very positive, and it is not difficult to believe that such progress in course design has resulted in a real improvement in the speed and quality of language learning.

And yet ... A dogma remains a dogma, and in this respect the 'communicative revolution' is little different from its predecessors in the language teaching field. If one reads through the standard books and articles on the communicative teaching of English, one finds assertions about language use and language learning falling like leaves in autumn; facts, on the other hand, tend to be remarkably thin on the ground. Along with its many virtues, the Communicative Approach unfortunately has most of the typical vices of an intellectual revolution: it over-generalizes valid but limited insights until they become virtually meaningless; it makes exaggerated claims for the power and novelty of its doctrines; it misrepresents the currents of thought it has replaced; it is often characterized by serious intellectual confusion; it is choked with jargon.

In this article I propose to look critically at certain concepts which form part of the theoretical basis of the new orthodoxy, in an attempt to reduce the confusion which surrounds their use, and which unfortunately forms a serious obstacle to sensible communication in the field. I shall discuss in particular: (1) the idea of a 'double level of meaning' associated with such terms as 'rules of use' and 'rules of communication', and the related concept of 'appropriacy'; and (2) some confusions regarding 'skills' and 'strategies'. In [Article 2], I shall deal with: (3) the idea of a semantic ('notional/functional') syllabus, and (4) the 'real life' fallacy in materials design and methodology.

I shall find it convenient to argue as if the Communicative Approach were a coherent and monolithic body of doctrine. This is, of course, far from being the case. Individual applied linguists and teacher trainers vary widely in their acceptance and interpretation of the different ideas which I shall discuss here. Some of the views quoted are becoming outmoded, and would not necessarily be defended today by their originators. But whatever their current status in academic circles, all of these ideas are familiar, widespread, and enormously influential among language teachers, and they merit serious scrutiny.

Meaning and use

A basic communicative doctrine is that earlier approaches to language teaching did not deal properly with meaning. According to the standard argument, it is not enough just to learn what is in the grammar and dictionary. There are (we are told) two levels of meaning in language: 'usage' and 'use', or 'signification' and 'value', or whatever. Traditional courses, it appears, taught one of these kinds of meaning but neglected the other.

> One of the major reasons for questioning the adequacy of grammatical syllabuses lies in the fact that even when we have described the grammatical (and lexical) meaning of a sentence, we have not accounted for the way it is used as an utterance ... Since those things that are not conveyed by the grammar are also understood, they too must be governed by 'rules' which are known to both speaker and hearer. People who speak the same language share not so much a *grammatical* competence as a *communicative* competence. Looked at in foreign language teaching terms, this means that the learner has to learn rules of communication as well as rules of grammar.
> (Wilkins 1976:10, 11)

This line of argument is often illustrated by instances of utterances which clearly have one kind of 'propositional' meaning and a different kind of 'function'. The coat example and the window example are popular. If you say 'Your coat's on the floor' to a child, you are probably telling him or her to pick it up; a person who says 'There's a window open' may really be asking for it to be closed. However, examples are not confined to requests masquerading as statements. All kinds of utterances, we are reminded, can express intentions which are not made explicit by the grammatical form in which the utterance is couched.

> ... this sentence (*The policeman is crossing the road*) might serve a number of communicative functions, depending on the contextual and/or situational circumstances in which it were used. Thus, it might take on the value of part of a commentary ..., or it might serve as a warning or a threat, or some other act of communication. If it is the case that knowing a language means both knowing what *signification* sentences have as instances of language usage and what *value* they take on as instances of use, it seems clear that the teacher of language should be concerned with the teaching of both kinds of knowledge.
> (Widdowson 1978:19)

Put in general terms like this, the claim has a fine plausible ring to it—not least because of the impressive, if slightly confusing, terminology. There is of course nothing particularly novel about the two-level account of meaning given here. It has long been recognized that most language items are multi-purpose tokens which take on their precise value from the context they are

4   *Thinking about Language Teaching*

used in. What is perhaps more novel is the suggestion that the value of any utterance in a given situation can be specified by rules ('rules of communication' or 'rules of use'), and that it is our business to teach these rules to our students. Neither Wilkins nor Widdowson makes it clear what form such rules might take, and so it is a little difficult to deal adequately with the argument. However, let us try to see what might be involved in a concrete instance.

Widdowson asserts, effectively, that a student cannot properly interpret the utterance *The policeman is crossing the road* (or any other utterance, for that matter) if he knows only its propositional (structural and lexical) meaning. In order to grasp its real value in a specific situation, he must have learnt an additional rule about how the utterance can be used. Very well. For the sake of argument, let us imagine that an international team of burglars (Wilberforce, Gomez, Schmidt and Tanaka) are busy doing over a detached suburban house. Wilberforce is on watch. A policeman comes round the corner on the other side of the road. Wilberforce reports this to the others. Schmidt, who learnt his English from a communicatively oriented multi-media course in a university applied linguistics department, interprets this as a warning and turns pale. Gomez and Tanaka, who followed a more traditional course, totally fail to grasp the illocutionary force of Wilberforce's remark. Believing him to be making a neutral comment on the external environment, they continue opening drawers. Suddenly Wilberforce blurts out, 'The policeman is crossing the road', and disappears through the back door, closely followed by Schmidt. Gomez and Tanaka move calmly to the wardrobe. They are caught and put away for five years. Two more victims of the structural syllabus.

Although the argument about rules of use leads to some very extraordinary conclusions when applied to particular cases, it occurs repeatedly in the literature of the Communicative Approach, and there is no doubt that we are intended to take it literally. Here is Widdowson again, this time talking about language production, rather than comprehension.

> It is possible for someone to have learned a large number of sentence patterns and a large number of words which can fit into them without knowing how they are put to communicative use.
> (Widdowson 1978: 18, 19)

Well, no doubt this can happen. But is it necessarily or normally the case? One of the few things I retain from a term's study of a highly 'structural' Russian audio-lingual course is a pattern that goes something like this: *Vot moy nomer; vot moy dom; vot moya kniga*; and so on. I have done no Russian since, but I think I know when it is communicatively appropriate to say 'This is my room', 'This is my house', or 'This is my book' in that language, or most others. (And if I don't, it is not a communicative Russian course that I need; it is expert help of a rather different kind.)

Here is a final example of the 'usage/use' assertion; this time the term 'use potential' is introduced.

> Not until he (the learner) has had experience of the language he is
> learning as use will he be able to recognize use potential.
> (Widdowson 1978:118)

I've just looked up the Swedish for 'Something is wrong with the gearbox' in a motorist's phrase-book. It is (if my book is to be trusted) 'Någonting stämmer inte med växellåda'. I have no experience of Swedish 'as use'. However, I am prepared to hazard a guess that this expression's use potential is more likely to be realized in a garage than, for instance, in a doctor's surgery or a laundry (though of course one can never be certain about these things). I would also guess that this is true of the equivalent expression in Spanish, Tagalog, Melanesian pidgin, or any language whatever. And I know this, not because I am an exceptionally intuitive linguist, but because the fact in question is not just a fact about Swedish, or about language—it is a fact about the world, and the things we say about the world. A linguist may need, for his or her own purposes, to state explicitly that conversations about cars are likely to take place in garages, or that while 'The rain destroyed the crops' is a correct example of English usage, it is not an appropriate answer to the question, 'Where is the station?' But to suggest that this kind of information should form part of a foreign-language teaching syllabus is to misunderstand quite radically the distinction between thought and language.

Foreigners have mother tongues: they know as much as we do about how human beings communicate. The 'rules of use' that determine how we interpret utterances such as Widdowson's sentence about the policeman are mostly non-language-specific, and amount to little more than the operation of experience and common sense. The precise value of an utterance is given by the interaction of its structural and lexical meaning with the situation in which it is used. If you are burgling a house, a report of a policeman's approach naturally takes on the function of a threat or a warning—not because of any linguistic 'rule of communication' that can be applied to the utterance, but because policemen threaten the peace of mind of thieves. If you indicate that you are hungry, the words 'There's some stew in the fridge' are likely to constitute an offer, not because you have learnt a rule about the way these words can be used, but simply because the utterance most plausibly takes on that value in that situation.

Of course, cultures differ somewhat in their behaviour, and these differences are reflected in language. Although most utterances will retain their value across language boundaries (if correctly translated), problems will arise in specific and limited cases. For instance, there may be languages where all requests are marked as such (perhaps by a special particle or intonation pattern), so that a simple unmarked statement such as 'There's a window open' cannot in these languages function as a request. Speakers of such languages who study English (and English-speaking students of these languages) will need contrastive information about this particular point if they are to understand or speak correctly. Again, there are phrases and sentences in any language which conventionally carry intentional meanings that are not evident from their form. (English questions beginning 'Where's my …?' often function as demands; 'Look here!' is an expostulation; 'Why should I?' is not a simple request for information.) However, both the contrastive and the idiomatic aspects of language use have already received a good deal of attention in the past. Although the Communicative Approach may have some new information and insights to contribute (for instance about the language of social interaction), there is nothing here to justify the announcement that we need to adopt a whole new approach to the teaching of meaning. The argument about 'usage' and 'use', whatever value it may have for philosophers, has little relevance to foreign language teaching.

In a recent paper, Wilkins makes it clear that he has now come round to this kind of view.

> It seems reasonable to assume that the relation of linguistic and pragmatic features that we have referred to here is characteristic of all languages. If we consider second language learners, therefore, it appears that although there will be values, attitudes, norms and even types of information that are culturally restricted and consequently not known to the learners, they will be aware that such a relation does exist in principle and that much in their previous experience will remain relevant in the second language. What the learners have to learn is less that there is a connection between language and context than the forms and meanings of the second language itself, together with whatever differences there are in the society that might affect the operation of the pragmatic element in communication. The learners will also know that if they can convey the meanings that they wish, even without making their intentions (i.e. illocutionary forces) explicit, the hearer has the capacity to make appropriate inferences … Provided one understands the meaning of the sentences, in the nature of things one has every chance of recognizing the speaker's intention.
> (Wilkins 1983: 31)

Appropriacy

The argument about a second level of meaning often surfaces in a slightly different form involving the concept of 'appropriacy'. This is the notion that our choice of language is crucially determined by the setting in which the language is used, the speaker's relationship with the listener, and similar matters. So important is this (we are often told) that appropriacy is the real goal of language teaching.

> What we want to do through language is affected by (the) relationship of (the) speakers, setting, etc. Grammar and lexis are only a small part of this.
> (Alexander 1977)

> Structural dialogues lack communicative intent and you cannot identify what *communicative operations* the learner can engage in as a result of practice. The result of purely structural practice is the ability to produce a range of usages, but not the ability to use forms appropriately. This is true even in cases where it looks as if communication is being taught. For example, the exclamation form 'What a lovely day' might be covered. But the interest is in the form, not on when and where to use it or what you achieve by using it.
> (Scott 1981:70, 71)

Nobody would deny that there are language items that are appropriate only in certain situations, or (conversely) that there are situations in which only certain ways of expressing oneself are appropriate. English notoriously has a wealth of colloquial, slang, and taboo expressions, for instance, whose use is regulated by complex restrictions. In French, it is not easy to learn exactly whom to address by the second person singular. Getting people to do things for you is a delicate business in most cultures, and this tends to be reflected in the complexity of the relevant linguistic rules. Although there is nothing particularly controversial or novel about this, it is an area where the Communicative Approach (with its interest in the language of interaction) has contributed a good deal to the coverage of our teaching.

We must understand, however, that 'appropriacy' is one aspect among many—an important corner of linguistic description, but not by any means a feature of the language as a whole. 'Appropriacy' is not a new dimension of meaning, to be added everywhere to lexical and structural meaning. It is a category that applies to certain items only: the same kind of thing as 'animate', 'countable', or 'transitive'. Items such as the imperative, *had better*, *bloody*, *I want*, *get* are marked for appropriacy in one way or the other; students have to be careful how they use them. But most items are not so marked. The past tense, for instance, or the words *table, design, blue, slowly, natural*, or the expression to *fill in a form*, or the sentence *She was born in 1940*—these items, and the vast majority of the other words, expressions, and sentences of the language, are unmarked for social or situational appropriacy of the kind under discussion. Consequently they cause the learner no special problems in this area.

What has happened here might be called the 'new toy' effect. A limited but valuable insight has been over-generalized, and is presented as if it applied to the whole of language and all of language teaching. Unfortunately, this is a common occurrence in the communication sciences.

Interestingly, the discussion of appropriacy often obscures a perfectly valid point about the need for increased attention to the teaching of lexis.

> We might begin our consideration of communicative language teaching ... by looking at the discontent which teachers and applied linguists in the 1960s felt towards the kind of language teaching then predominant. This discontent is vividly expressed by Newmark ..., who speaks of the

'structurally competent' student—the one, that is, who has developed the ability to produce grammatically correct sentences—yet who is unable to perform a simple communicative task. His example of such a task is 'asking for a light from a stranger'. Our structurally competent student might perform this task in a perfectly grammatical way by saying 'have you fire?' or 'do you have illumination' or 'are you a match's owner?' (Newmark's examples). Yet none of these ways—however grammatical they may be—would be used by the native speaker.

Most of us are familiar with this phenomenon of the structurally competent but communicatively incompetent student, and he bears striking witness to the truth of the one insight which, perhaps more than any other, has shaped recent trends in language teaching. This is the insight that the ability to manipulate the structures of the language correctly is only a part of what is involved in learning a language. There is a 'something else' that needs to be learned, and this 'something else' involves the ability to be appropriate, to know the right thing to say at the right time. 'There are', in Hymes's ... words, 'rules of use without which the rules of grammar would be useless'.
(Johnson 1981:1, 2)

Now the 'structurally competent but communicatively incompetent student' pictured here certainly has a problem, but it is quite unnecessary to invoke nebulous abstractions such as 'appropriacy' or 'rules of use' to account for it. Newmark's student doesn't know enough vocabulary. He may be structurally competent, but he has not been taught enough lexis. He is unaware of the exact range of meaning of the word *fire* (and perhaps thinks it can be used in all cases as an equivalent of *feu* or *Feuer*); he does not know the expression *a light*; he is (implausibly) confused about the meaning of *illumination*; he has not learnt the conventional phrase used for requesting a light. These are all lexical matters, and all the information the student lacks can be found in a respectable dictionary. It is perfectly true that 'the ability to manipulate the structures of the language correctly is only a part of what is involved in learning a language', and that there is a 'something else' that needs to be learned. This something else, however, is primarily vocabulary, and the Communicative Approach can hardly take credit for the 'insight' that language contains words and phrases as well as structures.

The teaching of lexis has certainly been greatly improved by the recent concern with communicative competence. Teachers and course designers are more aware than before of the vast range of conventional and idiomatic expressions that have to be learnt if a student is to be able to perform ordinary communicative tasks (such as saying she has been cut off on the phone, asking a petrol pump attendant to check his tyre pressures, or indeed asking a stranger for a light). If we are now adopting a more informed and systematic approach to vocabulary teaching, that is all to the good. But we should understand clearly that this is what we are doing. Inappropriate references to appropriacy merely confuse the issue.

Skills and strategies

Discussion of language skills is no longer limited to a consideration of the four basic activities of reading, writing, understanding speech, and speaking. We are more inclined nowadays to think in terms of the various specific types of behaviour that occur when people are producing or understanding language for a particular purpose in a particular situation, and there has been something of a proliferation of sub-skills and strategies in recent teaching materials. As we have seen, it is often taken for granted that language learners cannot transfer communication skills from their mother tongues, and that these must be taught anew if the learners are to solve the 'problem of code and context correlation which lies at the heart of the communicative ability' (Widdowson 1978: 87–8). If, for instance, there is a special 'comprehension skill' involved in interpreting messages, then surely (it is claimed) we had better teach this skill to our students. Otherwise they will 'comprehend' the words they 'hear' as examples of 'usage', but will fail to 'listen' and 'interpret' messages as instances of 'use'; they will respond to 'cohesion' but not to 'coherence', and so on (Widdowson 1978 passim). (One of the most bizarre features of current terminology is the deliberate use of pairs of virtually indistinguishable words to illustrate allegedly vital distinctions. Faced with terms like 'use' and 'usage' or 'cohesion' and 'coherence', one really finds it extraordinarily difficult to remember which is which.)

One of the comprehension skills which we now teach foreigners is that of predicting. It has been observed that native listeners/readers make all sorts of predictions about the nature of what they are about to hear or read, based on their knowledge of the subject, their familiarity with the speaker or writer, and other relevant features. Armed with this linguistic insight (and reluctant to believe that foreigners, too, can predict), we 'train' students in 'predictive strategies'. (For instance, we ask them to guess what is coming next and then let them see if they were right or wrong.) But I would suggest that if a foreigner knows something about the subject matter, and something about the speaker or writer, and if he knows enough of the language, then the foreigner is just as likely as the native speaker to predict what will be said. And if he predicts badly in a real-life comprehension task (classroom tasks are different), it can only be for one of two reasons. Either he lacks essential background knowledge (of the subject matter or the interactional context), or his command of the language is not good enough. In the one case he needs information, in the other he needs language lessons. In neither case does it make sense to talk about having to teach some kind of 'strategy'.

Another strategy which we are encouraged to teach is that of 'negotiating meaning'.

> ... speakers and writers perform an unconscious guessing game, because they have to establish what the agreed goals are (and this is not always clear, especially at the beginning of the conversation), as well as how much knowledge, or past experience, or understanding is shared. Thus if you ask me where I live, I may answer 'Britain' or 'London' or 'Surrey', or the name of the exact road, depending on why I think you asked me and how well I think you know south-east England. If I answer 'London' and you answer 'Whereabouts in London?' you are telling me that you want more specific information: we are negotiating about the purpose of the conversation, for you are showing that you really want to know, rather than just making a general social enquiry.... It needs to be emphasized that everyone, in any language, needs to develop the skills of adjustment and negotiation.
> (Brumfit 1981: 6, 7)

The point is not always made with such unpretentious clarity.

> The shift towards a balance between form and function has had important methodological effects. If we see language as one part of wider social interaction and behaviour, deriving its communicative value from it, then we are compelled to introduce the process of interaction into the classroom. Learners now need to be trained and refined in the interpretive and expressive strategies of making sense amid a negotiable reality where the ground rules for understanding what partners mean are not pre-set entirely, nor unequivocal. In fact, learners have to come to cope with the essential problem of communication—to acquire the mutually negotiated and dynamic conventions which give value to formal signs. They have to learn how to agree conventions and procedures, for the interpretation of non-verbal and verbal language, with which they temporarily abide.
> (Candlin 1981: 25)

Now this is very impressive, but it is simply not true. Language learners already know, in general, how to negotiate meaning. They have been doing it all their lives. What they do not know is what words are used to do it in a foreign language. They need lexical items, not skills: expressions like 'What do you mean by ...?', 'Look at it this way', 'Whereabouts do you mean?', 'I beg your pardon', or 'No, that's not what I'm trying to say'. Of course, there will be cases where the mother-tongue and the foreign language differ in the detailed approach used for negotiation. Where this happens, we need to know specifics—at what point, and for what purpose, does language X operate a different convention from language Y? (Perhaps in language X it is rude to ask somebody what she means, for instance.) Such specifics can be incorporated in teaching programmes for speakers or learners of language X, and this can be very valuable. But in general there is not the least need to teach our students 'the interpretive and expressive strategies of making sense amid a negotiable reality', even assuming that we were able to define what this involves. And to talk in these terms contributes nothing whatever to our understanding of how to teach foreign languages.

Guessing, too, is something which learners are apparently unable to do outside their mother tongue.

> Clearly training in making intelligent guesses will play an important part in learning to understand the spoken form of a foreign language.
> (Brown 1977: 162)

Assertions like this regularly pass unchallenged at conferences. As one reads the quotation, one is inclined to nod in automatic assent from force of habit: the sentiment is so familiar, so much part of the accepted orthodoxy. And yet, why should language students need training in making intelligent guesses? Are they less intelligent people, less good at guessing, than other groups in the population? Than language teachers, for instance? Is there any reason at all to suppose that they do not already possess this skill? And if they possess it, do we have any real evidence that they cannot in general apply it to learning a foreign language? And if we do not have such evidence, what are we doing setting out to teach people something they can do already? Most of the readers of this journal [*ELTJ*] can probably understand the spoken form of a foreign language to some extent at least. How many of them have received systematic training in making intelligent guesses in the language in question?

It can happen, of course, that a learner has difficulty in transferring a skill from his or her mother tongue to the foreign language, especially in the early days of language learning. When this happens (as it can with comprehension skills), it *may* be worth giving specific practice in the 'blocked' skill in question. However, we need to know why the skill is blocked. If a learner seems to be understanding most of the words he or she hears but not really grasping the message (not seeing the wood for the trees), this may simply be due to anxiety. More often, perhaps, it is a matter of overload—the learner's command of the language is just fluent enough for him to decode the words, but this occupies all his faculties and he has no processing capacity to spare for 'interpreting' what he hears. The problem will go away with increased fluency; practice in 'global' comprehension may appear to go well and may increase the student's confidence, but I doubt whether a great deal can really be done to accelerate the natural progression of this aspect of learning. At higher levels, students may perform badly at classroom comprehension tasks (failing to make sense of texts that are well within their grasp) simply because of lack of interest; or because they have been trained to read classroom texts in such a different way from 'real life' texts that they are unable to regard them as pieces of communication. Here the problem is caused by poor methodology, and the solution involves changing what happens in the classroom, not what happens in the student. We cannot assume without further evidence that students lack comprehension strategies, simply because they have trouble jumping through the hoops that we set up for them.

This 'tabula rasa' attitude—the belief that students do not possess, or cannot transfer from their mother tongue, normal communication skills—is one of two complementary fallacies that characterize the Communicative Approach. The other is the 'whole-system' fallacy. This arises when the linguist, over-excited about his or her analysis of a piece of language or behaviour, sets out to teach everything that has been observed (often including the metalanguage used to describe the phenomena), without stopping to ask how much of the teaching is (a) new to the students and (b) relevant to their needs. Both fallacies are well illustrated in the following exercise (Figure 1). It will be observed: (a) that the purpose of the exercise, as stated, is to develop 'conversational strategies' (a therapeutic procedure which might seem more relevant to the teaching of psycho-social disorders than to language instruction); (b) that students are taught a piece of discourse analysis and its metalanguage; and (c) that the actual English language input seems to be the least important part of the exercise—it is in fact by no means clear what language teaching is going on here, if any at all.

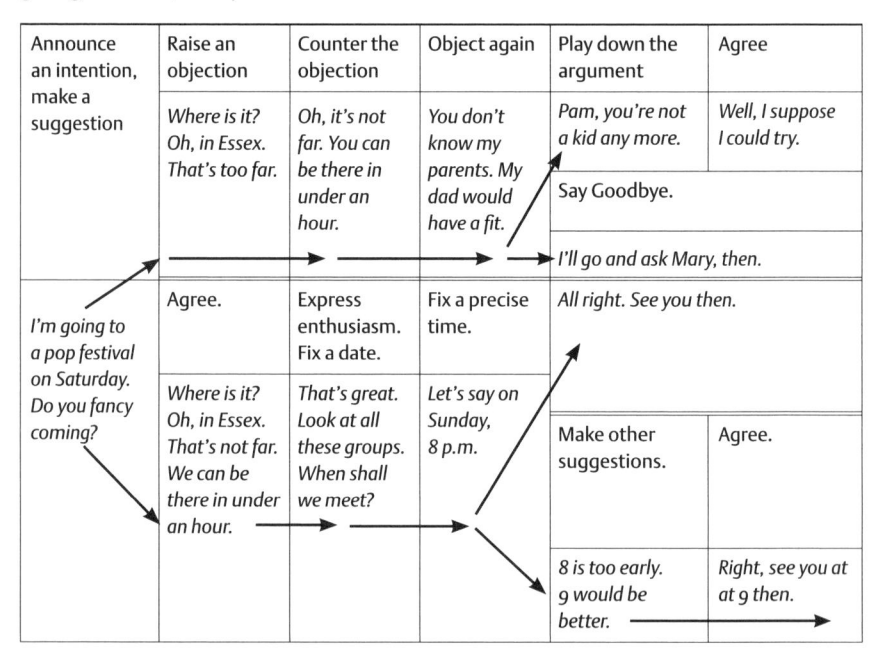

Announce an intention, make a suggestion	Raise an objection	Counter the objection	Object again	Play down the argument	Agree
	Where is it? Oh, in Essex. That's too far.	Oh, it's not far. You can be there in under an hour.	You don't know my parents. My dad would have a fit.	Pam, you're not a kid any more.	Well, I suppose I could try.
				Say Goodbye.	
				I'll go and ask Mary, then.	
I'm going to a pop festival on Saturday. Do you fancy coming?	Agree.	Express enthusiasm. Fix a date.	Fix a precise time.	All right. See you then.	
	Where is it? Oh, in Essex. That's not far. We can be there in under an hour.	That's great. Look at all these groups. When shall we meet?	Let's say on Sunday, 8 p.m.	Make other suggestions.	Agree.
				8 is too early. 9 would be better.	Right, see you at at 9 then.

Figure 1: A 'discourse chain' from an experimental teaching unit 'I wanna have fun' by Ulrich Grewer and Terry Moston, first published in the Protokoll of the 7th Meeting of the Bundesarbeitsgemeinschaft Englisch an Gesamtschulen: 'Teaching Kits, Discourse Structure and Exercise Typologies', Hessen State Institute for Teacher In-Service Training, Kassel-Fuldatal (1975); reprinted in Candlin (1981) and reproduced here by permission of the publisher.

Exercises like this treat the learner as a sort of linguistically gifted idiot—somebody who knows enough language to express the (quite complex) ideas involved, but who somehow cannot put the ideas together without help. Normal students, of course, have the opposite problem: they know what they want to say more often than they know how to say it.

Conclusion

I have argued that the 'communicative' theory of meaning and use, in so far as it makes sense, is largely irrelevant to foreign language teaching. These considerations may seem somewhat over-theoretical. 'After all,' it might be objected, 'what does it matter if the theory doesn't really stand up? Theories about language teaching never do. The important thing is that students should be exposed to appropriate samples of language and given relevant and motivating activities to help them learn. This is what the Communicative Approach does.' I think there is something in this, and I should certainly not wish to condemn the Communicative Approach out of hand because its philosophy is confused. No doubt its heart is in the right place, and in some ways it has done us a lot of good. But theoretical confusion can lead to practical inefficiency, and this can do a lot of harm, with time and effort being wasted on unprofitable activities while important priorities are ignored. In the second of these articles I shall focus more closely on these practical issues, considering in particular the validity of the 'notional–functional syllabus', the question of authentic materials, and the 'real life' fallacy in communicative methodology.

2

A critical look at the Communicative Approach (2)

(Originally published in *ELT Journal* 39/2, April 1985.)

> An English boy who has been through a good middle-class school in England can talk to a Frenchman, slowly and with difficulty, about female gardeners and aunts; conversation which, to a man possessed of neither, is liable to pall. Possibly, if he be a bright exception, he may be able to tell the time, or make a few guarded observations concerning the weather. No doubt he could repeat a goodly number of irregular verbs by heart; only, as a matter of fact, few foreigners care to listen to their own irregular verbs, recited by young Englishmen … . And then, when the proud parent takes his son and heir to Dieppe merely to discover that the lad does not know enough to call a cab, he abuses not the system but the innocent victim.
> (Jerome 1900)

Syllabus design

The incompetent school-leaver

Jerome K. Jerome was neither the first nor the last to observe that the language courses of his day were inefficient, or to propose ways of improving them. The learner who has studied the language for seven years, but who cannot ask for a glass of water, a cab, or a light for a cigarette, is regularly brought on to the stage to justify demands for a radical change in our approach to language teaching. Jerome's recommendations for reform were: more time, better qualified teachers, better coursebooks, a more serious attitude to language learning, and the application of common sense to education. These are modest, practical suggestions, but of course Jerome had no knowledge of linguistics. He would scarcely have expressed himself in such down-market terms if he had been writing today, with the benefit of an M.A. course in one of our better applied linguistics departments. Jerome would more probably have complained that his school-leaver knew grammar and words, but could not use them appropriately; could not express everyday notions, or perform basic communicative functions; lacked productive and receptive skills and strategies; was unable to negotiate meaning successfully; had learnt language on the level of usage rather than use; created text that was cohesive but not coherent; was not successful in relating code to context; and in general lacked communicative competence, which he could best acquire by following a good communicative course based on a scientific needs analysis. On the whole, I think I prefer the original formulation.

The communicative syllabus

Defective language learning is often attributed to defective syllabus design: the student does not learn the language properly because we do not teach the right things, or because we organize what we teach in the wrong way. Recently the attention of linguists has been focused on meaning, and it has come to be widely believed that the secret of successful language teaching lies in incorporating meaning properly into our syllabuses. We can perhaps distinguish four common versions of this belief:

a 'Older language courses taught forms, but did not teach what the forms meant or how to use them. We now do this.'
b 'Older language courses taught one kind of meaning (that found in the grammar and dictionary), but did not teach another kind (the communicative value that utterances actually have in real-life exchanges). It is this second kind that we really need to teach.'
c 'Older language courses failed to teach students how to express or do certain things with language. We must incorporate these things (notions, functions, strategies) into our syllabuses.'
d 'Even if older structure-based language courses taught meanings as well as forms, they did so very untidily and inefficiently. A communicative syllabus approaches the teaching of meaning systematically.'

The first version (a) is no longer as common as it used to be, and it is not really worth wasting time on. I have discussed version (b) at length in [the] previous article (Swan 1985), in which I argue that the kind of meaning referred to ('rules of use') does not need to be taught, and cannot in any case be codified. Here I should like to deal principally with the issues raised by versions (c) and (d).

Meaning in older courses

Traditional structure-based courses have had a bad press. Current mythology notwithstanding, they did not systematically neglect the teaching of functions, notions, and skills. Older courses may indeed have failed to teach people to do some important things with language, and more modern materials, whose authors have access to checklists of communicative functions, have plugged a number of gaps. It is also true that many traditional courses adopted a very mechanical approach to drilling what was taught—that is to say, meaning was often neglected during the practice phase of a lesson. Nonetheless, it is quite false to represent older courses as concentrating throughout on form at the expense of meaning, or as failing to teach people to 'do things with language'. I have in front of me a copy of a typical structure-based beginners' course of the 1960s (Candlin 1968). The course has many of the typical defects of books of its generation (though these may seem greater to us, with our sharpened hindsight and different priorities, than they did to its users). However, by the end of Lesson 8, students have been shown perfectly adequate ways of performing the following language functions: greeting, enquiring about health, leave-taking, thanking, expressing regret, eliciting and giving information, offering, requesting goods and services, proffering, self-identification, asking for more precise information, confirming what has been said, exhortation, identifying and naming, describing, narrating, giving informal instructions, agreeing to carry out instructions, and enquiring about plans. 'Semantico-grammatical categories' are not neglected: students learn to talk about place and direction, to refer to states and processes, to describe past, present, and future events, to express concepts related to quantification, and so on. (In other words, they learn prepositions, verb tenses, singular and plural forms, etc. Structures have meanings, and traditional courses usually made a reasonable job of teaching them.) And of course the book provides a year's work on lexis—words and expressions are taught, and the notions associated with them are on the whole clearly demonstrated. Finally, the course (like many of its kind) uses the meaning category of situation as an organizing principle. Even if each lesson is designed to teach a specific structural point, it sets out at the same time to teach the language that is appropriate to a common situation. *Present-Day English* (like any book of its generation) does in fact have a quite clear and carefully worked out semantic syllabus. There are perhaps reasons why one might not wish to teach from this book, but it should not be accused of failing to deal properly with meaning.

Putting meaning first

For many people, the central idea in 'communicative' teaching is probably that of a 'semantic syllabus'. In a course based on a semantic syllabus, it is meanings rather than structures which are given priority, and which form the organizing principle or 'skeleton' of the textbook. Lessons deal with such matters as 'greeting', 'agreeing and disagreeing', 'comparison', 'warning', 'point of time', and so on. So we do not (for example) give a lesson on the comparative forms of adjectives, but on a notion such as that of relative size or degree, which may be expressed not only by using comparative adjectives but also in many other ways. In the bad old courses, where grammar was tidy and meanings untidy, students might learn comparative adjectives in June and the *as ... as* structure the following February; they were never able to put together the various items they needed to express fully the notion in question. With a semantic syllabus, items which belong together semantically are taught together, even if they are structurally quite diverse.

The problem with this approach is obvious to anybody who has recently taught a beginners' class. Unfortunately, grammar has not become any easier to learn since the communicative revolution. If we set out to give a lesson to elementary students on the notion of relative degree, we are likely to run into difficulty straight away, for two reasons. First of all, the main syntactic patterns involved are complex (*as tall as, taller than, less tall than, not so/as tall as*, etc.), and if they are presented all together the students will probably mix them up, confusing *as* and *than* and so on. And secondly, it is not at all obvious to a learner how to form the comparatives of English adjectives: the rules are complicated, and can hardly be picked up in passing in the course of a notion-based lesson which introduces several other structural points at the same time. Experienced teachers often like to isolate and practise difficult structures (such as comparative adjectives) before combining them with others in realistic communicative work. They have excellent reasons for doing so.

Language is not *only* a set of formal systems, but it is a set of systems, and it is perverse not to focus on questions of form when this is desirable. Some points of grammar are difficult to learn, and need to be studied in isolation before students can do interesting things with them. It is no use making meaning tidy if grammar then becomes so untidy that it cannot be learnt properly. As Brumfit points out in his review of Wilkins's *Notional Syllabuses*, the teaching of functions and notions cannot replace the teaching of grammar.

> The point about the grammatical system is that a limited and describable number of rules enable the learner to generate an enormous range of utterances which are usable, in combination with paralinguistic and semiotic systems, to express any function. To ask learners to learn a list instead of a system goes against everything we know about learning theory.
> (Brumfit 1978)

Structural versus functional: a false dichotomy

We really need to question the whole idea that one syllabus, whether structural or functional, should be 'privileged', acting as the framework on which a whole course is built. Language courses involve far too many components, and the relationships between the components are far too complex, for us to be able to subordinate everything to a tidy progression of structures, functions, notions, or anything else. When deciding what to teach to a particular group of learners, we need to take into consideration several different meaning categories and several different formal categories. We must make sure that our students are taught to operate key *functions* such as, for instance, greeting, agreeing, or warning; to talk about basic *notions* such as size, definiteness, texture or ways of moving; to communicate appropriately in specific *situations* (for instance in shops, on the telephone, at meetings); to discuss the *topics* which correspond to their main interests and needs (for example tourism, merchant banking, football, physics). At the same time, we shall need to draw up lists of *phonological* problems which will need attention; of high-priority *structures*; and of the *vocabulary* which our students will need to learn. In addition, we must think about performance as well as competence: we will need a syllabus of *skills*, to make sure that our students are trained to become fluent in whatever aspects of speaking, understanding, reading, and writing relate to their purposes.

Rather than taking either meanings or forms as our starting point, therefore, we really need to look at the language from two directions at once, asking both 'What words and structures are needed to express meaning X?' (semantic syllabuses) and 'What meanings do we need to teach for word Y or structure Z?' (formal syllabuses). At first sight, it might seem as if semantic syllabuses and formal syllabuses ought ultimately to cover the same ground (so that if we have one we can do without the other). After all, if we have listed the meanings we want our students to express, and worked out what structures, words, and expressions are used to convey these meanings, this should surely provide us with a list of all the forms we need to teach, and it ought therefore to be unnecessary to list the forms separately. It is important to realize that this is not the case.

First of all, semantic syllabuses tend to list only items that are specifically related to the functions or notions included in the syllabus. More 'general purpose' items slip through the net. If we make a list of high-priority functions and notions and write down all the words and expressions that are needed to handle them, there is no guarantee that we will include, for instance, the words *umbrella*, *control*, *move* or *rough*. These words are, however, common and important, and will need to be included in most intermediate courses. To be sure of plugging gaps of this kind, we shall need to refer to a traditional lexical syllabus based on word-frequency. The same is true of structures. Grammar items that do not have an easily identifiable 'meaning' (such as points of word order) tend to get left out of notional syllabuses, though they may be of great importance for the correct learning of the language.

Secondly, and conversely, traditional structural/lexical syllabuses are not very good at catching sentence-length idioms and conventional expressions such as 'Can I just break in here?' or 'I'd like to make a reversed charge call'. They may also fail to pick up special uses of 'standard' structures which are important for the expression of certain functions: for instance, the English use of the co-ordinate structure in threats ('Do that again and I'm going home'). To be sure of getting such items into our teaching programme, we need to look at lists of functions and notions and their exponents.

It is, therefore, essential to consider both semantic and formal accounts of the language when deciding what to teach. Failure to do so will result in serious omissions on one side or the other. (There is a well known and deservedly popular 'communicative' beginners' course which gets through a whole year's work without teaching the names of the colours or the basic use of the verb *have*.) The real issue is not which syllabus to put first: it is how to integrate eight or so syllabuses (functional, notional, situational, topic, phonological, lexical, structural, skills) into a sensible teaching programme.

Integrating semantic and formal syllabuses

In discussions of communicative teaching, a good deal of confusion is caused by invalid generalizations. For instance, people often talk as if language courses had much the same shape at all levels from beginners' to advanced. In fact, the relative importance of the various syllabuses, and especially of the grammar component, varies crucially with level. It is fashionable to criticize old-style courses for being excessively concerned with teaching structure, and there is certainly some truth in the criticism. But it really applies only to lower-level courses (where grammar must in any case get a good deal of attention, even if this can easily go too far). At more advanced levels language textbooks have rarely given very much space to grammar: more typical concerns have traditionally been vocabulary-building, the teaching of reading and writing skills, literature and other 'cultural' matters, and the encouragement of discussion.

Equally, the role of 'grammar' in language courses is often discussed as if 'grammar' were one homogeneous kind of thing. In fact, 'grammar' is an umbrella term for a large number of separate or loosely related language systems, which are so varied in nature that it is pointless to talk as if they should all be approached in the same way. How we integrate the teaching of structure and meaning will depend to a great extent on the particular language items involved. Some structural points present difficulties of form as well as meaning (for example interrogative and negative structures; comparison of adjectives; word order in phrasal verbs). As I have already suggested, it may be best to deal with such problems of form *before* students do communicative work on notions or functions in which they will have to mix these structures with others. Other grammar points are less problematic, and can be taught simultaneously with work on a relevant notion or function. (For instance, students might learn to use *can* in the context of a lesson on offering, or requesting, or talking about ability, ease and difficulty.) Some functions and notions may be expressible entirely through structures which are already known: if students have learnt imperatives and simple *if*-clauses, and if they can make basic co-ordinate sentences, then they are already in a position to give warnings. Yet other functions and notions are expressed mainly through lexis, with no special grammatical considerations of any importance (for instance greeting, leave-taking, thanking, speed, size).

How we organize a given lesson will therefore depend very much on the specific point we want to teach. A good language course is likely to include lessons which concentrate on particular structures, lessons which deal with areas of vocabulary, lessons on functions, situation-based lessons, pronunciation lessons, lessons on productive and receptive skills, and several other kinds of component. Many lessons will deal with more than one of these things at the same time. Designing a language course involves reconciling a large number of different and often conflicting priorities, and it is of little use to take one aspect of the language (structures, notions/functions, or anything else) and to use this systematically as a framework for the whole of one's teaching.

The importance of vocabulary

There is a certain air of unreality about the whole 'structural/notional' debate. Assertions which look plausible and persuasive when they are presented in general terms ('We should teach units of communication, not structures') tend to dissolve and become meaningless when one tries to apply them to specific cases. Part of the trouble is perhaps that pragmatics (the study of what we do with language) is grossly over-valued at the moment, in the same way as grammar has been over-valued in the past. The 'new toy' effect is leading us to look at everything in functional terms: we see the whole of our job as being to teach students to convey and elicit information, to describe, to define, to exercise and elicit social control, to express approval, make requests, establish rapport, warn, apologize, and the rest of it. It is important to remember two things. First of all, these functional categories are not themselves the names of things that have to be taught (though they may help to define how we *organize* what we teach). Students can already convey information, define, apologize and so on—what they need to learn is how to do these things in *English*. And secondly, when we have taught students what they need to know in order to carry out the main communicative functions, we *still* have most of the language left to teach. Students not only have to learn how information is conveyed or elicited, or how requests are made: they also have to learn the words and expressions which are used to refer to the things in the world they want to talk about, ask about or request. However good a lesson on the function of warning may be, it will not in itself enable students to say 'Look out—the top half of the ladder isn't properly fixed on'. Functions without lexis are no better than structures without lexis. And referential lexis is a vast field—it certainly makes up the bulk of the learning load in any general-purpose language course.

Stereotyped and creative language

An earlier linguistic school saw language use as being largely a matter of convention, involving a set of predictable responses to recurrent situations. Although this view of language is discredited, it is not so much wrong as only partially correct. A great deal of language does involve knowing what is conventionally said in familiar situations—interrupting, asking for a light, complimenting, leave-taking, buying stamps, correcting oneself and so on. This stereotyped, idiomatic side of language accounts for a substantial proportion of the things we say, and this is the area with which the Communicative Approach is perhaps mainly concerned, investigating the meanings we most often express and tabulating (in semantic syllabuses) the ways in which we conventionally express them. (For all its attention to meaning, the Communicative Approach has a strong behaviourist streak.)

Not all language, of course, is stereotyped. Since Chomsky's ideas became widely known, we have become accustomed to seeing language as something that makes infinite (or at least indefinitely large) use of finite resources. As O'Neill points out in his article 'My guinea pig died with its legs crossed' (O'Neill 1977), most utterances are not conventional responses to familiar situations. Students need to learn to say new things as well as old things. A learner of English may need to be able to say 'Could you check the tyre pressures?'; but he or she may also find it necessary to say 'The car makes a funny noise every time I go round a left-hand bend', or 'I nearly ran over a policeman just by the place where we had that awful meal with your hairdresser's boyfriend'. Sentences like these are not predicted by any kind of semantic syllabus; they can be generated only by constructing sentences out of lexical and grammatical building blocks in accordance with the various rules of phrase and sentence construction.

Simplifying somewhat, one might say that there are two kinds of language: 'stereotyped' and 'creative'. Semantic syllabuses are needed to help us teach the first; only structural/lexical syllabuses will enable us to teach the second.

Methodology
The 'real-life' fallacy

Teachers usually feel guilty about something: translating, or explaining grammar, or standing up in front of the class and behaving like teachers, or engaging in some other activity that is temporarily out of favour. Currently teachers feel guilty about not being communicative. Mechanical structure practice is out: it would be a brave trainee teacher who used a substitution table in his or her RSA practical exam.[1] Language work, we are told, should involve genuine exchanges, and classroom discourse should correspond as closely as possible to real-life use of language. Old-style courses, it appears, failed to take this into account. (At this point in the lecture the speaker usually does his 'Is that your nose?' number, where he reads aloud some appalling piece of pseudo-dialogue from a bad structure-based course and waits for the laughs.)

Of course one can hardly quarrel with the suggestion that classroom language should be as lifelike as possible. All other things being equal, authentic or natural-sounding dialogues are better models than artificial dialogues; it is good to demonstrate structures by using them as they are typically used in the outside world; writing and speaking practice should if possible involve genuine exchanges of information. The more we can (in Widdowson's eloquent formulation) 'contrive to make the language we present less of a contrivance', the better. And this is an area where the Communicative Approach has without question made an important contribution to language teaching. Whatever the defects of the communicative theory of language and syllabus design, the last fifteen years or so have seen enormous improvements in our methodology.

None the less, the classroom is not the outside world, and learning language is not the same as using language. A certain amount of artificiality is inseparable from the process of isolating and focusing on language items for study, and it is a serious mistake to condemn types of discourse typically found in the classroom because they do not share all the communicative features of other kinds of language use.

A common target for criticism is the use of questions to elicit feedback or to cue practice responses. If you say 'Is this my book?' or 'What am I doing?', it is objected that you are asking a question to which you know the answer already; the response will not convey any information, and the conversation is therefore condemned as a piece of pseudo-communication which incidentally gives a misleading picture of how interrogatives are used in English. Now conversations of this kind may not be very interesting, and we may well be able to think of better ways of getting the responses we want, but it is not true that no communication is going on. The questions have the communicative value (common in classroom discourse) of eliciting feedback—of asking students to display knowledge of a piece of information; the answers show whether the student does in fact possess the knowledge in question. Students are always perfectly well aware of the illocutionary force of questions and answers in exchanges like these (they have been in classrooms before), and they are in no danger at all of going out of the classroom believing, for instance, that English-speaking people are always asking questions to which they already know the answers.

A great deal of learning takes place in settings which are remote from the situation where the skills or knowledge will ultimately be used. Kittens playing on a living-room carpet are learning aspects of hunting: stalking, hiding, pouncing, biting, reacting at speed. The fact that they are learning these things in the absence of any real-life prey does not seem to detract from the value of the practice that is going on. Again, in many kinds of learning there is an element of 'mechanical' repetition that makes the activity at times very different from the goal behaviour that is ultimately envisaged. A boy who takes up the violin may dream of one day playing the Beethoven violin concerto to a packed concert hall. But if he is to realize this aim, he is likely to spend much of his time in the intervening years working alone doing very 'uncommunicative' things: playing scales, practising studies, improving his bowing technique, gaining a mastery of positional playing, and so on. Somebody who wants to break the women's 1,500-metre record will train for a long time before her big race. But comparatively little of her training will involve running the full 1,500-metre distance at racing speed; and a lot of what she does (e.g. interval training, calisthenics) will seem artificial and remote from what she is training to do. Learning a language is not altogether the same thing as learning to play the violin, run races, or catch mice, and analogies can be dangerous. However, it should be clear that effective learning can involve various kinds of 'distancing' from the real-life behaviour that is its goal. We do not therefore need to feel that there is anything wrong if, among our battery of teaching activities, we include some (repetition, rote learning, translation, structural drilling) which seem to have no immediate 'communicative' value. If all our exercises are of this kind, of course, it is another matter.

Communicative practice and 'information gap'

I have suggested that methodology is perhaps the area where the Communicative Approach has done most to improve our teaching. It is surprising, however, how often 'communicative' courses achieve the appearance of communication without the reality. A basic concept in contemporary methodology is that of 'information gap'. When one student talks to another, we feel that it is important that new information should be transmitted across the 'gap' between them. To this end, ingenious exercises are devised in which half the class are provided with data to which the other half do not have access; those who lack the information then have to obtain it by using language in an appropriate way. I do not wish to belittle the value of such exercises; the technique is a powerful one, and (if used intelligently) can generate interesting, lively, and useful work. However, the information conveyed should ideally have some relevance and interest for the students. If (to take a familiar example) I give a student a paper containing the times of trains from Manchester to Liverpool, purely so that he can pass on the information to another student who is not in Manchester and does not wish to go to Liverpool, then we are perhaps still some distance from genuine communication.

Perhaps no classroom exercises can completely achieve the spontaneity and naturalness of real exchanges, but there are certainly more realistic and interesting ways of organizing information-gap work than by working with 'imposed' information of this kind. Each individual in a class already possesses a vast private store of knowledge, opinions, and experience; and each individual has an imagination which is capable of creating whole scenarios at a moment's notice. Student X is probably the only person in the class to know the number of people in his family, the places he has travelled to, what he thinks of a film he has just seen, whether he is shy, whether he believes in God, and what is going on in his head while the class is doing an information-gap exercise. If student X can be persuaded to communicate some of these things to student Y—and this is not very difficult to arrange—then we have a basis for genuinely rich and productive language practice. In many contemporary language courses, communication of this 'personal' kind seems to be seriously under-exploited. The tendency to get students to exchange unmotivating, imposed information can even go to the extreme where much of their 'communication' is about the behaviour of the fictional characters in their coursebooks ('You are George—ask Mary what she does at Radio Rhubarb'). Role play and simulation are all very well in their places, but there are times when the same language practice can take place more interestingly and more directly if the students are simply asked to talk about themselves.

Authentic materials

Like many of the other issues in this field, the question of using authentic materials has become polarized into an opposition between a 'good' new approach and a 'bad' old approach. Many teachers nowadays probably feel, in a vague kind of way, that there is something basically unsatisfactory, or even wrong, about using scripted dialogues or specially written teaching texts. These are (we have been told) 'unnatural', and contrived; they tend to lack the discourse features of genuine text; they are fundamentally non-communicative (since they were written essentially to present language data rather than to convey information). Often, of course, this is all too true, and the general quality of published EFL dialogues and prose texts is a powerful argument for the increased use of authentic materials, whatever problems this may entail. However, it is important not to lose sight of the principles involved. There is nothing wrong in itself with creating special texts for specific purposes, and illustrating language use is a purpose like any other. People use deliberately simplified language when writing for children; when adapting scientific articles for laymen; when creating advertising copy; when writing leading articles in the popular press. Why not, then, when writing for foreign learners? Of course, we must be careful about quality: the language found in older-style 'John and Mary' type dialogues, or in some elementary story-lines, is so far removed from natural English that it does nobody any good. But this is an argument against bad scripted material, not against the use of scripted material in general.

In fact, it is obviously desirable to use both scripted and authentic material at different points in a language course for different reasons. Scripted material is useful for presenting specific language items economically and effectively: the course designer has total control over the input, and can provide just the linguistic elements and contextual back-up he or she wishes, no more and no less. Authentic material, on the other hand, gives students a taste of 'real' language in use, and provides them with valid linguistic data for their unconscious acquisition processes to work on. If students are exposed only to scripted material, they will learn an impoverished version of the language, and will find it hard to come to terms with genuine discourse when they are exposed to it. If they are exposed only to authentic material, however, they are unlikely (in the time available for the average language course) to meet all the high-frequency items they need to learn. And elementary students, faced with authentic material that is not very carefully chosen, may find it so difficult that they get bogged down in a morass of unfamiliar lexis and idiom. Eddie Williams, in a recent article, draws attention to

> the paradox that the use of authentic text with learners often has an effect opposite to that intended; instead of helping the learner to read for the meaning of the message, an authentic text at too difficult a level of language forces the reader to focus upon the code.
> (Williams 1983)

The mother tongue in foreign language learning

As far as the British version of the Communicative Approach is concerned, students might as well not have mother tongues. Meanings, uses, and communication skills are treated as if they have to be learnt from scratch. Syllabus design takes no account of the fact that students might already possess some of the knowledge that is tabulated in a needs analysis. (Munby's *Communicative Syllabus Design*, for instance (Munby 1978) makes no significant reference to the mother tongue at all.) Communicative methodology stresses the English-only approach to presentation and practice that is such a prominent feature of the British EFL tradition. (Perhaps because this has made it possible for us to teach English all over the world without the disagreeable necessity of having to learn other languages?) This is a peculiar state of affairs. It is a matter of common experience that the mother tongue plays an important part in learning a foreign language. Students are always translating into and out of their own languages—and teachers are always telling them not to. Interlanguages notoriously contain errors which are caused by interference from the mother tongue; it is not always realized that a large proportion of the *correct* features in an interlanguage also contain a mother tongue element. In fact, if we did not keep making correspondences between foreign language items and mother tongue items, we would never learn foreign languages at all. Imagine having to ask whether *each* new French car one saw was called 'voiture', instead of just deciding that the foreign word was used in much the same way as 'car' and acting accordingly. Imagine starting to learn German without being able to make any unconscious assumptions about the grammar—for instance, that there are verbs and pronouns with similar meanings to our verbs and pronouns. When we set out to learn a new language, we automatically assume (until we have evidence to the contrary) that meanings and structures are going to be broadly similar to those in our own language. The strategy does not always work, of course—that is why languages are difficult to learn—and it breaks down quite often with languages unrelated to our own. But on balance this kind of 'equivalence assumption' puts us ahead of the game; it makes it possible for us to learn a new language without at the same time returning to infancy and learning to categorize the world all over again.

If, then, the mother tongue is a central element in the process of learning a foreign language, why is it so conspicuously absent from the theory and methodology of the Communicative Approach? Why is so little attention paid, in this and other respects, to what learners already know? The Communicative Approach seems to have a two-stage approach to needs analysis:

1 find out what the learner needs to know;
2 teach it.

A more valid model, in my view, would have four stages:

1 find out what the learner needs to know;
2 find out what he or she knows already;
3 subtract the second from the first;
4 teach the remainder.

Conclusion

Teachers do not always appreciate how much new approaches owe to speculation and theory, and how little they are based on proven facts. We actually know hardly anything about how languages are learnt, and as a result we are driven to rely, in our teaching, on a pre-scientific mixture of speculation, common sense, and the insights derived from experience. Like eighteenth-century doctors, we work largely by hunch, concealing our ignorance under a screen of pseudo-science and jargon. Speculation, common sense, and experience do not necessarily provide a bad basis to operate on, in the absence of anything better, and somehow our students do manage to learn languages. However, the lack of a solid empirical 'anchor' of established knowledge about language learning makes us very vulnerable to shifts in intellectual fashion. A novel piece of speculation can have an effect out of all proportion to its value, especially since the purveyors of new doctrines are rarely as humble or as tentative as the situation merits. As the theoretical pendulum swings from one extreme to the other, each exaggeration is followed by its opposite. We realize that we have been translating too much, so translation is banned completely. Grammar explanations are seen to have been over-valued, so grammar explanations are swept away. Generation A spends half its time doing structure drills; for generation B, structure drills are anathema. Contrastive studies promise the moon and the stars; when the moon and the stars are slow to arrive, contrastive studies disappear from syllabus design as if they had never been. One approach fails to give sufficient importance to phonetics, or modal verbs, or functions; the next approach does nothing but phonetics, teaches modal verbs for thirty minutes a day, or announces that functions are more important than grammar, vocabulary, and pronunciation put together. Arguments for the current view are invariably highly speculative, extremely plausible, and advanced with tenacious conviction; if one looks back fifteen years, one can see that the arguments for the previous approach (now totally discredited) were equally speculative, just as persuasive, and put forward with the same insistence that 'this time we've got it right'. Each time this happens, the poor language teacher is told to junk a large part of his or her repertoire of materials, activities, and methods (because these are no longer scientific) and to replace them by a gleaming new battery of up-to-date apparatus and techniques. The students, as a rule, learn about as much as before.

It is characteristic of the Communicative Approach to assess utterances not so much on the basis of their propositional meaning as in terms of their pragmatic value. We should perhaps apply this criterion to the Communicative Approach itself. As with a religion, it may be more sensible to ask, not 'Is it true?', but 'What good does it do?' This is not a difficult question to answer. The Communicative Approach has directed our attention to the importance of other aspects of language besides propositional meaning, and helped us to analyse and teach the language of interaction. At the same time, it has encouraged a methodology which relies less on mechanical teacher-centered practice and more on the simulation of real-life exchanges. All this is very valuable, and even if (as with religions) there is a good deal of confusion on the theoretical side, it is difficult not to feel that we are teaching better than we used to. By and large, we have probably gained more than we have lost from the Communicative Approach.

In the same way, we shall probably benefit from the next language teaching revolution, especially if we can keep our heads, recognize dogma for what it is, and try out the new techniques without giving up useful older methods simply because they have been 'proved wrong'. (The characteristic sound of a new breakthrough in language teaching theory is a scream, a splash, and a strangled cry, as once again the baby is thrown out with the bathwater.) Above all, we must try not to expect too much. New insights can certainly help us to teach more systematically and effectively, but it is probably an illusion to expect any really striking progress in language teaching until we know a great deal more about how foreign languages are learnt. For the moment, talk of 'revolution' simply does the profession a disservice, raising hopes that cannot be fulfilled, and soliciting an investment of time and money which is out of all proportion to the return which can realistically be expected from the new methods. (It is a shock to realize that, after more than ten very expensive years of 'communicative' teaching, we cannot prove that a single student has a more effective command of English than if he or she had learnt the language by different methods twenty years earlier. Our research depends to an uncomfortable degree on faith.) The Communicative Approach, whatever its virtues, is not really in any sense a revolution. In retrospect, it is likely to be seen as little more than an interesting ripple on the surface of twentieth-century language teaching.

Note

1 The examination leading to the Royal Society of Arts Diploma in TEFL.

The exchange

'Against dogma': A reply to Michael Swan by H. G. Widdowson

(Originally published in *ELT Journal* Volume 39/3 July 1985.)

Michael Swan's two articles are admirably provocative pieces, eloquently written and stimulating to read. This much should be acknowledged. It should be noted, however, that they are not to be read as dispassionate criticism of a careful analytic kind. They are, rather, an indictment, charged with feeling, almost as if Swan felt that the ideas he opposes were a personal affront. And the desire to have a dig at theorists and to pander to anti-intellectual prejudice at times reduces the discussion to farce. So with reference to their title, these papers are 'critical' only in the sense of being captious: they are not evaluative. Nevertheless, they do indicate areas of misunderstanding and misconception, and as such warrant a reply.

Dogma and enquiry

The first point I should like to make is a very general one about the purpose of intellectual enquiry. The ideas that have been put forward concerning a communicative approach to language teaching do not, as Swan himself acknowledges, constitute a 'coherent and monolithic body of doctrine', nor were they intended as a manifesto for revolutionary change. They cannot by definition therefore be a dogma. Swan represents them as such in order to make a better target for attack. This is, to say the least, regrettable, because these ideas were proposed (for the most part) in the spirit of positive enquiry and were intended to encourage teachers not to reject customary practices out of hand and embrace a new creed, but on the contrary to subject these practices and proposals to critical (i.e. evaluative, not captious) assessment. So the intention behind the enquiry was to act *against* the dogmatism of doctrine whether new or old, revolutionary or reactionary. Its purpose was to provoke, not to persuade; to liberate thought, not to confine it by the imposition of fixed ideas. Perhaps I might be permitted to give two quotations from my own work to correct the quite false impression of doctrinaire assertion that Swan, for some reason, wishes to convey:

> This book is not in any way intended as propaganda for a new 'communicative' orthodoxy in language teaching. It is, on the contrary, an appeal for critical investigation into the basis of a belief and its practical implications. I am not trying to present a conclusive case but to start an enquiry.
> (Widdowson 1978: x)

> Above all we must deny ourselves the comfort of dogma which deals in the delusion of simple answers.
> (Widdowson 1979: 262)

My reason for drawing attention to this misrepresentation is not (principally) to express my resentment at unfair treatment, but to point to a consequence which nullifies much of Swan's own argument. For the effect of creating a dogma on which to practise his polemic is that he is led into contradiction by committing precisely the same error that he unjustly attributes to the approach he is criticizing. What he does is to dismiss one set of ideas as if they constituted a single dogmatic creed, but then replace them with a dogma of his own. Again, as Swan might himself put it, we hear a strangled cry as the communicative baby this time disappears down the plughole.

Questions arising

What the Swan dogma amounts to essentially, it would seem, is a reassertion of the traditional view that what learners need to be taught is grammar, lexis, and a collection of idiomatic phrases: their effective use for communicative purposes can be left for them to work out for themselves by reference to common sense and the experience they have of using their own language. Ideas about use and usage, the realization of appropriate meaning, communicative strategies, negotiation, and so on that all these theorists prattle about in their impenetrable jargon are so much moonshine and nothing more. One can almost see the groundlings rolling in the aisles with glee. This dogma is then itself directly contradicted by other remarks in the two articles. Swan talks approvingly, for example, about the teaching of notions and functions: 'We must make sure our students are taught to operate key functions such as, for instance, greeting, agreeing or warning'. But why should this be necessary if the function of an utterance (use) can always be inferred by a common-sense association of sentence meaning (usage) and situation, as has previously been claimed, and, in the case of warning, so amusingly (if tendentiously) demonstrated by the anecdote of Wilberforce and his accomplices? And if Swan accepts that functions need to be taught as aspects of language other than structure and lexis, how does he propose that this should be done in a principled way without invoking the ideas about use and usage he has so summarily dismissed? Again, Swan tells us that we need 'to make sure that our students are trained to become fluent in whatever aspects of speaking, understanding, reading and writing relate to their purposes'. But, according to the dogma, students already know how to do these things: all they need is a knowledge of English structures and lexis and these abilities will come of their own accord. So why do they need any training? Why indeed do we need to bother with teaching these abilities at all?

Again we are told that one of the reasons for poor performance at classroom comprehension tasks may be that 'the learner's command of the language is just fluent enough for him to decode the words, but this occupies all his faculties and he has no processing capacity to spare for "interpreting" what he hears'. But how is this possible if the ability to understand, that is to say to provide language items with appropriate communicative value in context, follows automatically from a knowledge of language combined with the skills the learner has already acquired from the experience of using his own mother tongue? According to the dogma which denies any relevance to the use/usage distinction, decoding and interpreting should not be different processes at all. Fluency (whatever Swan might mean by this) in the one ought not to be distinct from fluency in the other. This problem of poor performance may also, we are told, be caused by the fact that the learners 'have been trained to read classroom texts in such a different way from "real-life" texts that they are unable to regard them as pieces of communication'. But how can this be? If they know the language, why can't they automatically apply this knowledge?

And what, anyway, does it mean to say that learners treat texts in a 'different way'? How then is this distinct from regarding them as 'pieces of communication'? These questions can be clarified by reference to the concepts of cohesion and coherence and strategies of prediction and negotiation, but this kind of 'jargon' is inadmissible, so all we are left with is a befuddled vagueness which, to use Swan's own expression, 'contributes nothing to our understanding of how to teach foreign languages'. We are told that the inability of learners to regard texts as pieces of communication is the result of poor methodology and that 'the solution involves changing what happens in the classroom, not what happens in the student'. What exactly is it that might lead us to assess one methodology as poor, another good? What sort of change in the classroom is called for? And anyway what is the point, we might ask, of changing what happens in the classroom unless it brings about changes in the student?

Questions of this kind (in so far as they make sense) need careful and *theoretical* consideration. They cannot be resolved by bland statement. Repeatedly we find in these articles assertions about teaching and learning which can be justified, or indeed understood, only by reference to the kind of idea that Swan ridicules with such relish. And not infrequently, as we have seen, such assertions actually presuppose the validity of these ideas even when they are intended to undermine them.

Approve with care

Elsewhere, what Swan conceives of as 'the communicative approach' is favoured with approving comment. It has, we are told, 'many virtues'. What are they then? It has 'new information and insights to contribute (for instance about the language of social interaction)'. What new information and what new insights? At times, Swan seems to suppose that the language of social interaction simply means the 'stereotyped, idiomatic side of language' to be learned as a collection of 'conventional and idiomatic expressions' of the kind provided by a notional/functional inventory. Even a cursory glance at the literature on the pragmatics of language use would disabuse him of such a simplistic notion. But then pragmatics, depending as it does on recognizing a distinction between usage and use, 'has little relevance to foreign language teaching' and is anyway 'grossly over-valued at the moment'. The communicative approach is, again, given credit for 'enormous improvements in our methodology'. 'Methodology is perhaps the area where the Communicative Approach has done most to improve our teaching'. What exactly are these improvements? On what principles are they based? And how have they come about, if they are based on ideas that are apparently so defective in theory and irrelevant in practice?

Unreasoned approval of the 'communicative approach' is no better than unreasoned condemnation. What we need is clear thinking and explicit, well-informed argument of the kind which Swan conspicuously fails to provide. He fails to provide it because he is more interested in attacking the 'communicative approach' than in seeking to understand and assess it, and so finds it convenient to invent a distorted version so as to present his own views more effectively. These views are represented as being in opposition to the ideas about communicative language teaching. But many of them, particularly those put forward in the second paper, have already been explored in relation to these ideas, although Swan, by ignorance or design, fails to acknowledge the fact. His discussion about the use of authentic data, for example, and the classroom replication of reality has long since been anticipated by others pursuing the implications of a communicative approach. Similarly there has long been a recognition of the importance of grammar and lexis and the need to teach them as an essential communicative resource. The difference is that these matters have been treated as issues to be thought out and not just pronounced upon. Most of those who have given any systematic consideration to the effective teaching of grammar, for example, would wish to question the proposal for a *separate* treatment of the formal and functional aspects of language which Swan (not very humbly or tentatively, I may say) puts forward with such apparent conviction:

> Simplifying somewhat, one might say that there are two kinds of language: 'stereotyped' and 'creative'. Semantic syllabuses are needed to help us teach the first; only structural/lexical syllabuses will enable us to teach the second.

This statement, we should note, presupposes both a theory of language and a theory of pedagogy. The least we might expect is that such theoretical presuppositions should be made as explicit as possible so that they can be brought out into the open and debated.

Of course it is more comfortable (and convenient) to deny the validity of theoretical enquiry and instead make easy appeals to prejudice in the name of experience and common sense. But if we claim that our activities have any professional status, then we have to accept the need for a careful appraisal of the principles upon which they are based. And this must require the exercise of intellectual analysis and critical evaluation not as specialist or elite activities, but ones which are intrinsic to the whole practical pedagogic enterprise. Naturally there are risks involved: ideas can be inconsistent or ill-conceived;

they may be misunderstood or misapplied; they may induce doubt. Some of us believe that such risks are worth taking. For others the delusion of simple answers will always be available as an attractive alternative to thought.

Michael Swan's response to Henry Widdowson's 'Against dogma'
(Originally published in *ELT Journal* Volume 39/4 October 1985, 'Correspondence'.)

I was disappointed by Professor Widdowson's reply, in the July 1985 issue of *ELT Journal*, to my articles on the Communicative Approach (*ELT Journal* 39/1, 39/2). I had hoped, in these articles, to stimulate rational debate on the ideas underlying the Communicative Approach. Up to a point, I should not have been sorry to have my arguments disproved, since the process would at least have led to a gain in clarity regarding the issues involved. These questions (whether 'rules of use' can be taught, how far we really need to teach communication skills and strategies, how meaning categories should be incorporated in syllabuses, how far the classroom should simulate 'real life') are not only of academic importance. A great deal of time and money is invested in current approaches to language teaching and learning, and the more clearly we understand what we are doing, the less likely we are to waste these precious resources. Professor Widdowson begins his reply by attempting to disqualify my arguments on the grounds that the style is inappropriate, the motives discreditable, and the approach intellectually unsatisfactory. The articles, he says, are not 'dispassionate criticism of a careful analytic kind'; they are 'an indictment, charged with feeling', written out of a 'desire to have a dig at theorists and to pander to anti-intellectual prejudice', to get the 'groundlings rolling in the aisles'. They are 'captious ... not evaluative'; they misrepresent the views they oppose 'in order to make a better target for attack'. In the articles I 'deny the validity of theoretical enquiry', he asserts, 'and instead make easy appeals to prejudice in the name of experience and common sense', seduced by the 'delusion of simple answers' which 'will always be available as an attractive alternative to thought'.

Professor Widdowson's dispassionate evaluative criticism does not confine itself to the generalizations quoted above. He also attempts to come to terms with some of the detailed arguments which I put forward in my articles (in the belief, I may say, that I was engaging in valid theoretical enquiry). Unfortunately, with a few exceptions, he either misrepresents my arguments or fails to understand them. This is no doubt because I have not made myself clear. I cannot deal here with all of the misinterpretations involved, but I should like to clarify (or reclarify) my position on three central issues:

1 I do not reassert the traditional view 'that what learners need to be taught is grammar, lexis, and a collection of idiomatic phrases: their effective use for communicative purposes can be left for them to work out for themselves by reference to common sense and the experience they have of using their

own language'. This is nowhere stated or implied in my articles. I take some trouble to discuss the integration of form and meaning in syllabus design and teaching, on [*ELTJ* 39/2] pages 79–80 and elsewhere.

2 As far as the teaching of meaning is concerned, I claim that rules can only be taught where there exist conventional associations between language items and meanings (as in the use of *Look out!* to warn, *Do you mind if…?* in requests, and so on). Where no such conventional association exists, I argue that no rule can be taught; the illocutionary force of an utterance will then be determined uniquely by the context (as with the use of *I'm cold* to mean *Please shut the window*). In suggesting, rightly or wrongly, that there are two different cases involved here—those where we can teach rules and those where we cannot—I am not contradicting myself, as Professor Widdowson claims, though I am certainly contradicting a commonly-held view about the existence of 'rules of communication' or 'rules of use'. Professor Widdowson's failure to grasp this point reveals a good deal about the confusion underlying his own position on the question of 'use' and 'usage'.

3 In my discussion of skills and strategies, I maintain that some mother-tongue communication skills can be transferred to a foreign language without needing to be taught (such as the ability to predict), while others cannot be so transferred (the ability to speak fluently is an obvious example). Again, Professor Widdowson claims to see a contradiction. If he believes either that all mother-tongue skills are automatically transferred to foreign language competence, or that none are, I think he should produce evidence for his unusual view.

Not everything Professor Widdowson says in his reply is mistaken. In particular, I believe that he is to some extent justified in complaining that my accusations of dogmatism are unfair. I also accept his criticisms of my discussion of the communicative attitude to authentic materials and classroom 'replication of reality'. It is clear, too, that the strongly polemic tone of my articles has upset him, and I must take some responsibility for this. However, I do not think that his response to what I say has greatly advanced our grasp of the issues involved. By dismissing serious and detailed theoretical arguments as 'easy appeals to prejudice', and by rejecting wholesale all criticism of his and his colleagues' views, Professor Widdowson has shown a profound reluctance to modify his intellectual position, or to admit that he might at times be wrong. At the end of his article, he says '… if we claim that our activities have any professional status, then we have to accept the need for a careful appraisal of the principles upon which they are based'. It is a pity that, when faced with an opportunity to carry out such an appraisal, Professor Widdowson turned it down.

Henry Widdowson to Michael Swan 2011: 'Against dogma': an afterword

The editors of a volume that included an earlier reprint of this exchange (Rossner and Bolitho 1990) describe my response as 'an angry paper', and so it was. I was provoked by what seemed to me to be an intention to dismiss ideas by ridicule rather than to give them the serious attention I thought they deserved. It was no doubt this that prevented me from giving the points that Michael Swan raised in his articles the 'careful appraisal' that he refers to in his letter. But as I saw it, the way these points were raised did not itself amount to careful appraisal and so did not warrant one. Twenty-five years on and with the anger long since faded, I can now focus on these points without being distracted by the manner in which they are made. As he says, he would not express himself in the same way today, and nor would I.

But to matters of substance and the points themselves. In my 1978 book that Michael cites I argue the need for teachers to take into account not only how the encoded properties of language are manifested but how they are realized as communicative use. *How* they take it into account is another matter. It certainly does not imply the explicit teaching of 'rules of use' and I do not suggest that it does. What I do suggest is that relating linguistic form to communicative function associates the language being learned with the learners' own linguistic experience whereas too exclusive a focus on form has a dissociating effect and makes the foreign language more foreign. A quotation that Michael might have cited to indicate my position would be:

> By effectively denying the learner reference to his own experience the teacher increases the difficulty of the language learning task. A methodology which concentrates too exclusively on usage may well be creating the very problems which it is designed to solve.
> (Widdowson 1978:18)

As Michael says 'Foreigners have mother tongues: they know as much as we do about how human beings communicate'. Very true—there is no disagreement about that. But the issue is how such knowledge can be most effectively activated in learners. Michael seemed to argue that learners would automatically activate it for themselves and no pedagogic inducement was called for. The crucial issue he raises here for language teaching, or for the teaching of anything if it comes to that, is what makes for the most effective pedagogic investment: what needs to be taught and what can, and can only, be left for learners to learn for themselves. I do not think that activation will just happen and I see it as the primary purpose of language pedagogy to create activating conditions by contriving ways of getting learners to realize the foreign language by relating it to their own linguistic experience. One way of doing this that I propose in my 1978 book is 'to associate the teaching of a foreign language with topics drawn from other subjects' which are customarily taught through the medium of the mother tongue—a proposal that anticipates the currently fashionable approach that goes under the name of CLIL. Another is to give overt recognition to the covert presence of the mother tongue in the classroom in the form of translation activities—another proposal that is now beginning to enjoy new found pedagogic favour.

Whether these proposals would have found favour with Michael in 1985, I do not know. Although they are intrinsic to the case for a communicative approach that I outline, he does not refer to them. They are exemplified in the last chapter of the book by various task-based activities, in which chapter I again make it clear that I am making the case to stimulate critical debate about principles not to promote 'a whole new approach'. I also concede that:

> It may be that many of my conclusions will turn out to be mistaken in the light of actual teaching experience.
> (Widdowson 1978:162)

I took particular care to be tentative, which is why I was offended at the suggestion that I was dogmatic. But that was a quarter of a century ago. Since then, though I know there are still areas of disagreement between Michael and me, they are no longer the site of adversarial confrontation. We have both mellowed with age, we have got to know each other, we have worked together, and these days we exchange poems. The past is another country and we did things differently there.

References

Rossner, R. and **R. Bolitho.** 1990. *Currents of Change in English Language Teaching.* Oxford University Press.

Widdowson, H. G. 1978. *Teaching Language as Communication.* Oxford University Press.

3
Where is the language going?

(Originally published in *English Today* 3, July–September 1985.)

In a small way, this article anticipated later discussions of English as a Lingua Franca.

> Lord Airedale (L) said there was no question that if there was to be a world language it would be English, but whether it would be English English or American English was uncertain. He was prejudiced in favour of English English.
> The Americans, although they economised a little in their spelling, undid this good work by always preferring the longer word to the shorter.
> An Englishman left his flat by the lift and got into his car to go and see a film.
> An American left his apartment by the elevator and got into his automobile to go and see a motion picture.
> Lord Kings Norton (Ind) said that to develop brevity and preciseness was more important than to reform spelling. They should start rather than commence, leave and not depart and spit rather than expectorate. Anglo-Saxon since 1066 had been neglected. When new words had been needed they had built on Norman-French and Latin. The result of the Battle of Hastings dealt a blow to brevity from which the English language had never recovered. It was time they went back to 1065.
> Viscount Barrington (L) said it was not so easy to simplify the language as people thought. As the language went out into the world it was important that it should not only remain a language, but remain English.
> Lord Davies of Leek (L) said he did not think there was a child today who could parse or analyse. They could not tell a preposition from a leg of pork.
> (From a debate in the House of Lords on January 27, 1981, reported in *The Times* of London)

The noble lords' view of the future of the language contains two main ideas:

1 English is going to the dogs. This is due to the decline of grammar teaching, and to the sinister influence of alien cultures (Latin, Norman-French, American). We must fight to preserve our language, and restore it to an earlier state of (Anglo-Saxon?) purity.
2 English belongs to us. We must not lose control of it as it becomes a world language. If, despite all our efforts, we cannot stop English going to the dogs, let us at least ensure that the dogs are of a traditional British breed.

Many people hold views of this kind (though not always in such a crude form). How reasonable are they?

Whenever new or foreign cultural influences are strong, people tend to become uneasy about the way these influences are reflected in language. Renaissance literature contains frequent criticisms of the contemporary fashion for using French and Italian words. Spenser complained in *The Shepherd's Calendar* that 'now they have made our English tongue a gallimaufry or hodgepodge of all other speeches'. In *Romeo and Juliet*, Mercutio comments scathingly on Tybalt's affected way of speaking:

> The pox of such antick, lisping, affecting fantasticoes, these new tuners of accents! ... Why, is not this a lamentable thing, grandsire, that we should be thus afflicted with these strange flies, these fashion-mongers, these *pardonnez-mois*, who stand so much on their new form that they cannot sit at ease on the old bench? Oh, their *bons*, their *bons*!

Today, of course, British English is changing under the influence not of a foreign language, but of another variety of English. For half a century British people have been exposed to American speech through the cinema, radio, and television, so that we are all, at least receptively, British-American bilinguals. Although anti-American attitudes are not uncommon in Britain, American English enjoys generally high prestige here, both because of the political and economic power of the United States, and because of America's dominance of the cinema and the popular music industry. People tend to imitate the usage of high-prestige speakers, in order to associate themselves with values that they admire and thus gain status. So it is not really surprising that British people (especially younger people) often try to sound like Americans. The other day, I heard a teenager referring to a friend of hers, in a strong Oxfordshire accent, with the words 'He thinks he's a real cool dude'. (Despite my carefully cultivated descriptive linguist's neutral non-moralistic stance, I have to admit that this made me twitch a little.) And of course, many British popular singers use an American accent when performing: it seems somehow more appropriate.

When people deplore changes in their language, they are in fact nearly always worried about something else. If a man writes to *The Times* complaining about the way another man uses *hopefully*, he is obviously not simply concerned about a trivial change in usage (to which he does not in any case need to conform himself). When a mother tells her daughter to say *as if* instead of *like*, it is not just a grammatical detail that is involved. A social critic who attacks the way advertising debases the language, a feminist who complains that English is male-dominated, or a political commentator who objects to the military use of the word *pacification* to mean 'killing everybody in sight'—such people are worried about more than linguistic questions. What is at issue here, of course, is the belief that language embodies important social values, and that changes in one involve changes in the other. This seems to lead many people to feel—mistakenly—that they can prevent or bring about social change if only they can control its linguistic expression.

Languages tend to look after themselves, despite interference from Academies, teachers and people who write to the newspapers. If English had really been going to the dogs since 1066, it would have arrived there centuries ago. In fact, regardless of all the changes that it has undergone, the language is basically what it always has been, and what any language is—a reasonably efficient means of communication which is wide and flexible enough to serve the multifarious and contradictory purposes of its users. If standards are dropping in some areas—so that, for instance, schoolchildren no longer spell or write as well as they used to—this is not necessarily because English is decaying. It may simply be because priorities are being revised. Whether we like it or not, the nature of communication is changing, so that correct spelling and writing are less important then they used to be for most people, while other uses of language (for instance speaking on the telephone, computer programming) have become much more important. Teaching children to parse is unlikely to reverse the process.

Nobody can stop language change, though when the forces of linguistic conservatism are powerful and society is static it may slow down somewhat. So (assuming its speakers survive), British English will be rather different in two or three hundred years. In what ways? Nobody can really tell where the language is going, of course; but one can make informed guesses about at least some aspects. Here are a few modest predictions:

- British English will continue to be influenced by other high-prestige varieties of English, and by culturally and politically influential foreign languages. In the short term, at least, it will become more Americanised.
- The influence of the present southern British standard and of 'received pronunciation' inside Britain will continue to decline, and a new standard will emerge, perhaps based partly on working-class speech from the south-east ('Estuary English').
- Writing will become less important. Literary usage will no longer be regarded as an ideal to which other forms of the language should aspire, and the influence of writing on speech will diminish.
- The grammatical system will go on tidying itself up in small ways. The battle between *like* and *as (if)* will be won by *like*, *shall* will disappear as a first-person future auxiliary; *whom* will become obsolete. The complex distinctions between the present perfect and past tenses, and between the various structures used for talking about the future, may break down, and the lines may be redrawn more simply. Conditional sentences may come

Where is the language going? 39

to be regularly constructed with 'parallel' verb forms, as already happens quite often in speech (*If I'd have known, I'd have told you*). Changes are possible in other areas where English grammar is complex and unstable: for instance, the distinctions between *can*, *may* and *might*, and between *must* and *have to*; adverb position; article usage; adjective order; relative clauses. And the problem of our 'sexist' personal pronouns (we have no simple way of saying *he* or *she*) may finally solve itself.
- Vocabulary will change as social and technological progress provides new things to talk about. However, there will still be fierce arguments about 'correct' usage, and people in the year 2200 will bitterly condemn ways of speaking which were not current in 2180; by 2220, many of these will be well established in the standard language.
- Older people will still resist linguistic development; younger people will still recreate the language in their own way; the balance between the two forces will result, as usual, in a manageable rate of change.

Whatever happens to British English, it is unlikely to be widely used for international communication in centuries to come. We cannot of course be sure that any variety of English will perform this function. There are certain to be great political changes—and perhaps catastrophic wars—over the next few hundred years. If we could come back in the year 2200, we might for instance find the whole world speaking a variety of Chinese; or it might turn out that developments in automatic translation had made a world language completely unnecessary.

The most likely scenario, though (at least in the short term), shows English serving as the vehicle of international communication. What kind of English will this be? My tentative guess is that it will be a greatly modified derivative of American English. English is already widely used, for instance, by Japanese to sell cars to Turks, by Venezuelans to communicate with Chinese engineers, by scientists from all over the world to talk to each other at conferences. As this kind of use expands, we could see the development of a standard simplified language which will have shed many of the phonological and grammatical complexities that make present-day English difficult to learn. British and American English have an inconveniently large inventory of vowel distinctions (southern British has 21); we might expect the new international English to get by with fewer. This could, however, create an uncomfortable number of homophones (imagine *had*, *head*, *hard* and *heard* all being pronounced the same), and grammatical devices (such as part-of-speech markers) might develop to reduce the confusion. Verbal grammar might be greatly simplified, with *do* disappearing from questions and negatives, and our complex battery of tenses being reduced to a three-tense system.

What about the various local varieties of English which exist today? Will they converge, diverge, or be replaced by the hypothetical new international standard? One possibility is that cultural differences will be reflected in linguistic divergence, so that for instance Indian English, Nigerian English, and Singapore English will develop independently, getting further and further away from each other and from the 'white English' of Britain, North America, Australia, and New Zealand, until we end up not with different varieties of English but with different languages.

So the final picture might be not unlike what happened in the Middle Ages in Southern Europe, where one form of Latin evolved into a number of highly differentiated regional languages, while at the same time another form of Latin served as a vehicle for international communication.

And if, in those far-off days, British people find themselves teaching English as a foreign language, things will not be so easy for them as they are today. Because the chances are that the kind of English they are called on to teach will be a foreign language for *them* too.

4
The textbook: bridge or wall?

(Originally published in *Applied Linguistics and Language Teaching* 2/1, 1992.)

This article has been quoted more than once in support of the idea that teachers should reject textbooks and produce their own custom-made courses for their students. This is not at all what I believe. I am critical of bad or unsuitable textbooks, and I believe that any textbook needs adaptation and supplementation to make it appropriate for a particular group of students. However, producing full-scale language courses is a complex, demanding, and highly-skilled job. As I argue in a later article, to expect a practising teacher to do this is like expecting the first violinist to compose the orchestra's repertoire in his or her spare time.

> Oh, cuckoo! Shall I call thee bird
> Or but a wandering voice?
> State the alternative preferred.
> Give reasons for your choice.
> (F. H. Townsend)

I once watched a lesson whose declared aim was to present and practise the meaning and use of six words. They were not words whose meaning was particularly elusive or context-bound, and left to themselves the students in the class could probably have learnt them in five or ten minutes. Needless to say, the students were not left to themselves; instead, they were required to read a text in which the six new words were embedded. (As we all know, vocabulary should always be contextualized.) The text was not easy, and it naturally slowed the students down somewhat: without the teacher's help, the time needed to do the careful reading required and learn the new words was probably something of the order of twenty-five minutes. However, the teacher did help, using her well-practised technique for 'going through' texts. And so a piece of work that should have occupied ten minutes took fifty. The textbook, originally conceived as a bridge across which information about vocabulary would travel, had turned into a wall, with the teacher and her knowledge on one side and the students on the other.

Of course, the students in the lesson in question did not just learn six words. There were a certain number of side-benefits from the teacher's decision to use a text as her presentation vehicle. The students got whatever you get out of intensive reading—some more contact with written English, perhaps a bit more vocabulary and grammar, and possibly (just possibly) a slight improvement in their reading skills. And as the teacher did her 'going through the text' number, they had practice in listening comprehension. What they did not get, unfortunately, was fifty minutes' worth of well-focused cost-effective work on anything.

I am not, obviously, questioning the value of text-based teaching. Texts, like garlic, gypsy violins, sparking plugs, or anything else, are all right in their place, and indeed it would be very difficult to teach without them. The trouble is that if we are not careful they take over. Instead of using a text, where appropriate, as a vehicle for the presentation and practice of particular language items or skills, it is all too easy to shift one's focus and to treat the text as a destination, 'going through' it as if this were a valuable enterprise by definition, regardless of any possible result. As so often in language teaching, the activity tends to take over from the aim, and we end up doing things instead of teaching things.

The very name of our central piece of teaching material—textbook—betrays the superstitious reverence that so many educational systems have for texts. Perhaps this is because texts have traditionally functioned as the repository of the wisdom of the past, society's prime means of cultural transmission, and its source of religious instruction. Be that as it may, texts are the classic presentation vehicle for new language, and most textbook lessons still start automatically with a story, dialogue, newspaper article, literary extract, or some other text, followed, as day is followed by night, by questions. (I have often wondered why a teaching text always has to have questions with it. And why do teachers ask so many questions anyway? Watch six-year-olds playing schools. The one playing the teacher keeps asking questions, and gets cross because the others don't know the answers. That's what teachers do, isn't it? There is something deeply sinister about this.) It is, of course, possible to present new language without texts in very many interesting ways, and it is possible to use texts constructively without asking any questions at all; but I am not optimistic about progress in this area. Like death and taxes, texts and questions will always be with us.

The danger with ready-made textbooks is that they seem to absolve teachers of responsibility. Instead of participating in the day-to-day decisions that have to be made about what to teach and how to teach it, it is easy to just sit back and operate the system, secure in the knowledge that the wise and virtuous people who produced the textbook knew what was good for us. Unfortunately this is rarely the case. Even with the best teaching materials it is an inefficient approach—no coursebook contains exactly what is required for a particular individual or class. And textbooks are sometimes a very long way indeed from reflecting the needs and interests of one's students.

The textbook: bridge or wall? 43

I have always been interested in the image of the learner that is reflected by the distorting mirror of the textbook. Texts, after all, tell you a lot about what kind of people the writers think their readers are. And educational texts also tell you what the writers—or the system they work in—are prepared to allow the readers to be, say, and do. It can be instructive to write down the four or five things one thinks secondary school students are most interested in—the things they talk about among themselves when teachers and parents aren't listening—and then to check how many of these topics are touched on in their textbooks. Do the students get to read and talk about sex, human relationships, fairness, or conflicts with authority, for example—things that most adolescents are passionately interested in—or does the book give an unrelieved diet of safe bland topics like sport, pop music, and travel? Are students allowed to tell the truth—can they say whether or not they are interested in the topic of the lesson, or what they think about school—or does the book only leave room for good conformist people to say good conformist things?

Elementary textbooks with storylines are often an extreme case of refusal to deal with reality. All too frequently, the learner—even the adult learner—is treated as a retarded child who will only learn if he/she is constantly entertained by silly jokes, accompanied by those dreadful ELT illustrators' pictures of funny fat men with big noses. (I have nothing against humour, if it is successful—it makes a very important contribution to class dynamics and motivation. But of course in general the best classroom humour comes from the students, not from the book.) Even where fiction-based course material is less deliberately silly, it is often desperately bland. In the language textbooks I grew up with, none of the characters ever got seriously unhappy or worried, felt unfairly treated, was desperately poor or homeless; nobody fell deeply in love, felt homicidally jealous, got badly hurt in a relationship; nobody burst into tears without knowing why or started singing because the sky looked so beautiful; nobody had a serious accident, go an incurable illness or died. (All of that was left for the literature lesson, which had its own highly sophisticated techniques for disinfecting reality.)

A woman I knew who was teaching adults in Denmark with one of those elementary books worked bravely through Lessons 1 to 4 ('Bill comes to London', 'A day on the river', 'Bill and Alice go to the cinema' and 'Alice gets a new job'). When she reached Lesson 5, however, ('Tea at Alice's house') something snapped, and she got her students to rewrite the episode on the basis that halfway through the tea-party Alice announces, to the consternation of Bill and her parents, that she is pregnant. The students had a wonderful time adapting the language of the episode to the new situation: they dramatized it in groups, performed it for each other, and fell about laughing. From then on the class never looked back. They had done exactly what one should always do with unsuitable teaching materials: instead of respecting the textbook as something engraved on tablets of stone, they saw it as a vehicle that wasn't going where they wanted it to, and simply hijacked it to a more suitable destination.

There are fewer dull courses around these days, and many modern courses contain interesting and motivating material, with good texts, attractive visuals, and well-chosen recordings. Paradoxically, however, interesting materials can be dangerous precisely because they are, in one sense, so good. It is important to remember that the textbook must not only be good itself; it must leave room for the learners to be good too. There is something deeply unsatisfactory about the kind of lesson which starts with a fanfare of trumpets, so to speak (as the teacher, the recording, or the book does something exciting), and finishes with a flabby deflating sound (as the students do something much less exciting like answering comprehension questions or filling in prepositions). In the race for who is going to be best at English, the students are bound to come last, a long way after the book, the recordings, and the teacher. If they always come last, as well, in the race for who is going to be most interesting, they are unlikely ever to develop much confidence or independence. The best lessons are those in which the book may do something interesting, but the students end up by doing something even more interesting, as they use their newly-learnt language to inform, amuse, entertain, persuade, or even move each other. And really good textbooks make this possible: instead of erecting walls between teacher and student, student and student, student and language, human beings and the world, they build bridges across which creative movement is possible and even easy. In the end, it is not what the textbook does that matters, in itself—it is what the learners do.

5
Design criteria for pedagogic language rules

(Originally published in *Grammar and the Language Teacher* (eds.) Bygate, Tonkyn and Williams. Prentice Hall/Pearson Education Ltd., 1994.)

After spending 20 years or so trying to write explanations of the unconscious rules we follow when we use language, I found myself wondering what unconscious rules I was following myself as I drafted my explanations. This article is the result.

Introduction: pedagogic and non-pedagogic rules

In this paper, I shall discuss the characteristics which distinguish pedagogic language rules from other kinds of language rule. By 'pedagogic rules' I mean rules which are designed to help foreign-language learners understand particular aspects of the languages they are studying (whether these rules are addressed directly to the learners, or to teachers and materials writers who are expected to pass on the rules to the learners in one form or another, is immaterial). I shall refer to a collection of such rules, unoriginally, as a 'pedagogic grammar'. This term can also reasonably be applied to a collection of rules designed for students who are learning about the structure of their own language, and much of what shall I have to say is relevant to mother-tongue language instruction.

'Pedagogic' rules can be more or less pedagogic. At one extreme, we can conceive (with some idealisation) of a rule designed for one specific learner, whose background, stage of development and preferred learning styles are all known. (This is the kind of rule that a good teacher might aim to give to an individual student.) Such a rule would probably be very different from a standard reference grammar's description of the same linguistic facts. At the other extreme is the type of broad-spectrum rule which one might find in a pedagogic grammar designed for teachers and advanced students from a variety of backgrounds; rules of this kind do not always differ in many respects from the equivalent non-pedagogic descriptions.

Implicit in this discussion is the belief that pedagogic rules can be useful to language learners. The question is notoriously a controversial one: it is of

46 *Thinking about Language Teaching*

course possible that teaching language rules contributes nothing to learners' development. This issue is, however, outside the scope of my paper.

Six criteria

Assuming, then, for the sake of argument, that language rules are useful to learners, good rules must be more useful than bad rules. But what makes a 'good' rule? I believe that one can identify at least six 'design criteria' for pedagogic language rules: truth, demarcation, clarity, simplicity, conceptual parsimony and relevance. (Not all of these terms are transparent, but I hope that the following discussion will make it clear what I mean by them.) The first three criteria are relevant to any kind of rule, while the others are especially important to the design of pedagogic rules. Some of them overlap; none the less, I feel that they are sufficiently distinct to merit separate consideration. Not all of them are compatible; indeed, I shall argue that some of the criteria necessarily conflict.

Truth

Rules should be true

It is obviously desirable to tell learners the truth. However, as Oscar Wilde said, the truth is rarely pure and never simple: it can be difficult to be sure exactly what the facts are, and to decide how much of the truth to tell. This criterion, therefore, is likely to conflict with others, and one will often need to compromise with truth for the sake of clarity, simplicity, conceptual parsimony or relevance. All other things being equal, though, it is best if language rules correspond reasonably well to the linguistic facts; since grammarians are fallible human beings like everybody else, this does not always happen. Readers may like to decide what is wrong with the following rules, taken from well-known pedagogic and general-purpose reference works. (For comments, see the end of the paper.)

1 The past tense refers to a DEFINITE time in the past.[1]
(Leech and Svartvik 1975)

2 *In case* is a subordinator referring to possible future conditions: *Do this in case a fire breaks* out means 'Do this in the event of a fire breaking out'. However, in British English *in case* in this sentence could also have the meaning of negative purpose: 'Do this to prevent fire breaking out'.[2]
(Quirk et al. 1985)

3 Unlike the simple genitive, the double genitive usually implies non-unique meaning ... Compare:

He is my brother (suggests I have one, or more than one brother)
He is a brother of mine (suggests I have more than one brother)[3]
(Leech and Svartvik 1975)

4 When the main verb of a sentence is in a past tense, verbs in subordinate clauses must be in a past tense also.[4]
(Thomson and Martinet 1980)

5 The plain infinitive is used with *had better; had rather; had sooner*.[5]
(Zandvoort 1957)

6 Spelling: *-ise* and *-ize* ... It is safer to write *-ize*: with a very few exceptions, this is always correct.[6]
(Swan 1984)

In the interests of telling the truth, a pedagogic grammarian must of course try to suppress his or her own prescriptive prejudices and resistance to language change. One may for instance personally disapprove of the use of *like* as a conjunction (as in *It looks like the tickets are sold out*), or one may feel that many people use *hopefully*, *refute* or *disinterested* in undesirable ways, but one is doing no service to learners by telling them, as some writers do, that such things are incorrect (though one may well want to point out that some people believe them to be so). If educated native-speaker usage is divided, the grammarian's job is to describe and account for the division, not to attempt to adjudicate.

Demarcation

A pedagogic rule should show clearly what are the limits on the use of a given form

Telling the truth involves not only saying what things are, but also saying what they are not. If you ask me what a pika is, and I tell you that it is small and furry, has four legs and is found in the United States, you have grounds for complaint. My answer is descriptive, in that it gives you some accurate information about pikas, but it has no defining or predictive value, because it does not enable you to distinguish between pikas and other creatures such as squirrels, martens, weasels, prairie dogs, chipmunks, moles, rats or cats. If I want to do better than this, I must, so to speak, demarcate the territory occupied by the concept of 'pika' from that occupied by similar concepts, by telling you what makes pikas unique.

In the same way, a pedagogic rule, however true and well-expressed, is useless unless it demarcates clearly the area within which a given form is appropriate, so that a learner will know when to use the form and when not to. Here is an example of a rule that does not meet this criterion.

> The PERFECT OF EXPERIENCE expresses what has happened, once or more than once, within the speaker's or writer's experience.
> (Zandvoort 1957)

One can see what Zandvoort has in mind, but his description does not distinguish between different ways of talking about 'experience', and so fails to provide a basis for predicting whether or not the present perfect will be appropriate in a given case. As formulated, in fact, Zandvoort's rule could be interpreted as meaning that one uses the present perfect to refer to everything that has happened in one's lifetime!

Here is another rule which fails to demarcate.

> The present perfect continuous tense ... [This tense] is used for an action which began in the past and is still continuing, or has only just finished.
> (Thomson and Martinet 1980)

What is said here is perfectly true, as well as being admirably clear and simple. The problem is that the present perfect continuous is not the only verb form that is used to talk about actions which began in the past and are still continuing. The present continuous is also used for this purpose—much more often, in fact, than the present perfect continuous. The rule does not list the features (e.g. specification of duration) which demarcate the use of the present perfect continuous from that of the present continuous, and so provides no basis for predicting which of the two forms will be appropriate in a given case.

The demarcation criterion is particularly important, and notoriously difficult to satisfy, in pedagogic lexical definition. Learners of English often have enormous difficulty in distinguishing close synonyms such as *evil* and *wicked*, *box* and *tin*, *shut* and *close* or *begin* and *start*. Dictionary definitions do not usually help—indeed, ordinary dictionaries are not designed to settle demarcation disputes between synonyms. (One of the learner's dictionaries on my shelf defines *evil* as 'causing harm and morally bad', and *wicked* as 'immoral and harmful'; the others do no better.) Perhaps as computerised corpus studies make more usage data available, it will at last become possible to give really helpful rules about the distinctions between words.

Clarity

Rules should be clear

Teachers tend to be good at making things clear. Their professional training and experience make them skilled at presenting information in an orderly fashion, using examples constructively, putting proper emphasis on what is most important, eliminating ambiguity, and so on. Modern pedagogic grammars, which are often written by people with teaching experience, do generally put things clearly, and it is much easier to find rules that are clear but untrue than rules which are true but unclear.

Where rules are unclear, it is often because of the use of unsatisfactory terminology, and this may conceal the fact that the writer does not himself or herself really understand the point at issue. Vague terms like *emphasis*, *definite*, *habitual*, *pronoun*, *condition*, *modality* or *style* can give the illusion of explanation without really conveying very much. When formulating pedagogic explanations, it is always worth asking oneself if one really understands exactly what is meant by the terms one is using; and assuming one does, whether one's audience is likely to understand the same things by them as one does oneself.

Here are two examples of rules where the writer has perhaps failed to put a premium on clarity.

> The perfect tense usually denotes an action that falls within the time-sphere of the present.
> (Zandvoort 1957)

> La modalité est le filtre coloré de notre subjectivité, au travers duquel nous voyons le réel. [Modality is the colour filter of our subjectivity, through which we perceive reality.]
> (Charlot, Hocmard, and Morgan 1977)

Zandvoort's time-sphere and the French authors' filter are both striking images, but neither of them successfully conveys the relevant information to someone who does not already possess it. After studying these rules, the learner is no better able than before to make valid choices of tense or modality. (How can we decide, after all, whether a given past action is 'within the time-sphere of the present' or whether facts that we wish to refer to are or are not seen through the 'colour filter of our subjectivity'?) The concepts are evocative, but they simply do not have enough precision to give them predictive value. Perhaps metaphors are better avoided in pedagogic grammar.

Simplicity

A pedagogic rule should be simple. There is inevitably some trade-off with truth and/or clarity. How much does this matter?

Simplicity is not quite the same thing as clarity (though it may contribute to it). Clarity, as I have used the term, relates above all to the way an explanation is worded; simplicity to the way it is constructed. Clarity is the opposite of obscurity, and means the avoidance of ill-defined concepts and vague or misleading terminology. Simplicity is the opposite of complexity—simplifying a description involves trimming it to make it more manageable, for example by reducing the number of categories or subdivisions or by leaving out inessential details.

One of the things that distinguish pedagogic rules sharply from general-purpose descriptive rules is the requirement that they be simple. The truth is of no value if it cannot be understood, and since ordinary language learners tend to have limited prior knowledge and are not usually natural grammarians, some degree of simplification is nearly always necessary. In addition, clear and simple rules are psychologically valuable: they make students feel that they can understand and control the very complex material that they are faced with. How much one can reduce complexity without excessive distortion is a matter for individual judgement: one person's skilful simplification is another person's irresponsible travesty, and teachers' journals are consequently full of articles in which pedagogic grammarians take each other to task for giving over-simple rules of thumb. In some cases, of course, a point of grammar may be so complex that a successful simplification is actually impossible: there are aspects of language which cannot be taught (though they can be acquired).

The following rule, on article usage, seems to me an excellent example of a carefully-thought-out trade-off between truth, clarity and simplicity.

> The best simplification is that the form of the article is determined by the interplay of the features 'definite' and 'known to the listener', thus giving four possible realizations:
>
> 1 Both definite and known to the listener   *the*
> *Look at the sun!*
> 2 Definite but not known to the listener   *a/an*
> *I passed through a village.*
> 3 Indefinite but known to the listener   *the/a/o+s*
> *The lion is dangerous.*
> *A lion is dangerous.*
> *Lions are dangerous.*
> 4 Neither definite nor known to the listener   *a/an*
> *If a person wants something …*
>
> (Todd and Hancock 1986)

Some clarity has been lost in the simplification—*definite* is not explained, and *known to the listener* is used as something of a catch-all term. The authors have also cut one or two corners—in particular, they have decided not to deal with the use of articles to make *general/specific* distinctions. But what is left gives a good deal of the truth about the use of articles, and gives it in a form that makes this very complex point accessible to the average advanced student or teacher.

Here is another impressive simplification, from an article on teaching the present perfect.

We often think that there are endless rules for this tense. In fact these can be boiled down to just two simple precepts:

1 To describe actions beginning in the past and continuing up to the present moment (and possibly into the future): *I've planted fourteen rose bushes so far this morning.*
2 To refer to actions occurring or not occurring at an unspecified time in the past with some kind of connection to the present: *Have you passed your driving test?*

Every use of the present perfect (for example with *since*, *for* and so on) will fit into one of these rules. Proliferating rules without end makes this tense sound more difficult than it actually is.
(Alexander 1988b)

Whether or not a particular simplification is valid depends ultimately on who it is addressed to, how much they already know, how much they are capable of taking in, and what value they and their teachers place on complete accuracy. None the less, one can reasonably ask whether Alexander, excellent pedagogic grammarian though he is, has not on this occasion paid too high a price for simplicity. It is easy to share his impatience with the jungle of rules that are often supplied in a desperate attempt to pin down the use of the present perfect. On the other hand, the point is a difficult one; that is why grammarians make such heavy weather of it. (Defining the use of the present perfect is rather like trying to fit a balloon into your pocket—as soon as you manage to get one bit in, another bit bulges out again.) It is interesting that, in his *Longman English Grammar* (1988a), Alexander actually devotes quite a lot of space—over 140 lines—to the point. In comparison, *Cobuild* (Sinclair, ed., 1990) has 58 lines and Greenbaum and Quirk's *Student's Grammar* (1990) has 80. Thomson and Martinet (1980), locked in a fight to the death with this most elusive of tenses, have over 380.

Conceptual parsimony

An explanation must make use of the conceptual framework available to the learner. It may be necessary to add to this. If so, one should aim for minimum intervention.

Simplicity and clarity may not be enough. One can drastically reduce the complexity of an explanation, use terminology that is perfectly precise in its reference, and still be left with something that is difficult for the non-specialist to grasp. When new information is communicated, there is often a conceptual gap between writer/speaker and reader/listener. Not only does the former know more than the latter; he or she may also analyse the material using concepts and categories which, though clearly defined, are unfamiliar to the recipient. In order to communicate effectively, it can be important to take into account the conceptual framework available to one's reader or listener, and to try to work within this as far as is reasonable. If the way in which one analyses a topic is too far removed from the analysis which one's audience initially brings to it, communication is likely to break down.

A professional grammarian writing for colleagues or well-informed amateurs does not of course need to make too many concessions to this principle of conceptual parsimony. He or she can assume that most readers will be familiar with the concepts and terminology used; if they are not, they can be expected to do the work necessary to grasp precisely what is meant by, say, 'theme and 'rheme', 'ergative', 'raising' or 'NP-trace'. On the other hand, a pedagogic grammarian or a teacher giving learners a rule can usually assume very little conceptual sophistication on the part of his/her readers or listeners. He or she must try to get things across using the simplest possible grammatical notions. Terminology will be chosen for its familiarity rather than for its precision. It will sometimes be necessary to provide students with new concepts in order to get a point across, but one must aim for minimum intervention. This will often mean compromising—perhaps quite seriously—with the truth.

Which of the following rules is more likely to be understood by the average learner?

1 We use *much* with uncountable nouns and *many* with plural countables.
2 We use *much* with singular nouns and *many* with plurals.

It seems to me that, in this instance, the added precision gained by referring to countability is not worth paying for, unless the student to whom the rule is addressed is already totally familiar with the concept. (Students who can distinguish between singular and plural are unlikely to try to use *much* with countable singulars anyway, because phrases like *much horse* do not make sense, so 'singular nouns' will effectively direct them to uncountable nouns in this case.) Similarly, one might (possibly gritting one's teeth) decide that it was more cost-effective with a particular student or class to talk about 'possessive adjectives' rather than 'possessive determiners', 'infinitive' rather than 'base form', 'tense' rather than 'tense plus aspect', or 'conditional' rather than '*would* + infinitive', however unsatisfactory these labels might be from a strictly descriptive point of view. (If one's students speak a language in which the equivalent of *would go* is an inflected verb form with a name such as *conditionnel* or *condizionale*, it is surely perverse not to use the cognate term when talking about the English structure.)

Relevance

A rule should answer the question (and only the question) that the student's English is 'asking'

Pedagogic grammar is not just about language; it is about the interaction between language and language learners. A good pedagogic rule does not present a neutral analysis of a set of linguistic data; it answers a question, real or potential, that is asked by a learner, or that is generated by his or her interlanguage. Consider the following concocted examples.

1 My sister Ksenija lives in Belgrade. She is hairdresser.
2 My sister Marie-France lives in Lyon. She is hairdresser.

Despite the surface equivalence, the two instances of 'She is hairdresser' can be seen as reflecting totally different interlanguage rules. In the first case (given the fact that Slav languages have no article systems), the learner's interlanguage rule—if this sentence is typical of his/her usage—might be paraphrased as 'There are no indefinite articles in English' or 'English articles are too hard to understand, so don't use them'. The second learner's interlanguage rule is more likely to be something on the lines of 'Articles are not used in English before classifying complements such as the names of professions'. In a teaching situation, one could regard each of the sentences as generating a question, or a request for a rule: respectively 'How are (indefinite) articles used in English?' and 'How does English article usage differ from French in the case of classifying complements?'. Clearly the pedagogic rules that will be appropriate in each case will be totally different one from the other. While the [Serbian] speaker will need a good deal of information about the meaning and use of the English articles, there is no point in giving a French-speaking learner a similarly complete account, since he/she already knows in general how article systems work.

The following rather fanciful examples show how failure to produce an English plural inflection might reflect four different interlanguage rules (so that four different pedagogic rules would be potentially relevant to the correction of the mistakes).

1 *I run an import-export business in Taipei with my two brother.*
   (Chinese does not inflect for number.)
2 *I run a carpet factory in Teheran with my two brother.*
   (Farsi nouns inflect for number, but singular forms are used with numerical determiners.)
3 *I run a call-girl network in Dijon with my two brother.*
   (Although written French commonly adds -s for plural, like English, the -s is not pronounced. This carries over into the spoken English of French-speaking learners, and—because of subvocalisation—quite often into their written English.)
4 *I run a brewery in Heidelberg with my two brother.*
   (Many German nouns form their plural by adding -er; many others have both singular and plural in -er. German-speakers quite often drop -s off the plurals of English words ending in -er: presumably this is because the ending already 'feels plural' to them.)

Because it is important to focus closely on a learner's point of difficulty and to exclude information that is irrelevant to this, it can sometimes be useful to present what is, objectively speaking, a thoroughly bad rule. Conditional structures are a case in point. The standard pedagogic analysis of sentences with *if* into 'first', 'second' and 'third' conditionals is, from a strictly descriptive point of view, total nonsense. (All sorts of possible combinations of verb forms are possible with *if*; in so far as it makes sense to categorise them, they can more usefully be divided into two main groups—those with 'ordinary' tenses, and those in which 'special' tenses are used to express a hypothetical kind of meaning.) However, given that students do tend to have trouble with the three structures that are presented in the standard pedagogic analysis, and that they can generally manage the others without difficulty, one could argue that—whatever its theoretical defects—this analysis gives students what they need.

Similar considerations apply to the teaching of indirect speech. This is very nearly a pseudo-category in English. Despite the monstrous apparatus of rules about backshift, deictic changes and so on that appear in many pedagogic grammars and course books, nearly all English indirect speech utterances are constructed in accordance with the general rules that determine the form of most other English sentences. A few kinds of indirect speech sentence do involve tense usage that is specific to this grammatical category (e.g. *Are you deaf? I asked you how old you were*), but these are the exception. On the other hand, indirect speech is very definitely a live category for many learners of English, either because in their languages it does follow special syntactic rules, or because their mother-tongues have no equivalent of the structure at all. This being so, it may after all be appropriate for a pedagogic grammar to provide a full-scale account of indirect speech as a separate topic, even if this would arguably be out of place in a purely descriptive grammar.

Failure to focus on the learner's linguistic state as well as on the language itself is responsible for a good deal of bad grammar teaching. In old-style mother-tongue English lessons in secondary schools, a great deal of emphasis was put on parsing: identifying parts of speech and their syntactic roles, labelling clause types and so on. This effectively amounted to saying 'Their grammar is defective; therefore we must teach them grammar', without consideration of whether the grammar they were allegedly getting wrong and the grammar they were being taught bore any relation to each other. But there is not much value, for instance, in teaching people to identify noun clauses, if the ways in which their language is unsatisfactory do not include failure to operate the category of noun clauses. This is like saying 'Jake got lost on the way back from the pub last night; he needs geography lessons' or 'Annie put salt in her tea this morning instead of sugar; she needs chemistry lessons' or (in the immortal words of *Yes, Minister*) 'Something must be done; this is something; therefore let us do it'.

Effective grammar teaching, then, focuses on the specific problems (real and potential) of specific learners. This will necessarily mean giving a somewhat fragmentary and partial account of the grammar of the target language, rather than working through a 'complete' grammar syllabus giving 'complete' rules. There is nothing at all wrong with this, though the approach may look messy and unsystematic: the grammar classroom is no place for people with completion neuroses. To quote a very apposite old American saying: 'If it ain't broke, don't fix it'.

Crossing linguistic categories: grammar, lexis or pragmatics?

When we formulate fine-tuned pedagogic rules, the need to focus on the learner as well as the language not only affects the shape of the rules; it may even determine whether a particular language element is seen as involving grammar, lexis, or pragmatics. Consider the various possible ways of handling *because* clauses. In a general-purpose reference book, these will be unambiguously classified under grammar. Whether a pedagogic rule treats them as grammar, however, will depend on who the rule is for. A learner whose language does not have clause subordination—or does not express cause through subordination—will certainly approach *because* clauses as an aspect of grammar. But a speaker of a European language is likely to have few problems with simple subordination; for such a student, the relevant information about *because* will be that it is the equivalent of *weil, parce que, porque, fordi, potamou sto* or whatever. He or she will learn *because* as a vocabulary item, and may well need no grammatical information at all in order to begin using it correctly.

Or consider ways of asking for help. For some learners, the English use of a negative declarative question structure to make requests (as in *You couldn't give me a hand for a minute?*) will correspond closely to what happens in their own languages, and their task will be the relatively simple one of mastering the English version of the form. For speakers of other languages, in contrast, the very fact of asking for help by means of a direct question may be quite alien, so that they will not only have to learn a new point of grammar—how to construct this kind of interrogative—but also an aspect of pragmatics—how to associate questions with a new kind of speech act. In pedagogic grammar work, therefore, the very way in which items are assigned to linguistic categories may depend as much on what the learner knows as on the structure of the target language.

Conclusion: in defence of rules of thumb

'School grammars' is a term that is often given a pejorative edge (sometimes with good reason). But it is easy to forget what it is like to know little about a subject and to have little aptitude for it. People who are inclined to be dismissive of popular pedagogic grammars might usefully consider in what form they themselves would like to be given information about quantum mechanics, laser technology, plant genetics, crystallography, or the physics of black holes. A little truth goes a long way when one is off one's own ground.

Teachers often give students explanations of a kind that they would not dream of producing if an inspector was in the room. And yet the teacher's corner-cutting rules of thumb, half-truths, and unscientific terminology might on occasion work better than anything that the inspector would be capable of. Good teaching involves a most mysterious feat—sitting, so to speak, on one's listener's shoulder, monitoring what one is saying with the listener's ears, and using this feedback to shape and adapt one's words from moment to moment so that the thread of communication never breaks. This is art, not science, and there is a great deal of such art in the production of successful pedagogic language rules. These rules may on occasion be very different from those found in a standard reference grammar; but it may be this very difference—the fact that they satisfy specifically pedagogic criteria such as simplicity, conceptual parsimony, and relevance—that makes them succeed where more descriptively 'respectable' rules would fail.

Notes

[On the quotations under 'Truth']
1 What is a 'definite' time? How definite is *once upon a time*? How about *an indefinite time ago*? How about *Nobody knows when ...*?
2 Suppose you insure a house in case fire breaks out. This doesn't mean either 'in the event of fire breaking out' or 'to prevent fire breaking out', but 'to guard against the consequences of fire breaking out'.
3 What about 'How's that brother of yours?' The 'non-unique' meaning in Leech and Svartvik's example comes from the indefinite article, not from the 'double genitive', whose function is simply to circumvent the English constraint on the co-occurrence of possessives with articles and demonstratives.
4 This is only true of certain kinds of subordinate clause in certain kinds of structure.
5 *Had rather* lives on in grammars, but is virtually obsolete in normal usage.
6 [For British English] The opposite is closer to the truth.

6

Language teaching is teaching language

(Originally published in IATEFL Annual Conference Report, 1996.)

In 1996 I was asked to deliver the Hornby lecture at the annual IATEFL conference. This was a particularly welcome invitation: I had long admired Hornby as a grammarian as well as a lexicographer, and his ground-breaking Guide to Patterns and Usage in English (OUP 1954) had been extremely useful to me in my own work. The talk, and the article to which it gave rise, reflected Hornby's concern with language, along with my own recurrent concern that language teaching can easily drift away from teaching language itself into the easier option of simply doing things with it.

> Something must be done; this is something; therefore let us do it.
> (From *Yes, Minister*)

Knowledge and skills: prioritising

I should like to start by putting forward a rather unoriginal view of the task facing us as language teachers, teacher trainers or course designers. This is that.
- Language use involves: 1) a knowledge base, and 2) skill in performing operations which draw on this knowledge base. These are equally important.
- Compared with, say, music or driving, the knowledge base required for effective language use is vast.
- Both the knowledge base and the associated skills take a great deal of time and (for most adults) considerable work to assimilate.
- Most learners only have time to master a small part of a foreign language.
- Our task is therefore 1) to prioritise, selecting the language and skills which are most important for our learners, and 2) to ensure that our learners engage with the language and skills selected in ways which will ensure that they are effectively learnt.

Most people in ELT are, of course, well aware of these considerations, and plenty of very effective teaching goes on all over the world as a result—I don't wish to suggest that everybody is getting it all wrong. However, there does seem to be a perennial tendency for the balance to tip over too far to one side or the other of the knowledge/skills divide; and also for means—teaching activities—to supplant ends—the knowledge and skills that the activities are supposed to be teaching. I shall argue that this is happening now, and indeed that, in some corners of the profession at least, we may be so concerned with the teaching of skills—language as process—that we are in danger of seriously neglecting the knowledge base—language as product.

Doing things and teaching things

When I was taking my first steps in EFL, language teaching seemed a relatively simple business. We taught—and we took it for granted that students learnt—grammar, vocabulary, and pronunciation. The fluent deployment of these elements was practised through work on receptive and productive skills. (It was well known that there were four of these.) Everything was neatly packaged in the textbook. There were, it is true, occasional hints that we might be overlooking something (as when students asked us to 'teach them conversation' and we shuffled our feet and told them uneasily that conversational fluency would just 'come with practice'.) But by and large the system worked smoothly: we gave our lessons and students' English got better.

Something that worried me even in those early days, though, was a feeling that we tended, without realising it, to slide from teaching things into doing things. This happened most obviously after one left the simple certainties of the elementary syllabus. If you stopped a beginners' teacher on the way to the classroom and said 'what's going to happen in your lesson?', you were likely to get an answer in terms of goals: 'colour words', 'the present perfect', 'things to say in shops'. But if you tried the same thing with an intermediate teacher, the answer was much more likely to describe activities: 'dictation', 'reading', 'doing a dialogue', 'making a radio programme'. While one told you what she was going to teach, the other said what she was going to do.

In itself, this change of emphasis is quite understandable. As students become more proficient, their needs become more varied and diffuse, and it becomes harder to define one's aims in terms of a list of specific linguistic products. At the same time, skills practice inevitably takes on increasing importance—intermediate students typically know a lot of language which they can't use, and more advanced students may need training in special uses of language relevant to their professional needs. So it is natural that, from intermediate level upwards, types of activity become important elements in teaching syllabuses.

But the change of emphasis brings with it a serious danger of losing focus on goals. The activities we select can become ends in themselves, while the language they are supposed to be teaching gets pushed into the background. We can easily end up simply doing a lot of things which seem vaguely related to language teaching, keeping students happily occupied with tasks that involve enough interactive use of language to reassure us and them that we are doing our jobs. (Surely, we feel, if they're speaking/reading/writing/hearing English they must be learning it?) So while we may intend, in theory, to give equal importance to the knowledge base and the associated skills, our students may actually spend a great deal of their time doing rather ill-defined fluency practice, and not very much time systematically learning new language.

Everything is getting more complicated

Since my early days in the profession, language teaching has progressed enormously. We know much more about language, we have more sophisticated ideas about how people learn it, and we have far better ways of teaching it. Work done by researchers in discourse analysis, in particular, has made it possible to tabulate the ways in which real-life exchanges work, to discover how different kinds of texts are structured, and to describe language and its use in terms of semantic categories such as 'notions' and 'functions'. (So if students ask us now to 'teach them conversation', we know what the request means and we have a good idea of how to go about meeting it.)

Unfortunately, as we learn more about language, and as our methodology develops to keep up with our knowledge, it becomes even harder to define clear aims and to choose appropriate activities by which to achieve them. There is so much to teach, and so many things to do. Teachers, trainers, and materials writers who wish to be properly informed have to battle their way through a dense jungle of facts and theory, often impeded by thickets of vicious terminology. And with all of this, we don't seem much nearer to answering the central question: 'What happens in people's heads when they learn languages, and how can we make it happen more effectively?' In moments of gloom I have sometimes been reminded of Mark Twain's words: 'The researches of many commentators have already thrown much darkness on this subject, and it is probable that, if they continue, we shall soon know nothing at all about it'. As we despair of ever getting a clear overview that would enable us to make rational decisions, we are naturally tempted to stop trying and unconsciously take refuge in a cocktail of language-practice activities.

Language as process

The perennial tendency to seek refuge in user-friendly activity has received a powerful boost from one current in contemporary linguistics which has had a good deal of influence on language-teaching—the move towards seeing language as 'process' rather than 'product'. This has helped to legitimise a skills-centered view of what we are doing: our job (as many people now see it) is not to supply the learner with a product (the language); it is to enable him or her to engage in processes which will inculcate the skills he or she needs for successful language use (or some similar formulation). Many current language courses are based on what one might call the 'battery of skills' approach, in which the principal focus is not so much on teaching language as on training people to do things with it. When I started teaching, reading was a skill. Fifteen years later, in one well-known analysis, reading was alleged to comprise nineteen separate skills. Inventories of skills may be supplemented by equally complex inventories of strategies—learning strategies, communication strategies, and so forth—and it is often suggested that these too should be taught.

> Although 'strategy' has never been adequately defined in the learner language literature, and although some bizarre labels are given to learner behaviour, such as 'the strategy of incorrect application', it has been widely exemplified, and it comes over as an altogether positive concept: learners deploying strategies or teachers encouraging learners to use their existing strategies and add more to their strategy repertoires, seem assured of receiving an accolade.
> (James 1990)

This is not the place for a detailed criticism of the 'skills and strategies' view of language, but I should at least like to suggest, as a useful operating principle, that we should avoid teaching any 'skill' or 'strategy' unless we are reasonably certain 1) that it really exists, 2) that the learner needs it, 3) that the learner does not already possess it and 4) that it can actually be both taught and learnt.

A process view of language, then, with its skills-centered view of aims as well as methodology, moves us further in the direction of doing things rather than teaching things. Classroom activity, in this view, is now no longer a means to an end which includes the acquisition of the knowledge base; it can become virtually an end in itself, with the accompanying risk that the language itself gets swept even further under the carpet.

Simplification: the search for a quick fix

With so many things to teach, and so many things to do, it is natural that teachers and course designers should look for ways of simplifying their task. At the same time, researchers are under considerable pressure to come up with practical solutions to the language-learning problem. An enormous amount of time and money is spent worldwide teaching languages to children and adults; in general, the results are not spectacular. Anybody who can make this massive investment more cost-effective by finding ways of speeding up language-learning will earn the gratitude of nations and achieve fame and funding—or at least, in these hard times, have a better chance of surviving the next round of staff cuts. It is not surprising, then, that new 'methods' and 'approaches' appear at regular intervals. Up to a point this is desirable and indeed necessary: at the very least, new approaches generate new energy, and often they result in real, if modest, progress. The danger is that in our search for greater efficiency, and for simple routes through the conceptual jungle of language-teaching, we may latch onto the latest development and turn it into a 'quick fix' that will solve all our problems, creating one homogeneous 'method' or 'approach' that, at last, we can use to teach the language twice or three times as effectively as before. (I was recently shown a description of a well-known 'method', by no means new, that is alleged to teach languages up to 'six times as fast'. I was discouraged from trying it out by the reflection that if somebody had invented a fuel, twenty years ago, that was six times as efficient as petrol, nobody would be trying to convert us to it today—we would all be using it.)

Looking back over the last few decades, it is disturbing to realise how many methods, approaches, and technologies have been perceived as 'the key': structure drilling, the language lab, the audiovisual approach, the input hypothesis, the silent way, humanistic approaches such as counselling learning, suggestopaedia, the use of authentic materials, the notional/functional syllabus, the communicative approach, total physical response, learner-centered approaches, task-based syllabuses—to name but a few. In the seventies (the heyday of gurus and miracle methods), Catherine Walter and I published an article in *ELT Journal* on 'Teaching English by Sensory Deprivation' [see pages 203–7 of this collection]. Such was the climate of the times that more than one reader took the paper seriously, and references to it started turning up in bibliographies.

I think it is probably wise to beware of any philosophy of language teaching that has a name: 'the X method' or 'The Y approach'. The very fact that the method is delimited in this way means that its proponents are focusing primarily or exclusively on one aspect of language; inevitably, therefore, other aspects will be neglected. New approaches and technologies are good servants (because of what they add to our professional repertoire), but generally bad masters (because of what they make us leave out). When I was first learning my trade, we were good at teaching grammar but bad at teaching conversation. More recently, the opposite has often been the case. A few weeks ago somebody told me 'We've all gone over to the Lexical Approach now—we hardly do any grammar at all'. I doubt if Michael Lewis would have been pleased to hear that his ideas had been allowed to fill somebody's whole horizon in this way.

As each new panacea turns out not, after all, to be the miracle cure, disillusionment sets in, and another pendulum swing starts; so that too much of our energy goes into reacting to our mistakes, and not enough into simply trying to achieve our basic language-teaching aims. As Ian Stewart put it in *New Scientist*, talking about a topic remote from language teaching:

> It has been known for a long time that control systems can behave chaotically ... if they are 'over-driven' ... the whole system thrashes, spending nearly all of its time reacting to its own errors and very little time reacting to the reality it is supposed to be controlling.
> (Stewart 1995)

'The language will take care of itself': task-based syllabuses

Neglect of the knowledge base is not always an accidental side-effect of a concern to teach skills; it can be a matter of deliberate policy. Prabhu (1987) refers to 'a strongly-felt pedagogic intuition that the development of competence in a second language requires *not* systematisation of language inputs or maximisation of planned practice, but rather the creation of conditions in which learners engage in an effort to cope with communication'. Many people working in this perspective hold the view that teaching and learning can be organised according to a purely task-based syllabus. According to some versions of this model, if one analyses the 'target' tasks that learners will have to perform in real life, and if one then takes learners through examples of similar tasks in the classroom, the language (often described, significantly, as 'skills') that is needed will be generated in the process: it will emerge naturally from the materials used for the task, or from the teacher's input, or from the classroom interaction. There is therefore no need to draw up explicit formal or functional language syllabuses: if the tasks are correctly chosen, the language will take care of itself.

Well, will it? Will a specification of behavioural objectives automatically generate, as an incidental payoff, a specification of the knowledge base that learners will need for an adequate command of the language? If you take learners through a set of carefully selected tasks, will all the high-priority grammar, pronunciation, and vocabulary points show up and be learnt?

Let us make the precarious assumption that all the grammar that students are likely to need in real life will indeed be thrown up, without special planning, by a course consisting only of tasks; and that this grammar will be learnt effectively either during the task-based activities or during additional follow-up 'form focus' sessions. Let us also, for the sake of argument, accept Tom MacArthur's memorable definition of pronunciation as 'that part of a student which is the same at the end of a language course as at the beginning'. That leaves vocabulary.

In discussions of task-based learning, vocabulary tends to be invisible. (In two recent books by Nunan (1988, 1989), there are no index references to either 'vocabulary' or 'lexis'.) This is strange, because it seems obvious that, at least after elementary level, the largest part of a language learner's task is to build up an adequate stock of high-priority words and lexicalised phrases, including both knowledge of their forms and an awareness of their more important meanings, the major collocational and syntactic constraints on their use, and so on. If a purely task-based syllabus is to do its job, it should then provide learners not only with the grammar, but also with the vocabulary they need. Unfortunately, it seems clear to me that there is no way in which it can do this effectively: any task-based syllabus must be supplemented, I believe, at least by a separately-planned lexical syllabus.

The need for a lexical syllabus

In order to see why separate lexical syllabuses are necessary, we must consider questions of extent and frequency. Let us take the case of a typical learner—call her Sophia. Sophia is a reasonably well-motivated intermediate student, moving into her third year of English in a secondary school in a non-English-speaking country where task-based language-teaching syllabuses have been introduced. She has already learnt the commonest two thousand-odd vocabulary items, and she would like to finish her third year knowing the next thousand or so high-priority words and expressions. Now some of the vocabulary items in this frequency-range will be 'task-bound', and are sure to be learnt if the relevant tasks form part of the syllabus—for example, if Sophia and her fellow-students work on business negotiations, then one does not need to worry about whether they will learn *contract*, *meeting*, *negotiate*, *confirm*, *delivery date* and so on, because these are virtually certain to come up in one way or another. Unfortunately, however, the bulk of intermediate vocabulary is not task-bound in this way: there is a great deal of what you might call 'general-purpose' material. The 'third thousand' items include, for example, *calm*, *noisy*, *swallow*, *take trouble*, *rubbish*, *lane*, *genuine* and *out of sight*—but it is hard to see what tasks could be guaranteed automatically to throw up these words and expressions.

Perhaps, though, even the general-purpose items that Sophia needs are frequent enough to come up automatically in her year's work, whatever the tasks covered. In order to see whether this is a reasonable supposition, we need a little mathematics. During the school year, assuming a fair amount of written and recorded material, plenty of classroom activity, a teacher who talks a lot and some reading outside class, Sophia might be exposed—on a very generous estimate—to around 350,000 words of input: 10,000 words a week. Now words like *calm*, *noisy*, *swallow*, *rubbish*, *lane* and *genuine* tend to have frequencies between 7 and 30 occurrences per million running words. This means that any one of them, taken singly, is very likely to come up at least once in a corpus of 350,000 words. Using the frequency figures from the LOB Corpus, and applying some probability theory, *calm* would have better than a 99.9% chance of occurring; *noisy* a 95% chance; *swallow* a 90% chance. However, things that each have a good chance of happening separately have a far less good chance of all happening together (this is why one or two of your numbers often come up in the lottery, but never all six). The chance of twenty-five specific words at this level of frequency all coming up in our hypothetical year's work is in fact not much better than evens—50% or so. Assuming that 600 of our 'third thousand' high-priority items are general-purpose vocabulary, not automatically thrown up by the tasks chosen, then the chance of their all coming up anyway, without being artificially fed in, is quite remote—of the order of a million to one against. Sophia will not learn her thousand words.

Vocabulary, then, will not take care of itself. If students with limited time available for study are to learn high-priority lexis, this needs to be deliberately selected and incorporated into learning materials or activities. If this is not done, students will not be exposed—even once—to numerous important vocabulary items, and they will finish their courses with serious gaps in their knowledge. In earlier times we provided students, so to speak, with the necessary bricks, tiles, timbers, mortar, and so on, and assumed that they could build their own houses. Exclusively task-based approaches fall into the opposite error: they get learners building houses right away, but assume that the various supplies needed will magically materialise—as if delivered by elves—at the right times and in the right quantities. Unfortunately elves are scarce in ELT: we need lexical syllabuses.

Unlike the hypothetical third-year student in our example, some learners follow language courses in the country where the target language is spoken, and here the issues are of course somewhat different. The massive exposure to the language which such learners can get outside the classroom will guarantee that they acquire high-priority vocabulary, and class time can be used for other things. Whether purely task-based approaches are any more suitable for this environment is another question: on the face of it, it would seem that outside exposure will also equip students, on the whole, to do the things in English that they need to learn to do. One is led to ask what a language course in the target-language country is actually for; and this is not, perhaps, an easy question to answer.

Learner independence

> Language teaching and learning have frequently been beset by techniques in which the tail wags the dog. Thus the language laboratory—essentially a useful technique—became a controlling factor in some methodologies, so that language learning and teaching was organised around the language laboratory. Self-instruction and self-directed learning may pose a similar threat of a particular learning mode taking over the whole of the learning programme and distorting it so that the covert aim becomes the success of self-directed learning rather than the successful learning of the target language.
> (Dickinson 1987)

Current resistance to pre-planned language syllabuses often arises from an understandable desire not to impose external constraints on the very personal business of language learning. Each learner is unique, with his or her own goals, learning styles, and so on, and it is natural to feel that the more we can involve learners in the decisions that affect their learning, from personalisation of exercises right up to overall syllabus design, the more chance we have of providing courses that are sensitive to their needs.

It is of course true that only the learner really knows exactly what he or she wants. It is, however, equally true that only the teacher knows what there is to be learnt. In other branches of teaching we are not usually so diffident about imposing direction and constraints on the learners—I would not, for instance, encourage my seventeen-year-old son to adopt a discovery approach to learning to drive my car; nor would I want my rock-climbing instructor to leave me to find out for myself how to rappel down effectively.

It is not altogether clear, in fact, that all learners want the degree of autonomy that some teachers think is good for them. In two Australian studies investigating learning preferences quoted by Nunan (1988), while teachers gave most importance to conversation practice, self-discovery of errors and pairwork, learners gave higher ratings to pronunciation practice, explanation by the teacher, error correction, and vocabulary development. There was, indeed, some evidence of irritation with activity-rich approaches: as one student expressed it, 'I don't want to clap and sing, I want to learn English.'

Natural acquisition versus instruction

Recent years have seen a good deal of research on first and second language acquisition, and on the similarities and differences between them. This has led many researchers to ask whether 'instructed learning' can really achieve the same kind of results as 'natural acquisition'. A well-known extreme view is Krashen's 'no interface' position: that conscious learning of grammar rules provides learners, at best, with a kind of knowledge that can be used to monitor their own production when there is time to do so, and that this knowledge cannot be used to generate spontaneous grammatically-accurate utterances. Subsequent studies have tended to rehabilitate grammatical instruction up to a point, showing that rule-learning can have at least a modest effect on accuracy (see Ellis 1994 for discussion). However, there is still quite a widespread feeling that rule-learning is 'artificial', and that the more we can approximate the conditions of natural acquisition in our teaching, the better we are likely to do.

Strangely, the 'instruction versus natural acquisition' debate has concentrated almost exclusively on the learning of grammar, and on the question of *how* grammar is learnt. In fact, it seems to me that this question is almost irrelevant to a comparison between instructed learning and natural acquisition. The crucial difference between the two, surely, has to do with vocabulary, and far more with *what* is learnt than with *how* it is learnt.

According to a study carried out in the 1970s (Carey 1978), English-speaking children have learnt on average 14,000 words by the age of 6. This works out at about 6.3 words a day. Adults learning a second language at this rate would need around 10,000 hours' exposure to acquire a vocabulary of 5,000 words—a fairly time-consuming way to reach an intermediate level. Unaided natural acquisition, then, works slowly; and, as we have already seen, teaching approaches which simulate the conditions of natural acquisition cannot even present learners with the vocabulary they need in the time normally available for language courses.

The point about instruction is that, properly organised, it can do two things. First of all, it can *select* the language which will be presented to the learner, making sure that, in the short time available for a language course, as many high-priority items as possible occur in the input. Secondly, it can supply *concentrated exposure to*, and *concentrated practice of* the items presented, by providing activities which force the learner to engage intensively with the new material. Whether or not this is effective depends on too many factors to list, but at least planned instruction provides learners with some chance of acquiring essential vocabulary; whereas an approach which does not even get this vocabulary into the input simply abdicates responsibility for teaching core aspects of the language.

Summary and conclusion

I would, then, like to see something of a 'return to basics' in our profession (without wishing the expression to carry the obscurantist overtones that it has recently acquired in the context of political crowd-pleasing). Despite the enormous progress that has been made in language analysis, syllabus design, and methodology, it seems to me that our teaching aims are not actually very different from those that were identified when I first went into the classroom. That is to say, our task is to provide learners with a command of selected high-priority aspects of grammar, vocabulary, and pronunciation, and with facility in using these accurately and appropriately. (Though of course we do not mean quite the same by words like *grammar*, *vocabulary*, or *appropriately* as we did thirty years ago.) This return to basics would involve, among other things:

- A rehabilitation of instruction, in the quarters where this is needed, together with a clear understanding of the need to select and present input, especially lexis, in a principled way, and of the consequent limitations of learner autonomy and of approaches that emulate 'natural acquisition'.
- The realisation that a trained language teacher needs a thorough knowledge of the structure of the language that he or she is teaching—native-speaking teachers of English today are often surprisingly ignorant of grammar.
- An acceptance that language learning is hard, and sometimes dull, and that it will remain so—there are no quick fixes. Of course we must find ways of making it interesting, but we must remember that what the bored teacher wants is not necessarily what the student needs. We naturally don't want to be doing the same things in our twentieth year of teaching as in our first; but our learners' needs may not be very different today from those of their parents. And if in our first year we were teaching vocabulary efficiently, and in our twentieth year we are training learners in autonomous interactive discourse negotiation strategies, we need to ask if this really represents progress, and if so, for whom.
- A sharpened focus on product as well as process. There are an enormous number of good things to do in language lessons, but we do need to be sure

that the activities we choose actually teach something useful. 'Product' is not a dirty word—it is what our learners are paying for. When we walk out of a classroom, if the lesson was successful, we ought to be able to say what important bit of language the learners now know that they didn't know before; or what important skill they can now operate a little better than they could before. If we can't do this, there may be something wrong.
- A rejection of the view that communication is an absolute good. The more we can integrate real communication into language practice the better, but it does not follow that because students are communicating they are learning English; and some activities (such as learning by heart or mechanical structure-practice), unfashionable because they are totally uncommunicative, may none the less be very valuable.
- A common-sense attitude to what we are doing. It can be helpful, in evaluating a fashionable approach, to ask how we would like it applied to ourselves. If we were learning Chinese, Greek or Swahili, how many of our own methodological assumptions would we put up with? (Not all that long ago, teachers in Britain regularly forbade their students to translate or use bilingual dictionaries. Guess what kind of dictionaries they all took on holiday abroad.)

Kenneth Tynan, reflecting on his own profession, said that a good drama critic is one who perceives what is happening in the theatre of his time, but that a great drama critic is one who perceives what is not happening. Our conference programmes, journal articles, and publishers' catalogues show evidence of a great variety of concerns, pursued with enormous creativity and impressive energy. As we find ever more interesting, motivating, and professionally rewarding things to do, we, too, need to look carefully at what is not happening.

7
The influence of the mother tongue on second language vocabulary acquisition and use

(Originally published in 'Vocabulary: description, acquisition and pedagogy', in Schmitt and McCarthy (eds.), Cambridge University Press. 1997.)[1]

Mother tongues have been out of favour for a long time. Their use in the classroom was well-nigh criminalized in the early 20th century, and this taboo still has a powerful hold on many teachers and teacher trainers, despite its complete lack of support in theory or research. Later in the century, some scholars attacked the very notion that the characteristics of learners' first languages might shape their acquisition of others, although it must be clear to any experienced language teacher that this is the case. For a brief discussion of this episode in intellectual history, see Article 13: 'History is not what happened.'

Introduction

> ... contrastive analysis, error analysis, etc., are not simply unrelated to linguistic theory in particular, they are dead meat in general.
> (Gregg 1995: 90, reviewing Cook 1993)

Oh, well ...

In this [article] I shall consider the ways in which the mother tongue can support, fail to support or actively hinder someone who is learning or using the vocabulary of a second language. This may happen:

1 when a learner acquires[2] new vocabulary
2 when he or she tries to recall and use previously-learnt vocabulary
3 when he or she tries to construct a complex word or expression that has not already been learnt as a unit.

> As a **learning process,** transfer supports the learner's selection and remodelling of input structures as he progresses in the development of his interlanguage knowledge. As a **production process,** transfer is involved in the learner's retrieval of this knowledge and in his efforts to bridge

The influence of the mother tongue on second language vocabulary 69

linguistically those gaps in his knowledge which cannot be side-stepped by avoidance.
(Kohn 1986: 22)

Before looking at these three areas, it will be useful to consider briefly how languages differ in the ways they encode the world through lexis, and to settle on a definition of crosslinguistic influence.

How languages differ

It is quite an illusion to think, as even literate people sometimes do, that meanings are the same in all languages, that languages differ only in the forms used for those meanings.
(Lado 1957: 77)

The vodka is all right, but the meat is bad.
(Alleged computer translation, into Russian and back, of 'the spirit is willing but the flesh is weak.')

The world contains too many things for us to have one word for each; we economise by using words in more than one sense, leaving context to disambiguate. Unfortunately, different languages parcel up meanings into words in different ways; and so a word in language A may have various equivalents in language B, depending on exactly what is meant. There are several different typical patterns of relationship between words in different languages:

1 We may find a relatively exact fit: Swedish *växellåda* = English *gearbox*; French *chamois* = Italian *camoscio*; English *re-proof* = French *réimperméabiliser*. This happens most often where words relate to concepts that are firmly grounded in physical reality. Even here, though, there may be differences of use (*scarpe di camoscio* are *chaussures en daim* or *suede shoes*, not *chaussures en chamois* or *chamois shoes*.)

2 Sometimes, although speakers of two languages seem to divide the world up conceptually in the same way, they stick the linguistic labels on in different places.

Conceptual organization and its component concepts are not the same as the meanings for the lexical items of a language. For example, English speakers typically make do with just one verb in talking about dressing, namely *put on*. This verb serves for all clothing, headgear, socks and shoes, jewellery, glasses, everything. Yet ask a group of English speakers to demonstrate, with gestures, how to put on a shoe, a glove or a sweater, and they will offer clear and consistent actions based on their conceptual knowledge. They know more about dressing, in other words, than the one lexical item *put on* would suggest. And speakers of other languages in fact use a much more elaborate lexicon for talking about dressing. Japanese speakers use one verb for garments on the upper body, another

for those on the lower body, yet another for garments on extremities like feet and hands, another for articles that go on the head, and another still for jewellery like earrings or a watch ... At the conceptual level, though, these speakers will represent the same actions as speakers of English. Conceptual knowledge, in other words, is not identical to our knowledge about word meanings.
(Clark 1993: 10)

3 Unlike gearboxes, chamois and dressing, many aspects of the world have unclear boundaries, and categorisation is more subjective. In such cases, both lexical and conceptual organisation may vary from one language to another. Different languages notoriously divide up the colour spectrum in quite different ways (see for example Taylor 1989: 1–20). English distinguishes streams from rivers, rather unclearly, on the basis of size; French, unlike English or Italian, distinguishes rivers which run into the sea (*fleuves*) from rivers which are tributaries of others (*rivières*). The following diagram (after Arcaini 1968) shows how French, Danish and Swedish refer to what English calls *a tree*, the material *wood*, *a wood* (collection of trees) and *a forest*.

English	French	Danish	Swedish
tree	arbre		träd
		træ	
wood (material)	bois		trä
wood (small forest)	bois		
		skov	skog
forest	forêt		

Extreme cases of such semantic relativism are sometimes reported; for instance, one often reads that Eskimos have a vast number of words for different sorts of snow. These claims need to be treated with caution, however—see Pullum's entertaining paper *The Great Eskimo Vocabulary Hoax* (1991: 159–171).

Very often this pattern involves prototypicality: languages may have exact translation equivalents for words when these are used in their central senses, but not when they are used in more marginal or metaphorical ways. English *bite* and French *mordre* correspond closely when they refer to cutting with teeth, but outside this use they go their separate ways: one is *piqué*, not *mordu*, by a mosquito, while *la balle a mordu la ligne* means *the ball just touched the line*. No doubt most languages have a word which corresponds to *read*; but how many of these equivalents can be used not only transitively and intransitively, and to refer to reading aloud as well as silent reading, but also to talk about a machine reading a credit card, or about

The influence of the mother tongue on second language vocabulary 71

a person reading a balance sheet, a meter, music, a map, somebody's lips, people's minds or between the lines?

4 More problematically, people with dissimilar cultures may classify things (especially abstract concepts) so differently that it becomes very difficult to establish crosslinguistic equivalences at all. Words like *guilt, shame, remorse, apology, repentance, penance*, for instance, reflect concepts that may not be in anything like a one-to-one correspondence with the ways in which another culture analyses notions of blame and guilt. Here it is not just a matter, so to speak, of putting the labels in different places on the same picture; the picture itself may be so different that it is hard to relate the labels to each other in any meaningful way.

5 Differences of conceptual organisation may be reflected in differences in the very way words are assigned to part-of-speech categories. The Japanese equivalents of many English adjectives are effectively nouns or verbs.

6 Related languages abound in cognates—e.g. German *Buch*, Danish *bog* and English *book*, or Greek *duo*, Portuguese *dois* and English *two*. Where the meanings have diverged, as is often the case, the formal similarity can be very misleading: French *agenda*, Italian *morbido* and Spanish *embarazada* mean respectively *diary, soft* and *pregnant*.

7 Even where words in related languages 'mean the same', they may be false friends from the point of view of permissible grammatical context or collocation. French *expliquer*, unlike English *explain*, can be followed by an indirect object without a preposition (*expliquez-moi* …). English *want* can be followed by an 'object + infinitive' construction, as in *I want her to start tomorrow*; corresponding verbs in most other European languages cannot be used in this way.

8 Questions of formality and style are also relevant. English *get* (before a direct object) corresponds quite well to German *kriegen*, which is also casual in tone, but less well to the closest French equivalents (*prendre, obtenir*), neither of which is marked as informal. French has a slang word for shoes (*godasses*), for which there is no stylistically congruent counterpart in English. Some non-European languages differ radically from English in their ways of expressing formality through the lexicon, to the extent of virtually having separate word-lists in their 'high' and 'low', or 'respectful' and 'intimate' styles.

9 The way vocabulary is organised in discourse may differ from one culture and its language to another. According to Bartelt (1992: 103), for instance, Navajo uses types of repetition for emphasis which would be regarded as inelegant and redundant in English.

10 Finally, the very notion of a 'word' is far from constant across languages. The French for *gearbox* is not a single noun, but a three-word phrase; the German word *Erzeugerabfüllung*, common on wine labels, has to be rendered into English as *chateau bottled*, while its Spanish equivalent has four words and its French counterpart six. Comparisons between less closely related languages are even more striking. As Ringbom points out:

> ... the word has a different status as a linguistic unit in synthetic and analytic languages ... average Finnish words contain more semantic information than English or Swedish words. So for instance the single Finnish word *autostammekin* corresponds to the English phrase *from our car, too*.
> (Ringbom 1986: 155, 1987: 20)

Crosslinguistic influence and ease or difficulty of learning
Interlingual or intralingual?

Recent research has confirmed more and more strongly what language teachers have always known: that the mother tongue has a strong influence on the way a second language is learnt and used (e.g. Kellerman 1984, Kellerman and Sharwood Smith 1986, Ringbom 1987, Odlin 1989, Perdue 1993).

> There is obviously one critical way in which L2 acquisition cannot be compared with L1: children can experience no 'transfer' or 'interference' from a previously acquired language. All of the reports of the ESF [European Science Foundation] project are rich with documentation of SL [source language] influence ... I have claimed that each native language has trained its speakers to pay different kinds of attention to events and experiences when talking about them. This kind of training is carried out in childhood and is exceptionally resistant to restructuring in ALA [adult language acquisition].
> (Perdue 1993, vol II: 245)

The pioneers of contrastive analysis believed that by making crosslinguistic comparisons one could predict learning difficulty:

> We assume that the student who comes in contact with a foreign language will find some features of it quite easy and others extremely difficult. Those elements that are similar to his native language will be simple for him, and those elements that are different will be difficult.
> (Lado 1957: 2)

This view, though productive, was a serious over-simplification: not all crosslinguistic differences cause learning problems, and some things turn out to be more difficult than predicted by contrastive analysis.[3] The notions of crosslinguistic influence and learning difficulty later came to be more clearly distinguished, and learners' errors were seen as falling into two possible categories: 'interlingual' confusions, caused by interference or transfer from the mother tongue, and 'intralingual' confusions, caused by complexities in the second language itself.

A notorious problem with this model, which is still current, is that it is difficult to classify certain kinds of error. If an English-speaking learner of French confuses *fenêtre*, *vitre*, *vitrine* and *vitrail* (words for different types of window), is this an interlingual error (because the learner is misled by the simpler English system for referring to windows), or does it make more sense to call it an intralingual error (because the French lexical system is complicated in this area and English provides nothing useful to transfer)? The same question arises in relation to the omission of English articles—if a learner's mother tongue has no article system, is it realistic to consider his or her failure to use articles in English as an instance of transfer?

There are perhaps two reasons for the confusion. First of all, there is the mistaken view that errors have to be analysed in either-or terms: they must *either* be attributable to the mother tongue, *or* to features of the second language. And secondly, there is a common tendency to see mother-tongue effects, too narrowly, in terms of the 'transfer' of a detectable feature of the mother tongue into the second language.

> As Kellerman (1987) has pointed out, researchers tend to reflect their theoretical biases in what they interpret as transfer effects. He notes that Arabski (1979) made the somewhat surprising assertion that the 974 article errors in his Polish-English corpus were not transfer errors on the grounds that, because Polish does not have articles, there is nothing to transfer. Clearly, though, the absence of a structural feature in the L1 may have as much impact on the L2 as the presence of a different feature.
> (Ellis 1994: 311–312)

Relating intrinsic difficulty and crosslinguistic influence

Intrinsic difficulty and crosslinguistic influence are not alternative sources of error. For all the elements of a second language, we clearly need to consider:

1 how difficult they are in themselves (in terms of factors like transparency, complexity and processing load)
2 what sort of position the mother tongue puts a learner in when he or she approaches them: does it help, hinder, or simply stand aside?

The notion of difficulty in language is elusive. None the less, one can readily think of lexical features that seem intuitively to be intrinsically easy or hard. English and German words for numbers are quite straightforward; French number-words between 70 and 99 are slightly more complicated; one of the Japanese systems of number-words is relatively elaborate. Vietnamese has a very complex system of personal pronouns. English has a daunting array of verbs in the area of 'shine/gleam/sparkle/glitter' etc, but not many different words for tastes. Of the two Czech words *srdce* and *mi*, the first is clearly more difficult to say than the second. An English child will learn to use the words *postman*, *fat* and *run* earlier and more easily than *collateral*, *metaphysical* or *denigrate*.

Independently of the intrinsic ease or difficulty of items, however, a learner's mother tongue can greatly affect the way he or she is able to approach them. For instance:

- The Italian word *attuale* (= *current, topical*) is reasonably easy for most learners to grasp; especially easy for speakers of several European languages (*aktual* [Russian], *actuel* [French], *aktuel* [Danish] etc mean the same); but a confusing false cognate for an English-speaker.
- German numbers, though intrinsically unproblematic, are 'the wrong way round' from an English point of view: English-speaking learners typically mix up pairs like *fünfunddreissig* (35—literally 'five and thirty') and *dreiundfünfzig* (53—literally 'three and fifty').
- The English structure *I like X* is structurally and semantically straightforward, but problematic if one is coming at it from Spanish or Italian: *me gusta X* and *mi piace X* have a misleadingly similar word order to the English structure, but require the liked thing rather than the 'liker' as subject.
- Different learners approach the difficult French gender system from different starting points. Italians get enormous help from a mother tongue which assigns gender to nouns much as French does, though there are of course problems with particular words. German has three genders as against the French two, and knowledge of German is of little help in predicting the gender of a French noun; on the other hand, German-speakers are at least psychologically prepared for nouns to have genders, and this may well help them to notice and store the genders of French nouns as they learn them. English- or Turkish-speaking learners of French do not even have this advantage, and find French genders very difficult.
- Serious problems arise where the second language contains whole classes of word which are not shared by the mother tongue. Finnish uses case-endings to express the meanings which are communicated by prepositions in most European languages. Consequently Finnish learners of English have substantial trouble with prepositions as a class: they find them not only difficult to learn, but difficult to notice.

It may be assumed that a Swedish learner does not perceive the category of English prepositions as either particularly salient or non-salient: he simply recognizes them as prepositions and soon knows roughly how they function ... a Finnish learner, on the other hand, perceives the category of prepositions to be clearly non-salient, since they are redundant according to his L1 code. This perception often makes him omit them in production to a surprising extent even after many years of English.
(Ringbom 1986: 155)

The article systems of western European languages are similarly non-salient for speakers of languages which do not have articles: it is not unusual, for instance, to encounter Russians who have a relatively good command of English, but who use articles rarely or not at all.

Language distance, transfer and learning

Language distance clearly has some effect on the amount of transfer that can take place between languages, and therefore on the extent to which transfer can support or hinder learning. Related languages often share a great deal of cognate vocabulary, and even where vocabulary is not cognate, there tend to be close translation equivalents: this can give learners an enormous advantage. Where languages have less common ground, word forms will generally be quite different; more information about word meaning and use also has to be acquired from scratch. Studies have demonstrated, for instance, that Swedish- and Spanish-speaking learners of English acquire vocabulary faster and more successfully than Finnish- and Arabic-speakers (see Odlin 1989: 77–80 for details and discussion). Transfer from third languages seems to depend very much on relative language distance (Ringbom 1987: 113–14, 119). Difference of phonological structure also has an effect on vocabulary learning. It has been shown that, as one might expect, those foreign words which conform more or less to the phonetic and orthographic patterns of the mother tongue are the easiest to assimilate (Laufer 1990, Ellis and Beaton 1993). English has a large inventory of phonemes, permits quite elaborate consonant clusters, and reduces unstressed vowels. These features make many English words hard to handle for speakers of languages, like Spanish or Japanese, which have a different type of phonology.

Cultural distance, as well as language distance, can greatly affect ease or difficulty of learning. A Hungarian learner of Spanish, for example, will find that, though there are virtually no cognates (Spanish and Hungarian are unrelated), the new words in general express familiar concepts and are often semantically congruent with mother-tongue roots; so that a good deal of semantic transfer is possible. This will be far less the case for a Hungarian learning Chinese: not only are the words quite different in the two languages, but there is also far less overlap between the concepts that they express.

Types of error are therefore likely to vary somewhat with language distance. Where the first and second language are closely related, there may be fewer errors resulting from the intrinsic difficulty of what has to be learnt, since the mother tongue will provide support in more areas. At the same time, since more can be transferred, there is more scope for the type of interference errors which arise when items in two languages are similar but not identical in form or use. Conversely, where languages are unrelated, more errors are likely to result from the intrinsic difficulty of second-language items, whereas the role of interference will be somewhat reduced.

Learning vocabulary

> I shall always regret your lessons.
> (C. Ducarme, personal communication)

Generalisation

Words (other than proper names) mostly refer to classes of things, events, properties etc, not to individuals. When a baby learns a word, a major part of its task is to find out where the boundaries of the relevant class lie: does *cat* refer to all four-legged creatures, all domestic animals, all felines, all furry things or just the family pet? As small children learn vocabulary, in fact, they are simultaneously learning the world, as it is categorised and described by the culture into which they have been born. To some extent, children seem to have built-in strategies for fitting categories to words—for instance, they take it for granted that if nouns refer to objects, these will be discrete whole objects (Clark 1993: 49–66). Nonetheless, the process involves a good deal of trial and error, and young children typically overgeneralise or undergeneralise.

Second language learners, too, face the problem of establishing the range of reference of new words and expressions that they meet, and a good deal of exposure may be needed before they have enough experience of the way words are used to be able to do this accurately.

> By being familiar with collocations *like a convenient situation* and *a convenient time*, but not with ones like *a convenient person* or *a convenient cat*, [students] will realise, however subconsciously, that the adjective *convenient* is only used with inanimate nouns.
> (Carter and McCarthy 1988: 75)

However, second language learners have one great advantage over infants: they have already learnt how one culture categorises and labels the world. Whatever the differences among human cultures and their perceptions, there is also massive common ground, so we already know a lot about the scope of much second language vocabulary before we learn it. We can take it for granted, for example, that another language will have ways of talking about dogs, babies, pain, drinking, sleeping, work, heat and cold; if we are told that a particular train is *Zug*, *poyezd* or *treno*, we know the chances are that the foreign word can be applied, more or less, to the whole class of things that we call *train* in English.

A second language learner is likely, then, to short-cut the process of observing a new word's various references and collocations, by mapping the word directly onto the mother tongue. He or she may well learn from experience what kind of words *convenient* collocates with; but this may do little more than confirm and refine a prior identification of convenient with *comodo*, *gelegen* or whatever.

> We may assume that wherever possible the beginning foreign learner tries to operate with simplified translation equivalences between lexical items ... In the learning of related languages, simplified equivalences work

> well for the development of a receptive competence, even though these equivalences will have to be modified by later learning.
> (Ringbom 1986:154)

Often, indeed, the translation equivalence is made explicit at the outset, as when a learner says 'What's the Japanese for …?', or looks up an unknown word in a bilingual dictionary. Even when this does not happen, though, an immediate association with a mother-tongue word is likely to be set up as soon as possible. (At one time it was considered essential to avoid the mother-tongue in foreign-language teaching, and teachers would go through contortions to explain or demonstrate the meanings of words without translating. What often happened, of course, was that, after the teacher had spent ten minutes miming, say, *curtain* to a class of baffled French students, one of them would break into a relieved smile and say 'Ah, *rideau*'.)

Different kinds of equivalence hypothesis

> What the beginning Swedish learner [of English] takes to be self-evident is the basic, even trivial fact that an English preposition normally corresponds to some other preposition in Swedish and that the concept of (in)definiteness is expressed by articles.
> (Ringbom 1986: 154)

The simplest version of the learner's equivalence hypothesis might be stated as follows: 'Foreign words look different from mother-tongue words, but work in the same way (semantically and grammatically)'. Naive though this view is, it is not uncommon among people who know little about languages, and it is sometimes found even among more experienced learners. (I was at school with a boy who, working for an important Latin examination, was convinced that all he needed to do was to memorise words and their translations from a Latin-English dictionary.)

A more reasonable version of the equivalence hypothesis, then, might be 'Regard everything as the same unless you have a good reason not to'.

> The learner tends to assume that the system of L2 is more or less the same as in his L1 until he has discovered that it is not.
> (Ringbom 1987: 135)

This is probably the way most people approach language learning (though they may not all draw the 'good reason' line in the same place). According to research by Naiman, Fröhlich, Stern and Todesco (1978, quoted in Skehan 1989: 76–77), one of the strategies typical of good language learners is to 'refer back to their native language judiciously … and make effective cross-linguistic comparisons at different stages of language-learning'. Experienced learners, then, are likely to have some sense of the limits of translation equivalence, and to realise, for instance, that idiomatic uses of mother-tongue words are less likely than others to carry over into the second language. Kellerman carried out several interesting experiments (e.g. 1978, 1986) to test learners' intuitions about transferability. He found that, while the Dutch students he tested were prepared to use English *break* and *eye* to translate core meanings of Dutch *breken* and *oog*, more advanced learners were generally reluctant to extend the equivalence into more peripheral, irregular or idiomatic uses. So, for instance, his subjects were happy to translate *Hij brak zijn been* as *He broke his leg*, but doubted whether *break* could be used (as *breken* can) to talk about breaking one's word, strike-breaking or breaking a ceasefire. Kellerman's students turned out to be wrong in these particular cases, because the idiomatic uses chosen for the experiment were ones which do happen to coincide in English and Dutch. However, their caution probably stood them in good stead in general in their approach to English, and would certainly have paid off handsomely if they had been learning languages less closely related to Dutch.

Learners' perceptions of linguistic or cultural distance may also affect their readiness to transfer. As we have seen, there is more scope for successful transfer between closely related languages than between languages which are not related, and most learners seem to develop some sense of where they stand in this respect. Kasper (1992) cites evidence that Danes transfer mother-tongue usages more freely to German than to English. Ringbom, working in Finland, found that monolingual Swedish speakers are far more likely to transfer mother-tongue forms into English than are moniligual Finnish speakers (though Finns who know Swedish may transfer Swedish forms into English).

> Apparently Finnish learners are aware that their mother tongue is so different from the target language that they do not normally expect formal similarity between L1 words and L2 words, at least not to an extent that would guide them very often when they make their approximations.
> (Ringbom 1978: 90)

Readiness to transfer may also be affected by such factors as personality profile, type of education, and personal and cultural attitudes to language.

Some kind of equivalence hypothesis is probably indispensable in second language learning, especially during the early stages. Mother-tongue influence is responsible not only for errors, but also for much of what is correct in an interlanguage. If we did not keep making crosslinguistic correspondences, we might never manage to learn new languages at all. (Imagine having to ask whether each new Spanish house one saw was called *casa*; whether the new word was used by both men and women; whether a different word was needed for centrally-heated houses; whether it was taboo to talk about houses where people had recently died; and so on—instead of just provisionally deciding that the foreign word was probably used in much the same way as *house* and acting accordingly.) The strategy does not always work, of course—that is why languages are difficult to learn—and it is effective in inverse proportion to language distance, breaking down much more often, as we have seen, with languages unrelated to one's own. But on balance the equivalence hypothesis puts us ahead of the game: it enables us to learn new languages without at the same time returning to infancy and learning to categorise the world all over again.

When the equivalence hypothesis fails: errors and avoidance

The equivalence hypothesis can fail simply because the learner misinterprets a word or expression. There is an apocryphal story about a school class who thought that their French teacher's regular greeting 'Bonjour, mes enfants, asseyez-vous' meant 'Good morning, boys, sorry I'm late'. And one also hears of African trees whose native 'names', meticulously copied down from local informants by nineteenth-century explorers, turn out to mean things like 'It's a tree, you fool' or 'Go home white man'.

Even when the learner correctly interprets the reference of a new word, he or she is unlikely to grasp all of its semantic and structural characteristics immediately, and the correspondence with the mother-tongue 'equivalent' is almost certain to break down somewhere. As we have seen, when words in two languages are not exact equivalents, each may have more than one 'translation', depending on the exact meaning or context. Learners often acquire one of the equivalents before the others, and use this 'primary counterpart' (Arabski 1979) in both appropriate and inappropriate cases. Conversely, where the mother tongue makes lexical distinctions that are not matched in another language, learners may undergeneralise. A French learner of English may use *door* for the door of a room or house (French *porte*), but not apply it to the door of a car (French *portière*).

Errors arising from the inappropriate use of partial translation equivalents are extremely common, and have been extensively catalogued in the literature. Dušková, for instance, in a study (1969) of the errors made by Czech science students, found that '... a major group of lexical errors comprises misuse of words due to the fact that a Czech word has several equivalents in English.' She cites, among other cases, confusions between *do/make* (Czech *dělat*); *way/journey* (*cesta*); *repair/correct* (*spravit*); *include/involve* (*zahrnout*); *page/aspect* (*stránka*); she also reports receptive confusion between pairs of abstracts such as *suppose/suggest* and *involve/include*. Grauberg (1971), investigating the errors made by English-speaking students of German, found that in 35 out the 102 lexical errors he catalogued the student had 'attributed to the German word all the meanings of an English word, and not only the few correct ones'. Blum-Kulka and Levenston report on a study in which Israeli learners used *guilty* to cover a wide variety of related notions.

> To admit responsibility for an offense, the native speaker can choose from a range of expressions that vary according to the gravity of the offense, from *I'm guilty* for a capital crime, through *I'm to blame* to *It's my fault*

for a mere peccadillo. Some learners used *guilty* in all circumstances, even for denting a car in a parking lot.
(Blum-Kulka and Levenston 1987)

Contributors to Swan and Smith (1987) report numerous vocabulary confusions attributable to mother-tongue influence: for instance *think/hope, follow/accompany* (Swahili speakers); *definitely/exactly/completely, cut/kill* (Turkish speakers); *interesting/funny, careful/dangerous* (Japanese speakers); *why/because, also/even* (Italian speakers); *beat/hit/strike/knock, office/desk/study* (Greek speakers).

When equivalent words in related languages have different permissible grammatical contexts, this often causes error (e.g. **I want that you help me*; **Please explain me the problem*). More serious problems arise when crosslanguage 'equivalents' do not belong to the same part-of-speech category, as is often the case between mutually distant languages. Punjabi learners of English often treat prepositions as nouns, reanalysing English relational terms as names of locations on the pattern of the mother tongue and producing forms such as **Put the down chair* (Perdue 1993 vol II: 246). Some other examples of this type of error: *in upstairs, **I live with enjoy*, **It's belong to me* (author's files).

Interference can be from another foreign language. Dušková (1969) gives examples of characteristic German transfer errors in the English of her Czech students (e.g. *become* used for *get*, *also* for *then*, *will* for *want*.) Ringbom (1986, 1987) found errors in the English of Finnish learners that were due to their knowledge of Swedish false cognates. My son's school decided in its wisdom to teach him some Spanish three weeks after starting him on Italian; his Spanish interlanguage subsequently included the unusual greetings *buenas diores* (for 'good day') and *buenas nottes* (for 'good night').

When learners select and over-use one primary counterpart from among the options available in the second language, this is often the word or expression that most resembles the mother-tongue word in some way. Such resemblances can of course be misleading, and numerous errors, both receptive and productive, are caused by 'false friends' in related languages. I once seriously upset a French student by telling him that he had made dramatic progress (French *dramatique* = *disastrous*). Some examples from German learners' writing, cited by Gnutzmann (1973):
- * *take a place* (German Platz = *place* or *seat*)
- * *Very often he used to sit on that bank.* (German Bank = *bank* or *bench*)
- * *I am lucky that you have invited me.* (German glücklich = *lucky* or *happy*)
- *snake* misused for *snail* (German Schnecke).

Similar errors occur when learners re-export words which have been borrowed from other languages and changed their meanings, like French *baskets* (= *trainers*) or English *blitz* (German Blitz = *lightning*). Lists of English 'false friends' for various mother tongues can be found in numerous sources: see for instance Swan and Smith (1987); *Cambridge International Dictionary of English* (1995); Hill (1982).

Even when the preference for counterparts that resemble mother-tongue forms does not lead to error, it can result in stylistic infelicity, or in the systematic avoidance of common items which are less congruent with the mother-tongue equivalent. English learners of French, for example, tend to translate *Show me* by the structurally parallel form *Montre-moi*, rather than by the more idiomatic but structurally different *Fais voir* (= 'Make see'). English multi-word verbs are often under-used or avoided by foreign learners. French speakers use *enter* where English speakers would more naturally say *come/go in*; Tops et al (1987) report that Dutch learners are more likely to say *bear* than *put up with* (Dutch *verdragen*), or *seek* than *look for* (Dutch *zoeken*); Coe (1987) reports similar findings for Spanish and Catalan speakers, and Dagut and Laufer (1985) for Hebrew speakers. Wong (1983), quoted in Kellerman (1984: 120), found that Chinese learners, under the influence of the mother tongue, used large numbers of 'make + complement' structures (e.g. *They might make their friends get very upset*) in preference to lexicalised causatives (... *upset their friends*). Chang (1987), also studying Chinese learners, reports that they commonly avoid certain semantically diffuse English verbs:

> 'Small verbs' such as *be, bring, come, do, get, give, go, have, make, take, work* are characterised by the range of distinctive meanings each of them possesses and by the ease with which they combine with other words to form special expressions, many of which are highly idiomatic. These verbs do not have equivalents in Chinese and are very difficult to handle. Students tend to avoid using them. For instance, a Chinese learner is likely to say:
>
> 1 *Please continue with your work.*
> 2 *He finally yielded.*
>
> instead of:
>
> 1 *Please get on with your work.*
> 2 *He finally gave in.*

Japanese learners of English often under-use anaphoric pronouns, preferring to repeat noun phrases in a way which is more acceptable in their mother-tongue than in English. A typical example:

> My younger sister is junior high school student. My younger sister's junior high school is prefectural junior high school. That junior high school's provision of school meal is cooked rice and some subsidiary article of diet. My younger sister likes to eat cooked rice every day. But some another student doesn't like. So they take a box lunch. In Japan, box lunch is so popular.
> (Ian Thompson, personal communication)

Some words in the second language may not have mother-tongue counterparts at all, and these may be overlooked simply because learners do not expect them to exist, or avoided because they are felt to be difficult to handle. While a German-speaker may, for example, learn the French question-word 'combientième' (literally, 'how-manyeth') by asking for a translation of the German equivalent 'wievielter', an English-speaking learner does not have this route available, and he or she may therefore learn the word late or not at all. Blum-Kulka and Levenston (1983: 124) give an example of what they call 'void avoidance' by learners of Hebrew.

> Learners tend to avoid words for which no precise equivalents occur in their mother tongues, especially when the semantic components of such words require them to make distinctions they are not used to making at the level of single words. An example is the verb *šibec* (to insert in a suitable place). This is replaced by *hixnis* (insert) or *sim* (put), or by paraphrase.
> (Blum-Kulka and Levenston 1983)

And as we have seen, whole classes of words such as articles or prepositions may be avoided if they cannot easily be equated with mother-tongue categories.

Using vocabulary

Performance errors

> Many of the recurrent errors of systemic character, which we might be inclined to describe as errors in competence, reflect no real defect in knowledge, since most learners know the pertinent rule and can readily apply it, but the mechanism of application does not yet work automatically.
> (Dušková 1969)

> There finns a lot of racists in the world. (Swedish *det finns* = *there are*).
> (Quoted in Ringbom 1987: 149)

> 'I have done a mistake.' '*Made* a mistake, Wolfgang.' 'Oh, dear, I am always doing that mistake.'
> (Author's files)

Knowledge is not enough: people often make repeated mistakes with second-language material which they have learnt correctly. This was not a problem for behaviourist linguistics, which saw older (mother-tongue) habits as interfering with newer (second-language) habits. Early cognitive models of interlanguage had more trouble accommodating behaviour which conflicts with knowledge. Corder, for instance, felt that systematic errors must reflect the learner's current beliefs or 'transitional competence', and seems simply to

The influence of the mother tongue on second language vocabulary 83

have rejected the possibility that habitual errors might coexist with accurate knowledge of the relevant rules (e.g. Corder 1967: 10). Later conceptualisations involved for instance multiple-competence models (e.g. Tarone 1983, Ellis 1985), or consideration of the ways in which performance constraints can interact with competence (e.g. Bialystok and Sharwood Smith 1985, Bialystok 1994). For a detailed study of variability in interlanguage, see Tarone (1988); for an attempt to clarify some of the issues, see Swan (1987).

Common to many of these views is the notion of difficulty or effort: the learner produces a simplified form, or one closer to or identical with the mother-tongue pattern, because he or she has more fully automated control over it and can assemble it more quickly and easily than the correct target-language equivalent; or (in cognitive terms) because he or she cannot access the target-language form and retrieve it from storage quickly enough to use it for communication, and is driven back on more easily accessible material. While such views are plausible as far as second language syntax is concerned, they seem less satisfying when we consider lexical errors. *Make a mistake* is not obviously more difficult to assemble or retrieve than *do a mistake*; why does the learner, who 'knows' very well that one is correct, produce the other? And difficulty cannot account for 'backward interference', when people make mistakes in their mother tongues under the influence of other languages—mistakes which often seem identical to the transfer errors produced by foreign learners.

L2 influence on L1

It has been recognised for some time that backward interference occurs in the mother-tongue usage of people exposed to other languages: see for instance the discussion and references in James (1983), Johansen (1993) and Backus (1996). Sharwood Smith (1983) instances a Dutch speaker in his own country who, after a long English conversation, greeted a Dutch acquaintance with the words *Hoe ben je?* (literally *How are you?*, but not used in this way in Dutch). On a recent family holiday in France, I noted the following utterances, produced by three native English speakers in conversation with each other:

- *I should have commanded a cider.* (French *commander* = order.)
- *In the Dauphiné, high [mountain] huts get alimented by mule.* (French *alimenter* = supply.)
- *I'll unbranch the telly.* (French *débrancher* = unplug.)
- *Can I confide these trousers to you?* (French *confier* = entrust.)
- *That's very correct on his part.* (French *C'est très correct de sa part* = That's very punctilious/scrupulous of him.)
- *I shouldn't care to do it today. But the day after tomorrow—that's another business.* (French *affaire* = business; *une autre affaire* = another matter.)

Many people who are in frequent contact with foreign languages report the same phenomenon—it is common among expatriates, even those who use their mother tongue regularly.

Whatever causes this kind of effect, it seems reasonable to suppose that it is at least partly identical with the mechanism involved in transfer from the mother tongue—all six utterances just quoted could have been produced by a French learner of English. If this is so, however, neither older-established habits nor processing difficulty can completely account for transfer in second language production, since they are clearly not involved in backward interference of the kind we have been discussing. It seems that we need a more detailed understanding of what happens in the brain during bilingual storage and processing.

The bilingual lexicon

We know that words are not held in memory in isolation from each other. Storage of mother-tongue vocabulary involves networks of associations of various kinds, based on membership of semantic, phonological, graphical, syntactic and other classes (Aitchison 1994). Some of these relationships can be explored by word-association tests (Meara 1982, 1984); others are revealed when recall goes wrong and speakers produce slips of the tongue or malapropisms, or have words 'on the tip of the tongue'. Second-language lexicons, too, involve networks of associations, though second-language associative links may be less firmly established (Meara 1984) than mother-tongue links.

In the bilingual lexicon, the network of associations between words in one language is enriched by further associations with words in the other.

> It is clear that words in one language, and their translation equivalents in the other (when such exist) are related in the brain in a nonrandom way, much as a word and its synonym in the same language may be connected in an associational network.
> (Albert and Obler 1978)

How such relationships might be structured is not at all clear, although performance errors resulting from crosslinguistic interference obviously provide clues. As with monolingual associations, words seem to be related on several different linguistic levels which may operate simultaneously in complex ways. (Trying to think of the German for *nitrogen* (*Stickstoff*) recently, I first of all came up with *Klebstoff*, literally *sticky stuff*—the German for *glue*.) Data from error analysis, especially studies of unintentional code-switching, suggest that certain kinds of word may be more closely associated crosslinguistically than others in bilingual storage or processing. In some second language learners, for instance, function words such as conjunctions are particularly liable to importation from the mother tongue and other languages (see for example Vildomec 1963: 170, Poulisse 1993: 177).

And Ringbom (1986: 157), studying English examination papers written by Finnish-mother-tongue students, found that function words such as Swedish *och*, *men* and *fast* (*and*, *but* and *though*) were particularly liable to transfer from the learners' third language. For attempts to explain code-switching in terms of bilingual processing models, see for instance de Bot and Schreuder (1993) and Poulisse and Bongaerts (1994).

Laboratory experiments of various kinds (using procedures such as word-translation and repetition tasks involving cross-language semantic priming) have been carried out to clarify the nature of lexical storage and processing in bilinguals. Much of this work has focused on the question of whether words in two languages are linked to a common store of concepts, or whether each lexicon is associated with its own set of conceptual representations. Earlier research seemed to indicate that fluent bilinguals access semantic representations that are shared between languages. However, recent work suggests a more complex situation, with concrete nouns more likely than abstract words to involve shared concepts, and with the level of proficiency, the distance between languages and the nature of the experimental task all affecting the research findings (see Kroll 1993 for a survey).

Research by Meara suggests, interestingly, that different languages may have different preferred techniques for word-storage and handling. If this is so:

> ... then it is possible that learners will continue to use these strategies for handling words in their L2, even if the strategies are not particularly well adapted. This would lead to L2 words being stored with completely inappropriate entries if the L1 and L2 were ill-matched, and could account for much of the difficulty learners find with 'hard' languages such as Chinese and Arabic.
> (Meara 1984: 234)

This might explain the problems English learners have with French genders or Chinese tones, for instance: unlike native speakers, they may fail to store gender or tone information as part of the lexical entry for each relevant new word.

If the observational data from error analysis indicate that function words are particularly closely associated across languages, while findings from laboratory experiments suggest that it is concrete nouns that are most closely linked, we are obviously some distance away from an integrated view of what goes on in the bilingual brain during language use. Various attempts have been made to account for the observed facts in terms of schematic models of language storage and processing, such as that of Levelt (1989)—see for instance Poulisse (1993) and de Bot and Schreuder (1993). While this is not without value, there is a tendency for such box-and-arrow models to appear more explanatory than they are, by relabelling processes as if they were causal entities located in the brain. Saying that the brain contains a 'conceptualiser', a 'formulator' and an 'articulator' may amount to little more than using nouns instead of verbs to restate the fact that we think of things, put them into words and say them. (We do not explain what makes it rain by saying that the sky contains a 'rainer'.)

Constructing vocabulary

> Thank you for your unvaluable course.
> (F. González, personal communication)

Productive rules

Many lexical items consist of more than one element, arranged in rule-governed ways. The word *unfairness*, for example, reflects two common morphological rules: 'add *un-* to negate an adjective' and 'add *-ness* to form an abstract noun from an adjective'. The compound *toothbrush* follows an equally common rule: 'nouns can often be premodified by other nouns to express function or purpose; premodifying nouns are not usually marked for number'. The over-extension of such rules is a common cause of learner error. Jain (1974: 196) quotes mistaken coinages of agentive nouns like **witnesser* and **pick-pocketer* by Indian learners.

Rules of this kind can often be re-expressed, more or less accurately, in terms of translation equivalence: 'English *un-* = French *in-*' or 'French noun$_1$ + *à* + noun$_2$ = English noun$_2$noun$_1$'. To the extent that such rules have psychological reality for a learner, they allow the mother tongue to contribute to the generation of second-language forms, both correct and erroneous. So, for example, an English learner of French may exploit the fact that English adjectives and nouns ending in *-ive* tend to have French cognate counterparts ending in *-if*. (It was this strategy that led a friend of mine, who wanted to buy jam without artificial additives, to ask a French shopkeeper for 'de la confiture sans préservatifs'—jam without condoms.) Færch and Kasper (1986: 50, 58) quote Danish learners as producing, for instance, **employless* (Danish *arbejdsløs*) and **greens things* (Danish *grøntsager* = *vegetables*). Wilson and Wilson (1987) give examples of unidiomatic compounds produced by direct translation from Farsi: **work house* for *factory* (Farsi *kar khane*) and **book house* for *library* (Farsi *ketab khane*). Finnish learners' errors of a similar kind noted by Ringbom (1986: 158) include **home animals* (from the Finnish for domestic animals) and **swimming trousers*.

Technical terms are particularly susceptible to borrowing into cognate languages, and learners who are stuck for a technical word may simply import the mother-tongue word directly into the second language in the hope that it will be understood. Bongaerts, Kellerman and Bentlage (1987) report errors arising from the breakdown of this strategy, such as the unsuccessful use of Dutch *magnetron* to mean *microwave*.

Some learners seem more ready to 'coin' second-language words than others; this may correlate with personality-type, as was suggested earlier might be the case for readiness to transfer idioms. Ridley and Singleton describe an English-speaking learner of German who regularly makes up supposedly cognate German words to plug lexical gaps (for instance *gefastnet for stuck; *gelichen for leaked).

> She likes the sound of German, and 'positively enjoys making up words'. She describes it as 'tough luck' if her message is not always understood, saying that she 'can always point at something or get by' when communicating orally. ... Her language teacher describes her as an 'intuitive learner'. In a test designed for an evaluation of an impulsive/reflective approach to nonlinguistic tasks ... there is some evidence to suggest that her cognitive style is the least reflective among the four subjects.
> (Ridley and Singleton 1995: 145)

Multi-word items

Language use is not only a matter of applying generative rules. Many of the things we say are formulaic—fixed or semi-fixed expressions which are conventionally associated with recurrent situations and meanings, and which may be more or less idiomatic. Paradoxically, therefore, unpredictable utterances can be easier to produce in a foreign language than routine expressions. 'Why is there a dead cat on the floor of your shop?' can be constructed out of simple lexical and grammatical building blocks; 'Thank you, I'm being served' cannot be made in the same way—either you know how to say it or you don't.

There is a great deal of current interest in multi-word lexical items (also called, for instance, 'formulaic expressions', 'lexicalisations', 'lexical phrases', 'phraseology' or 'chunks'). In a much-cited article, Pawley and Syder (1983) describe 'native-like selection' as one of two 'puzzles for linguistic theory': how is it, they wonder, that a native speaker 'selects a sentence that is natural and idiomatic from among the range of grammatically correct paraphrases, many of which are non-native-like or highly marked usages'? How do we know, for instance, that *I'm so glad you could bring Harry!* is idiomatic, while *That you could bring Harry gladdens me so!* is not?

I am not sure why this is a puzzle. If we extend the notion of vocabulary to include formulaic multi-word items (as surely we must), then our knowledge that one formula is preferred over another seems no more mysterious than our knowledge that one sequence of phonemes rather than another realises a single word. The language has conventionalised, for example, *Can I look round?* rather than, say, *May I make a survey?* in the same way as it has conventionalised *optician* rather than *eye-doctor* or *asparagus* rather than *sarapagus*—that is just the way the idea has come to be expressed.

The inventory of formulaic or semi-formulaic multi-word items in a language is likely to stretch into the tens of thousands—there are probably conventionally preferred ways of saying all the things that come up regularly enough in interaction to be recognised as recurrent and predictable. Some such formulations cross linguistic boundaries very easily, behaving as if they were the property of a whole culture—you can 'save somebody's life' in twenty or so languages across Europe and America. Unfortunately for second-language learners, however, this kind of correspondence is the exception rather than the rule, even between related languages. Most such formulae cannot be successfully selected or constructed, either by literal translation from the mother tongue or by generalisation within the second language. There is no way of knowing, without learning the item itself, that the Italian for *Can I look round?* is *Posso dare un'occhiata in giro?* (literally *May I give a look round?*); or that a good English equivalent of *J'ai votre lettre sous le coude depuis pas mal de temps* (literally *I've had your letter under my elbow for some time*) is *Your letter's been sitting on my desk for ages*; or that the exasperated implication of English *That's all we needed!* is expressed by *Auch das noch!* (= 'that too, in addition') and *Il ne manquait que ça!* (= 'There was only that missing!') in German and French respectively. (But see Carter and McCarthy (1988: 37) for a note on patterns of collocation.)

Learners, of course, need ways of compensating for lack of knowledge—they must manage in one way or another to express themselves when they don't know the appropriate words—but there are few short cuts in this area. Attempts to match the idiomatic quality of mother-tongue formulae usually lead to error, and sometimes to absurd results. Grauberg (1971) found that 16 out of his 102 interference mistakes were caused by the complete transfer of English expressions into German. I tried—once only—to explain in German that a phone connection had failed by producing a literal translation of *I've been cut off*.

Implications for teaching

Clearly, the more aware learners are of the similarities and differences between their mother tongue and the target language, the easier they will find it to adopt effective learning and production strategies. Informed teaching can help students to formulate realistic hypotheses about the nature and limits of crosslinguistic correspondences, and to become more attentive to important categories in the second language which have no mother-tongue counterpart. In the case of related languages, it may be useful to integrate the systematic study of cognates into teaching programmes, as Meara (1993) suggests; it may also be possible to express some productive morphological rules in terms of translation equivalences. Learners need to realise that formulaic multi-word items cannot usually be literally translated; teaching may train them to identify such items, and to develop realistic paraphrase strategies to compensate for gaps in lexical knowledge where the mother tongue cannot provide support.

In this connection, Meara suggests equipping learners with:

a small metalanguage which allows them to cope with typical communication problems by negotiating the words they need to express their meanings.
(Meara 1993: 289)

For examples of teaching material which does this, see Swan and Walter (1990: 35 and 1992: 42).

Appropriate teaching and teacher-training can also help to dispel misunderstandings about the nature of error. It is important for learners and their teachers to realise that knowledge and control are not the same thing, and that continued failure to use learnt material accurately does not necessarily imply carelessness, lack of understanding or unsatisfactory teaching.

Conclusion

The mother tongue can influence the way second-language vocabulary is learnt, the way it is recalled for use, and the way learners compensate for lack of knowledge by attempting to construct complex lexical items.

1 Mapping second-language vocabulary onto the mother tongue is a basic and indispensable learning strategy, but also inevitably leads to error. How much the mother-tongue helps and how much it hinders learning depends, among other things, on language distance and on the realism of the learner's hypotheses about transferability.
2 Recall and use of learnt material—including mother-tongue lexis—can be interfered with by knowledge of another language; little is known at present about the storage and retrieval mechanisms involved.
3 Compensatory strategies involving translation equivalence can work successfully where morphological or other generative rules are involved; however, the mother tongue is usually of little help where formulaic multi-word items are concerned.

Appropriate teaching can help learners to develop realistic equivalence hypotheses, appropriate compensatory strategies and an understanding of the nature of error.

Notes

1 I am grateful to Michael McCarthy, Norbert Schmitt, and Catherine Walter for comments on an earlier draft of this paper, and to Ian Thompson for information about mother-tongue influence on the English of Japanese learners.
2 In this [article] I use the words *learn* and *acquire* in free variation. The same goes for *second language* and *foreign language*, and for *error* and *mistake*.
3 For a more accurate account of Lado's views, see Article 13, pages 138–142.

8

Legislation by hypothesis: the case of task-based instruction

(Originally published in *Applied Linguistics* 36/3, 2005.)

This article started out as an attempt to take issue with the noticing hypothesis: the idea that conscious noticing of a linguistic regularity is necessary for its acquisition. As I worked on the article, however, it escalated, turning into a full-scale criticism of hard-core task-based instruction, and of the hypotheses which are held to justify it. The introduction should make it clear that I was concerned only to address a relatively extreme approach to syllabus design, and not at all to question the general value of communicative tasks in language teaching. (How could one?) None the less, the article has sometimes been misunderstood in that direction. One or two scholars seem to have taken my criticisms of their views as personal attacks. This was certainly not my intention, and I am sorry if the sometimes polemic tone of the article gave this impression.

Abstract

Task-based instruction (TBI) is frequently promoted as an effective teaching approach, superior to 'traditional' methods, and soundly based in theory and research. The approach is often justified by the claim that linguistic regularities are acquired through 'noticing' during communicative activity, and should therefore be addressed primarily by incidental 'focus on form' during task performance. However, this claim is based on unproved hypotheses, and there is no compelling empirical evidence for the validity of the model. Many advocates of TBI reject proactive syllabus design on doctrinaire grounds, while commonly misrepresenting 'traditional' classroom practice. While TBI may successfully develop learners' command of what is known, it is considerably less effective for the systematic teaching of new language. This is especially so where time is limited and out-of-class exposure unavailable, thus making heavily task-based programmes inappropriate for most of the world's language learners. The polarization of meaning-based and form-based instruction is unconstructive, and reflects a recurrent pattern of damaging ideological swings in language teaching theory and practice.

1 Introduction

1.1 Definitions and focus

This paper examines a number of claims that are commonly made for, or in connection with, task-based instruction in second-language[1] learning. I am using the term 'task-based instruction' ('TBI') in a strictly circumscribed sense, following R. Ellis (2003). That is to say, I am concerned solely with an instructional approach that makes meaning-centred tasks the 'central planning tool of the syllabus' (Nunan 1991: 24) or 'the basis for an entire language curriculum' (R. Ellis 2003: 30), while rejecting alternative or complementary approaches to syllabus design. It is no part of my purpose to cast doubt on the pedagogic utility of tasks—communicative or otherwise—as such. Nor do I wish to question the value of the large body of task-directed research—both inside and outside the TBI framework—which has contributed substantially to our repertoire of pedagogic resources and to our understanding of second language acquisition.

1.2 Characteristics of TBI

While proponents of TBI naturally vary in their emphases and beliefs, there is broad agreement on the following principles:
- Instructed language learning should primarily involve 'natural' or 'naturalistic' language use, based on activities concerned with meaning rather than language (e.g. Prabhu 1987; Nunan 1989; J. Willis 1996; Skehan 1998; R. Ellis 2003).
- Instruction should favour learner-centredness rather than teacher control (e.g. J. Willis 1996; Skehan 1998; D. Willis 2003).
- Since purely naturalistic learning does not normally lead to target-like accuracy (Harley and Swain 1984), intervention is necessary, in order to foster the acquisition of formal linguistic elements while retaining the perceived advantages of a 'natural' approach.
- This can best be done by providing opportunities for 'focus on form', which will '[draw] students' attention to linguistic elements as they arise incidentally in lessons whose overriding focus is on meaning or communication' (Long 1991).
- Communicative tasks are a particularly appropriate vehicle for such an approach (Nunan 1989; J. Willis 1996; Skehan 1998; R. Ellis 2003).
- More formal pre- or post-task language study may be useful (J. Willis 1996; Skehan 1998; R. Ellis 2003). This may contribute to acquisition by priming or boosting 'noticing' of formal features during communication (Schmidt 1990, 2001).
- 'Traditional' approaches are ineffective and undesirable, especially where they involve proactive formal instruction and practice decoupled from

communicative work (e.g. Doughty and Williams 1998; Fotos 1998; Willis and Willis 2001; Robinson 2001).

TBI is frequently justified by the 'rehearsal rationale' (Nunan 1991: 282)—the view (common to all 'communicative' approaches) that language learning activities should directly reflect what learners 'potentially or actually need to do with the target language'. Equally important for many writers is the 'psycholinguistic rationale'—a consideration of the mechanisms underlying second language acquisition, and ways in which these can be activated in the classroom (Nunan 1991). Three hypotheses are associated with this perspective:

- An 'on-line hypothesis': language acquisition takes place solely or principally through communication (Schmidt 2001; Doughty 2001).
- A 'noticing hypothesis' (Schmidt and Frota 1986; Schmidt 1990, 2001): the conscious noticing of language elements is necessary to trigger acquisition.
- A 'teachability hypothesis' (Pienemann 1998): the acquisition of second-language syntax follows developmental sequences in ways which cannot easily be manipulated, thus rendering a predetermined structural syllabus unworkable.

1.3 Problems with TBI; structure of the paper

The TBI model is attractive, offering the possibility of combining 'the best insights from communicative language teaching with an organized focus on language form' (J. Willis 1996: 1), and thus avoiding the drawbacks of more narrowly form-centred or communication-centred approaches. Understandably, it has become popular with researchers and (in some teaching contexts) with practitioners.

However, I do not believe that TBI can fulfil its claims. In what follows, I take issue with the model on both theoretical and practical grounds. In Section 2, I argue that the hypotheses which underpin TBI provide no basis for decreeing that on-line focus on form should be the sole or determining way in which linguistic regularities are addressed—a view for which there is, further, no empirical evidence—and that other theoretical perspectives are pertinent. I also look critically at the way 'acquisition' is typically discussed largely in relation to interlanguage syntax. In Section 3, I argue that rejections of 'traditional' approaches are ill-founded and frequently tendentious. In Section 4, I suggest that naturalistically-biased approaches are in important respects pedagogically impoverished, favouring the development of what is already known at the expense of the efficient teaching of new language, and paying a heavy price for the 'downgrading' of the teacher. In Section 5, I suggest further that such approaches may be particularly inappropriate to the instructional contexts of most of the world's language learners, that in such contexts there is a powerful case for proactive teaching incorporating formal syllabuses, and that form- and meaning-based approaches should be integrated. I conclude by suggesting, in Section 6, that the exclusive advocacy of TBI reflects a perennial and damaging pattern of ideological swings in language teaching theory and practice.

2 The theoretical underpinnings of TBI

2.1 Three hypotheses

Arguments for a task-based methodology frequently invoke the hypotheses referred to above: that acquisition occurs on-line during communicative use of language, that the conscious 'noticing' of formal features is necessary for their acquisition, and that built-in developmental sequences render progressive structural syllabuses unworkable. Together with the belief that noticing needs to be boosted by deliberate focus on form, these hypotheses offer a theoretical rationale for TBI. Given the confidence with which many of the approach's proponents urge its superiority, and the firmness with which they reject 'traditional' methods, one would expect the hypotheses underpinning their recommendations and proscriptions to be supported both by solid theoretical reasoning and by sound empirical evidence. Is this the case?

2.2 Empirical support

Empirical support for the claims is sparse. Few studies have demonstrated the lasting retention and availability for spontaneous use of features acquired by incidental on-line focus on form, and there are no reports of successful long-term classroom implementation of the approach (Sheen 1993, 1994, 2002, 2003; Seedhouse 1999; R. Ellis 2003). Norris and Ortega's metastudy (2000) finds little advantage for on-line over off-line instruction. Schmidt (1990: 139) says that there is little evidence in the second-language literature that is directly relevant to the hypothesis that conscious noticing is necessary for acquisition; Schmidt (1990: 146) and Wray (2000: 473) make the same point for the related question of implicit rule acquisition. As far as developmental factors are concerned, evidence for inbuilt acquisition sequences currently lacks generality (Lightbown 1998: 179; DeKeyser 1998: 58); if such sequences exist, there seems no good evidence that they cannot be interfered with (DeKeyser 1998: 57–8).

2.3 Problems with the on-line hypothesis

The claim that acquisition only takes place on-line during communication, and the associated teaching recommendations, depend largely on extrapolation from work in areas distant from classroom SLA. Doughty (2001: 226–7), for instance, cites findings of working memory research by Cowan as an argument for the restriction of focus on form to the immediate context of the relevant linguistic feature, claiming that working memory makes available a 'cognitive window' of perhaps 40 seconds during which the mapping of form to function is possible and instruction can be 'seamless with processing for language learning'. While further research may strengthen such inferences, they do not seem currently to provide a very solid platform on which to base powerful and restrictive pronouncements about pedagogy.

The on-line claim is also undermined by the experience of the countless people who have apparently learnt languages successfully by 'traditional' methods incompatible with the hypothesis. And, if pushed to the limit, it is seriously counterintuitive. (Suppose I tell you that Japanese questions are made by adding the particle 'ka' to the corresponding statements, and suppose that a year later you start learning Japanese and remember what I told you. Are you really not able to ask questions until the rule has been acquired naturalistically in the prescribed way?)

2.4 Problems with the noticing hypothesis

The noticing hypothesis, propounded in a frequently-cited paper by Schmidt and Frota (1986) and discussed in subsequent papers by Schmidt (e.g. 1990, 2001) and others, suggests: 1) that all second-language learning requires the conscious noticing of linguistic elements; and 2) that what is noticed is surface features or exemplars 'at a very low level of abstraction' (Schmidt 2001: 5); more generalized knowledge of structural and other regularities is acquired through subsequent unconscious induction. The locus of noticing is typically a 'perceived [problem] with comprehension or production' (Long and Robinson 1998: 23), which may enable the learner to compare his or her interlanguage form with the target equivalent, and thus in addition 'notice the gap'. While this view has not perhaps achieved the status of 'conventional wisdom' attributed to it by Schmidt (1994: 195), it has become extremely influential, providing a psycholinguistic justification for the observationally-motivated need for 'focus on form', and constituting 'part of the rationale for a general reassessment of input-oriented approaches to language teaching' (ibid.); the hypothesis is commonly cited as an established principle in the pedagogical literature (e.g. Thornbury 1999: 85; Harmer 2001: 73–4).

The hypothesis is pedagogically benign: noticing linguistic features is surely a good thing for learners to do. However, it remains a hypothesis (Schmidt 1994: 176–7; 2001: 26), originating in Schmidt's relatively informal analysis of his experience of learning Portuguese (Schmidt and Frota 1986), and it is controversial. The idea that conscious attention is required for intake is certainly not universally accepted (Tomlin and Villa 1994; Truscott 1998; Cross 2002). It seems highly unlikely, in fact, that everything language learners acquire can derive from conscious noticing. Many non-native speakers of English, for example, produce the allophones of /p/ correctly; how many can have ever noticed that the /p/ in *spin*, unlike the /p/ in *pin*, is unaspirated? Constraints on linguistic generalizations constitute an even greater problem for the hypothesis. Many competent non-native speakers, for instance, are aware (not usually consciously) that not all transfer-of-possession verbs can be followed immediately by indirect objects: one can say *I offered/promised/ guaranteed Andrew £100*, but not *I donated/presented Andrew £100*. However such knowledge is arrived at, it cannot be by noticing exemplars, since there are no exemplars to notice: the non-use of a structure is not manifested through specific instances.

2.5 Problems with the teachability hypothesis

According to the teachability hypothesis in its current form, structures make differential demands on the learner's developing processing ability (Pienemann 1998); those that make heavier demands are acquired later. Acquisition of syntax is therefore thought to follow internally specified, relatively inflexible developmental sequences. Consequently, it may be pointless to follow predetermined structural syllabuses, since these cannot take account of individual learners' readiness to acquire particular structures (R. Ellis 2002: 19–20; Doughty 2001: 227–8). The hypothesis has generated much research and theoretical work. It is not clear, however, that theoretical arguments for pervasive and inflexible developmental sequences are currently powerful enough to compensate for the lack of wide-ranging empirical evidence.

It is also unclear why, if a fixed internal syllabus nullifies pre-planned structure teaching, it should not equally undermine opportunistic focus on form during task-based learning. If it is pointless to give a lesson on, say, relativization on Tuesday morning because we cannot tell who is developmentally ready for it, then surely it is equally useless to draw students' attention to an instance of relativization that arises during a task on Thursday afternoon. One can, of course, claim that task-based work enables teachers to deal with structures on an individual basis—particular problems will become salient for particular students as they are ready for them, and can be taught accordingly. But this argument conflates salience with readiness: learners may notice that they lack a difficult structure long before they are ready to learn it.

2.6 The acquisition of what?

> ... it is not clear that dealing with a lexical gap problem connects in any consistent way with the sort of change in the language system which is productive and which might lead to cumulative progress.
> (Skehan 1994: 179)

Perhaps because of long-standing concerns regarding the difficulty of achieving grammatical accuracy in a second language, TBI-related discussions of 'acquisition' often limit themselves to the acquisition of grammar, particularly syntax. On-line engagement with (grammatical) form through 'noticing' is held to trigger 'restructuring' of the 'interlanguage system'; 'pushed output' forces 'syntactic processing'; 'teachability' relates to (grammatical) developmental sequences. Researchers are of course entitled to address whatever aspects of language acquisition interest them most. But the frequent implicit equation of learning with syntactic development can encourage a serious bias in the way language learning and teaching are presented and evaluated, and contributes to a dangerous gap between what researchers mean by 'acquisition' and what language teachers and learners may understand by the term.

Schmidt's account (1983) of a Japanese learner, 'Wes', is frequently referred to in the literature. Wes was uninterested in grammatical accuracy, but in two years in Hawaii progressed from a very low level to a point where he was 'taken as a worthwhile interlocutor by native speakers who clearly reacted to him, at the end of the period of study, as a conversational equal' (Skehan 1998: 23). Skehan describes Wes as having spectacularly successful 'strategic capabilities', but as being 'very unsuccessful when judged in terms of development in his underlying interlanguage system', so that 'his improvement in terms of linguistic competence was minimal'. One can question a model of acquisition according to which learners who reach a new stage in their command of, say, verb-phrase negation are successfully 'restructuring' or 'developing' their 'interlanguage systems', while someone who increases his working vocabulary by several thousand items and reaches a point where he can communicate with native speakers on equal terms shows 'minimal' improvement in linguistic competence. The use of the 'system' metaphor, with its implications of interconnectedness, is perhaps partly to blame, suggesting that specific adjustments to syntax (but not lexis) somehow affect the whole of interlanguage. In fact, there is no reason or evidence to suggest that the acquisition of a particular syntactic feature such as English negation, third-person -s, or indirect question word order has any wider repercussions on interlanguage as a whole.

2.7 Skills

With occasional exceptions (e.g. R. Ellis 2002; Fotos 2002), emphatic condemnation of the syllabus-based teaching of discrete linguistic regularities is universal in the TBI literature. Such teaching, it is claimed, is unsupported by research in SLA or language teaching (Lightbown 1998: 188; Long and Crookes 1992: 30–31), and assumes a 'discredited' behaviourist model (Long and Robinson 1998: 16; Schmidt 1994: 167). Since research to date does not provide solid support for any language-teaching approach, this is not a very powerful argument. And in fact, instruction which takes as its starting point, where appropriate, a breakdown of what is to be learnt does seem reasonably compatible with skill-building theories, according to which declarative knowledge (however obtained) can serve as a platform for the establishment of proceduralized or automatized knowledge (Johnson 1996, 2001; DeKeyser 1998, 2001), even though the route from one to the other is not straightforward or well understood (Hulstijn 2002). Language learning is at least partly a matter of acquiring skills: 'a view of language as skill is persuasive, insightful, and useful for language teachers' (Johnson 1996: 38). This being so, instructed acquisition may reasonably include the presentation and practice of discrete elements of behaviour (Johnson 1996: 154–5); these elements (syntactic, phonological or other) constitute 'subskills' in the kind of 'skills syllabus' envisaged by Johnson (1996: 164).

The important role of practice in fostering automatization (DeKeyser 1998: 49; Johnson 1996: 154–161; Segalowitz 2003)—even, in certain contexts, of relatively mechanical practice (DeKeyser 1998: 54, 58)—is accommodated more easily in a skill-learning framework than in the models appealed to by TBI. The view that one can get from declarative to procedural knowledge of language 'by engaging in the target behaviour ... while temporarily leaning on declarative crutches' (DeKeyser 1998: 49), with a progressive reduction of conscious attention to form (Johnson 2001: 195), corresponds to what happens in other kinds of skill learning. Students of the violin typically master double-stopping or positional playing by working in the context of a progressive syllabus, often in ways that are far removed from 'natural' performance. Trainee airline pilots and surgeons similarly follow progressive courses of instruction involving relatively 'artificial' activities. (One would perhaps not wish to travel on a plane whose pilot had been left to acquire the skill of landing naturalistically, by focusing on the necessary formal manoeuvres when the need arose; nor would one want to undergo a heart operation from a surgeon whose training had been conducted on similar principles.) The fact that systematic practice is associated with 'discredited' behaviourist theory, and with a short-lived fashion for exclusively mechanical structure-drilling which perhaps only achieved 'false automatization' (R. Ellis 2003: 105), has led many scholars to dismiss its use as irrelevant to acquisition (e.g. J. Willis 1996: 135). But if practice aids learning, it aids learning. A fact is not invalidated by the place it has been given in an outdated theory—in the words of the biologist Jean Rostand, 'Theories pass, the frog remains'.

2.8 From theory to pedagogy

Advocates of TBI (and other researchers) differ, of course, in their acceptance of the stronger forms of the hypotheses discussed above. Views of what constitutes a 'natural communicative activity', of how far it is legitimate to 'seed' tasks with specific linguistic features, and of the difference between communicative 'tasks' and non-communicative 'exercises', vary somewhat; the distinctions can become rather scholastic, as in the discussion in R. Ellis (2003: 246–7). Interpretations of 'noticing' and 'focus on form' also vary widely, as do views regarding the extent to which they are sufficient for acquisition (see for instance the contributions to Doughty and Williams 1998). There is some agreement that, for the acquisition of complex syntactic or morphological systems, an 'occasional shift of attention to linguistic code features' (Long and Robinson 1998: 23) may not be adequate (e.g. Doughty and Williams 1998: 221). Many researchers such as Lightbown (1998), R. Ellis (1994,

2002) or J. Willis (1996) therefore accept the need to separate certain kinds of instruction, up to a point, from communicative activity, and to relegate them to pre-task or post-task work. This can generate some ideological agonizing: 'At what point does explicit segmentation cross over into linguistic isolation? This is a very fine line, indeed.' (Doughty and Williams 1998: 244).

Whatever compromises are made, however, TBI retains a powerful bias towards on-line learning at the expense of formal teaching. On the positive side, this brings learning and use under one roof, and encourages the exploration of ways in which task design and implementation can favour the rapprochement. Less constructively, it promotes a climate in which potentially useful pedagogic procedures are discouraged or outlawed on doctrinaire grounds: TBI learners are unlikely to spend much time, for instance, memorizing word lists, learning rules or examples by heart, or translating sentences. It can encourage a view of language instruction which overvalues noticing, in the belief that, with some exceptions, an adequate or even full control of structural features can generally be achieved by making target language forms in the input salient enough to be taken in and processed (R. Ellis 2002: 24). This can motivate reduced and potentially inadequate off-line attention to language problems, especially given the doctrine that off-line teaching must always be closely related to on-line activity:

> Although the requirement is that the target of focus on form must arise incidentally during the task, it is conceivable that the target be identified in advance through an analysis of learning problems. None the less, the teacher should wait until the problem actually does occur during the course of a communicative task (which may have been designed to increase the chances for use of a particular form).
> (Doughty 2001: 227)

The tendency to see acquisition in terms of grammar, discussed above, can encourage researchers to focus on ways of promoting accuracy and complexity (which are mainly to do with grammar) at the expense of the planned teaching of new language, and especially new lexis. This can have serious practical implications (see Section 4). Further, comparisons of TBI with 'traditional' methods are frequently made solely in relation to grammar teaching, and this can give a very misleading picture of the differences between approaches and of their relative merits (see Section 3).

These biases, I have argued, are not well supported by theory or research. When, for example, J. Willis justifies the need to prioritize certain kinds of input by referring to what has been established by 'research on second language acquisition' (1996: 13), or when R. Ellis suggests that traditional approaches do not 'conform to what is known about acquisitional processes' (2003: 210), and talks about 'the kind of communication ... which is required for acquisition to take place' (2003: 334), we need to remind ourselves that research has not in fact established what kinds of input or communication are required for acquisition to take place, and that the prescriptions and proscriptions that are common in the TBI literature are often based disturbingly on unproved hypotheses.

3 The rejection of traditional approaches

3.1 The scope and focus of criticism

As Lightbown (2000) reminds us, caution is needed both in rejecting the accumulated professional wisdom of teachers, and in applying research findings to the classroom. However, sweeping criticisms of 'traditional' language teaching are widespread in the TBI and SLA literature. The impression frequently given is of a paradigm shift in which discredited older methods, which have failed in practice and which are theoretically unsupported, have been replaced by approaches of a diametrically opposed kind based on sound theory and solid research findings. The methods especially under attack are those which incorporate proactive off-line teaching and practice following a progressive 'linguistic' (especially structural) syllabus. Fotos (1998: 301) talks of 'growing concern that a return to grammar instruction should not lead to a revival of "old ways" of language teaching—traditional grammar-based syllabuses, pattern drills and the like.' Similarly, Doughty and Williams, in their influential collection, reject 'discrete point grammar instruction' as 'inappropriate', and 'misguided' (1998: xiii). I have argued above that theory and research do not in fact provide a sound basis for rejecting the practices in question. Before dealing with the further claim that traditional teaching has failed (and the implication that it should therefore be replaced by TBI), it may be helpful to clear away some misconceptions which obscure the real issues.

3.2 'Straw man' attacks

The wish to pit 'good' new methods against 'bad' old methods can lead writers to present a caricature of traditional classroom practice with which currently favoured approaches are contrasted to their advantage. As Bruton puts it:

> Pedagogically, the typical justification for a move away from a [proactive] focus on forms has been to paint stereotypical pictures of straw teachers focusing only on irrelevant language features, in a rigid order, in a decontextualized and repetitious manner, with numerous tedious and meaningless exercises, where the language becomes an end in itself.
> (Bruton 2000: 54)

A characteristic example can be found in Willis and Willis:

> Most approaches to language teaching can be described as 'form-based'. Such approaches analyse the language into an inventory of forms which can then be presented to the learner and practised as a series of discrete items. There is an assumption that there is a direct relationship between

'input' and 'intake', that what is presented can be mastered directly and will, as a result of that mastery, become a part of the learner's usable repertoire. But second language acquisition research ... shows quite clearly that there is no such direct relationship between input and intake. (Willis and Willis 2001: 173)

Robinson (2001: 291), giving an almost identical account of teaching based on 'synthetic structural syllabuses', claims in addition that it relies on 'simplified classroom language and texts which are functionally and linguistically impoverished, prohibiting exposure to forms and functions learners may be ready to learn, or need to use'.

Such characterizations rarely refer to identifiable teaching situations or materials. They describe, if anything, aspects of an extreme form of behaviourist teaching which was favoured in a few contexts 40 or so years ago. Willis and Willis do not provide any evidence that the views they cite are held by the practitioners of 'form-based' teaching; these views are not incorporated in present-day teacher training programmes, and do not appear in the pedagogic literature. 'Synthetic' structural syllabuses, where they are used (mostly at lower levels), do not logically entail impoverished input. A glance at the major British-published English language courses of the last 30 years (e.g. Abbs and Freebairn 1975; Swan and Walter 1984; Soars and Soars 1993) will show that these balance controlled and free activity based on both simplified and 'rich' input and output, in parallel with the operation of progressive proactive syllabuses.

The conflation of language learning with the acquisition of grammar, referred to above, often causes traditional approaches to be characterized only on this dimension, as if pre-communicative teachers and materials had no concern, for example, with vocabulary, pronunciation, or receptive and productive skills. Thus Skehan (1998: 93–4), J. Willis (1996: 133–7) and R. Ellis (2003: 29–30) all contrast TBI with the allegedly inferior and 'discredited' PPP (presentation, practice and free production) technique. PPP is not however a language-teaching 'approach' or 'method' (Skehan's terms: 1993: 93), to which TBI can be opposed in some kind of ideological duel. It is a tool used by teachers for one of their many possible purposes: a useful routine for presenting and practising structural features until, ideally, they can be produced quickly and easily under semi-controlled conditions. In most types of language course, this is likely to form part of a programme which includes many other things, including communicative work. No doubt too much attention is often given to grammar, but there is no evidence whatever for the suggestion that 'traditional' teachers in general confine their work to the presentation and practice of structures, ignoring other types of activity and materials. (For a good account of PPP and ways in which it can be exploited, see B. Long and Kurzweil 2002.)

3.3 'Traditional approaches have failed'

Long and Robinson, discussing the rise of 'meaning-focused' approaches (1998: 18), describe 'a growing sense that something was wrong, recognition that traditional synthetic syllabi and teaching procedures were not working as they were supposed to'. R. Ellis (2003: 207) refers similarly to a 'continuing sense of the failure of traditional approaches'. The view that traditional approaches (however defined) have 'failed' and are 'discredited' (Skehan 1998: 94) is widespread, and seems almost axiomatic in the TBI literature. In the nature of axioms, it is not backed up by evidence: we are not generally told where, when or how seriously these approaches have failed, or by whom or for whom they have been discredited.

There is no evidence that traditional methods have 'failed'. (Indeed, it is hard to see what evidence there could be for such a sweeping assertion.) Countless people seem to have learnt languages over the centuries through the kind of instruction currently condemned in the TBI literature. The fact is simply that such methods have not done very well. No approaches work as they are 'supposed to': foreign languages are too hard for most people to learn well in classrooms in the time available. In addition, all approaches are vulnerable to circumstantial factors such as poor teaching, unsuitable materials or unsatisfactory syllabus design; and all approaches will fail in particularly unfavourable contexts such as large secondary-school classes of unmotivated adolescents.

The sense of failure no doubt relates partly to the apparently intractable carry-over problem: the difficulty of achieving fluent and accurate spontaneous production of what is taught, and especially of grammar. Consolidation of the teaching and practice of structures by continuing attention to accurate use during more communicative work is difficult to contrive, and will usually have disappointing results. As Johnson points out, however (1996: 171), it does not follow that the problem will be solved by eliminating the first two 'P's of grammar teaching—systematic presentation and practice—in order to stake everything on a more sophisticated exploitation of the comparatively neglected third 'P'—a focus on form during communicative activity. This is rather like saying that, because planting seeds does not guarantee growth, we should stop planting and concentrate on high-quality watering. It is of course theoretically possible that TBI, unlike traditional approaches, will be found to achieve spontaneous fluent error-free production in learners. If this is so, its proponents will certainly be entitled to talk of a paradigm shift. For the moment, however, as R. Ellis says (2003: 210), 'the rationale for task-based syllabuses is largely theoretical in nature, there being little empirical evidence to demonstrate that they are superior to linguistic syllabuses'.

4 TBI in practice: the problem of new language

4.1 The aims of language instruction

The purpose of TBI is to teach language. Any course of language instruction must establish an appropriate knowledge and skills base in the learner. This means solving three problems:

- *Selection and presentation*: The most important linguistic elements for learners' purposes must be identified and made available for learning.
- *Establishment of a knowledge base*: The forms and use of new language items must be fixed in learners' long-term memory.
- *Development of recall and deployment*: New material, once learnt, must become efficiently retrievable for comprehension or production. Where language use involves not only recall but also computation (for example applying a morphological or syntactic rule, matching a grammatical form to a meaning or situation), learners must acquire the ability to perform the operations required with reasonable accuracy in real time.

4.2 The naturalistic straitjacket

The third of the problems listed above is often the most intractable: advanced students, especially, may know far more language than they can use fluently and/or accurately. For such learners, appropriately designed TBI may be an ideal corrective, combining communicative practice with a focus on 'pushed output' which encourages them to process material syntactically, 'stretch' their interlanguage, and thus gain a genuine command of previously learnt material. For most learners, however, this is not enough, and solutions to the first two problems are also crucial. Progress means not only getting better at deploying what is known, but also learning more—there must be new language to 'push' and 'stretch', new forms to process. Here, the efficacy of TBI is more debatable. Despite its emphasis on the need to teach 'form', the approach retains the naturalistic orientation of earlier communicative theory, as well as its distaste (perhaps partly socio-political in origin) for control, whether personal or linguistic. Meaning-centred tasks, where acquisition can take place on-line, language is not prescribed and the teacher is not a dominant authority figure, are compatible with this perspective; the systematic off-line presentation and practice of elements in a progressive syllabus, involving the 'regurgitation of pre-arranged meanings' (Skehan 1998: 123) are not. This naturalistic slant constitutes something of a straitjacket, tending to limit the approach to doing what it does best—promoting more accurate, fluent and complex use of what has already been learnt—at the expense of a principled focus on new linguistic material. The bias is frequently made explicit in the literature. R. Ellis (2003: 16) characterizes communicative tasks as requiring students 'to make use of their own linguistic resources'. J. Willis, talking about the central 'task' phase of her 'framework' asks (1996: 135) 'How can production be "free" if students are required to produce forms which have been specified in advance?', and explains:

> An important feature of [TBI] is that learners are free to choose whatever language forms they wish to convey what they mean in order to fulfil, as well as they can, the task goals. It would defeat the purpose to dictate or control the language forms that they must use. As the need arises, words and phrases acquired previously but as yet unused will often spring to mind.
> (J. Willis 1996: 24)

4.3 Where does new language come from?

The question of where the 'words and phrases acquired previously' come from is not generally very clearly addressed in the TBI literature. Some researchers (e.g. van Patten and Cadierno 1993; R. Ellis 2001, 2003; Samuda 2001) discuss the task-based teaching of new material in interesting ways, but in general surprisingly little is said about the development of learners' knowledge, as Samuda (2001) points out. Comprehensive explorations of task design and operation frequently contrast with extremely sketchy discussions of the actual language which is supposed to be learnt, or the routes by which it is supposed to be provided. As a communication-centred, process-oriented approach, TBI is perhaps simply not very interested in linguistic product. R. Ellis (2003: 31), citing Kumaravadivelu, says 'methodology becomes the central tenet of task-based pedagogy, in that no attempt is made to specify what the learners will learn, only how they will learn'. It seems to be commonly taken for granted that structures and lexis will be made available for learning (and presumably learnt) through interaction, task materials, 'focus on form', teacher intervention, pre-teaching, or simply the rich input felt to be associated with TBI; but these assumptions are not for the most part given detailed attention or subjected to testing.

4.4 Interaction; learning from each other

Long (1988) says that 'negotiation of meaning' will produce 'more finely-tuned input' from a learner's interlocutor; J. Willis (1996: 11) makes a similar claim. For Skehan (1998: 118–9), extendable tasks generate 'complex, cutting edge language', and language 'emerges' from tasks. But while exchanges with native speakers may generate input which can be learnt from, it is difficult to see how, in many classrooms, interaction can reliably promote the acquisition of new material during task performance. Unless the teacher is the interlocutor, task-based interaction may more easily uncover gaps than bridge them. Several researchers (e.g. Foster 1998) have demonstrated that learners typically bypass communication problems during tasks with little or no negotiation of form (as against meaning) or language development.

(See Bruton 2002b, 2002c for discussion.) Indeed, task-based interaction can constitute a 'particularly narrow and restricted variety of communication' (Seedhouse 1999: 155). R. Ellis notes (2003: 82): 'there is very little research to show that meaning negotiation actually leads to grammatical development of any kind.' Tasks can certainly be structured to promote more complex and accurate interaction, and this aspect of task design and implementation has generated much valuable research (e.g. Skehan 1998; contributors to Bygate et al 2001), but there is no evidence that such interventions make unknown language 'emerge', and it is hard to see how they could do so. If some learners know things that others do not, limited cross-fertilization can no doubt occur, with students sometimes supplying vocabulary, correcting each other's errors, or working together to solve linguistic problems, especially in multilingual or mixed-level classes. However, successful transfer of knowledge in this context depends on a number of factors, and the knowledge transferred is not always correct (Storch 2002). Swain, who has carried out detailed and interesting work in the area, argues forcefully (2002) that students can learn from each other (or at least, the weaker students from the stronger) in group tasks in this way. But, whatever the interest of this framework for research, it seems a less than ideal basis for instruction. If one was seeking an efficient way of improving one's elementary command of a foreign language, sustained conversation and linguistic speculation with other elementary learners would scarcely be one's first choice.

At the most naturalistic end of TBI, it sometimes seems as if students are expected to develop their knowledge virtually on a bootstrap basis during interaction or task performance. J. Willis (1996: 18) explains: 'Tasks remove the teacher domination, and learners get chances to open and close conversations, to interact naturally, to interrupt and challenge, to ask people to do things and to check that they have been done.' But if students do not already know the linguistic conventions for opening and closing conversations, interrupting and challenging, etc., how are they supposed to learn them without input from the 'dominating' teacher? One cannot teach by eliciting what is not there.

Under these constraints, the concept of 'pushed output' can be stretched to breaking point. Swain (1998: 67) quotes Tarone and Liu (1995) to the effect that acquisition is most likely to occur in contexts 'where the learner needs to produce output which the current interlanguage system cannot handle ... [and so] ... pushes the limits of that interlanguage system to make it handle that output'. But this amounts to requiring students to invent non-target-like language in order to communicate. Swain's paper itself offers a striking example. She reports a think-aloud session with a student, in which her purpose was to explore the hypothesis that 'the activity of producing the target language ... may trigger cognitive processes that might generate linguistic knowledge that is new for the learner or consolidate the learner's existing knowledge'. The student was trying to work out the French for 'destruction', starting from his (inaccurate) knowledge of the word for 'destroy'. After considering *détruction, démolition* and *démolisson*, he settled for *détruision* (the correct form is *destruction*). Swain, commenting on this, seems quite satisfied that acquisition occurred, saying 'His final solution, "*la détruision*", is nontargetlike, but he has made use of his knowledge of French by using the stem of the verb he has just produced and by adding a French-sounding suffix. This example is revealing, because the incorrect solution allows us to conclude that new knowledge has been created through a search of his own existing knowledge.' 'New knowledge' seems an odd term for the acquisition of a non-existent noun form and the reinforcement of a belief in a phantom generative morphological rule.

4.5 Other sources: pre- and post-task work, materials, the teacher

Pre-teaching is widely cited as a way of priming on-line noticing (Schmidt 1990, 2001) and more generally as a source of new language (Skehan 1998:137; Skehan and Foster 2001: 199; R. Ellis 2003: 249). Texts (both spoken and written), information-sheets etc. can also expose learners to new material. As far as grammar is concerned, texts may provide a convenient locus for 'focus on form', both implicit and explicit, and there has been a good deal of research and discussion in this area (e.g. Doughty and Williams 1998). However, apart from J. Willis (1996), who makes detailed practical suggestions for pre-teaching and the use of texts, writers generally offer little more than a brief list of suggestions regarding the selection and presentation of new language. Skehan, for instance, quotes Long and Crookes (1992) who say that tasks 'provide a vehicle for the presentation of appropriate target language samples to learners' (1998: 97), but says little about how this 'presentation' might operate in practice; and many of his illustrative tasks provide no new linguistic input at all.

Pre-teaching, texts and other materials in fact seem to have a largely ancillary function in TBI: they are primarily a source of task-relevant language or information, rather than a vehicle for presenting new language that has been selected in accordance with task-external criteria. J. Willis, in her recommendations for pre-task work, specifies that 'The point of the introductory focus on topic and language is not to teach large amounts of new language' (1996: 43). Skehan is concerned that natural use of language in tasks cannot be predicted, and that pressurising learners to use particular structures renders tasks so unnatural that they are 'of dubious value for acquisition' (1998: 130). R. Ellis even feels that pre-teaching may threaten 'the integrity of the task' (2003: 246–7), causing learners (undesirably) to treat it as an 'exercise' for practising what has been pre-taught.

In J. Willis's (1996) framework, the important language focus element is reserved mainly for post-task work, and in practice neither the 'report' phase of her tasks, nor her other language-focus activities, necessarily recycle material from the input (Bruton 2002a: 7). Valuable new material is often introduced in Willis's post-task phase, but this is decoupled from the communicative activity which could have consolidated its acquisition.

The teacher is encouraged to keep a low profile in TBI: learners are not seen as progressing mainly because their teachers teach them what they need to know. Teachers can certainly act as sources of linguistic information, for example by supplying task-related vocabulary where necessary, offering recasts, or acting as 'interlocutors'. But the thrust of TBI is to cast the teacher in the role of a manager and facilitator of communicative activity rather than an important source of new language. D. Willis, comparing teacher-directed approaches unfavourably with experiential learning, says:

> Teacher-controlled and teacher-concocted examples increase the learner's dependence on the teacher. They tell learners: 'Your teacher is the guide and mentor, who will show you what to learn and how to learn it. Listen to your teacher and do as you are told. Then you will learn.' By recycling language which is familiar to them, we tell learners: 'Look at this. You have valuable experience of the English language. If you look at that experience and use it, then you will learn from it.'
> (D. Willis 2003: 167)

4.6 How rich is the input?

Underlying this lack of detailed concern with new language, there is perhaps a feeling that the 'rich input' (J. Willis 1996: 11) felt to be characteristic of TBI will automatically supply what is needed. This assumption, however, needs to be questioned. TBI puts great emphasis on output: the approach centrally involves learners deploying and refining their use of language to solve communicative problems. Inevitably, this means that TBI has less time available per class hour for new-language input than a conventional text-heavy course with its battery of reading and listening material. Conventional courses also typically supply 'analysed' new language material in the form of word-lists and examples of grammatical regularities; TBI does not do this. The term 'rich' is no doubt meant to imply quality rather than quantity: TBI favours authentic but comprehensible material, while modern conventional courses tend to provide a cocktail of authentic, simplified and scripted reading and listening material. However, even supposing one formula is superior to the other (which has not been established), it remains true that TBI provides learners with substantially less new language than 'traditional' approaches. This seems a serious weakness.

5 TBI and the world's language classrooms

> ... when researchers make strong claims that are at odds with the views teachers have developed through their experience with learners, and when those claims are made on the basis of research which has been done

in contexts which do not reflect reality as the teachers know it, they are likely to alienate teachers and lead them to dismiss researchers as ivory tower oddities.
(Lightbown 2000: 453)

5.1 The 3hpw learner: coverage and the case for planning

TBI is of obvious value to learners who do not need much new input from their language classes (either because they receive substantial out-of-class exposure, or because they have already been taught more language than they can use), and whose main concern is to improve the accuracy, fluency and complexity of their output. It is however not clear how TBI can fully meet the requirements of those learners—the vast majority—who fall outside these categories. Some researchers (e.g. Doughty and Williams 1998: 199–200; Lightbown 2000: 453–4) discuss the need to adapt 'focus on form' to different instructional situations; Fotos (2002: 139) recognizes the unsuitability of TBI for EFL contexts. More usually, however, as Klapper and Rees point out (2003: 285), it seems to be assumed that insights from research into exposure-rich learning are 'automatically transferable to other foreign language learning contexts'. This assumption ignores the problem of input coverage. Skehan (1998: 124) quotes D. Willis (1993) as suggesting that transacting tasks 'will, in an unforced way, generate the most significant lexis of a language'. But unless an enormous quantity of task-based input is provided, this is simply not so. As course designers discover, even at beginners' level a surprising amount of basic vocabulary is likely to fall through the net of a syllabus based purely on a communicative needs analysis; at higher levels ensuring coverage of the 'most significant lexis' in this way becomes increasingly problematic (Swan 1985: 79–80, 1996). While, clearly, in a task-based programme language relevant to the performance of the chosen tasks will be foregrounded, other important items that fall outside this framework cannot be guaranteed to occur naturally under normal time constraints, and may not therefore become available for learning. (What selection of tasks would reliably generate the occurrence of, or the need for, the following common lexical items: *control, rough, move, calm, noisy, swallow, take trouble, lane, genuine, out of sight, purple?*)

'Normal time constraints' can be very constraining indeed. A typical secondary-school pupil in many countries may have language lessons for three hours a week, 40 weeks or less a year, for perhaps five years—a total of 600 hours or so, very thinly spread. In such situations, as Fotos points out (2002: 139), the coverage problem becomes acute. In the tiny corpus of a year's task-based input, even some basic structures may not occur often, much core vocabulary is likely to be absent, and many other lexical items will appear only once or twice. Frequency of occurrence is important if noticing is to lead to acquisition (Schmidt 1990: 143; N. Ellis 2002), and adequate opportunities for the use of new material are necessary in order for retrieval and computation to become automatized. In the '3hpw' situation, a purely task-based approach can neither ensure that language learners encounter all the most common and useful language items, nor prevent much of what they do notice from being inadequately processed and rapidly forgotten. Satisfactory lexical coverage can only be ensured with the aid of a frequency-informed lexical syllabus, as Willis himself makes clear (1990: vi), and courses designed for use in exposure-poor contexts generally adopt this principle (e.g. Swan and Walter 1984, Willis and Willis 1988).

R. Ellis justifies TBI on the grounds that 'through tasks, we can engage learners in the kinds of cognitive processes that arise in communication outside the classroom' (2003: 336). However, acquisition cannot be left to the operation of such cognitive processes, if the circumstances in which they naturally operate—in particular, a high volume of input—are not present. The role of instruction in a typical language classroom is not, surely, to attempt the impossible task of replicating the conditions of natural acquisition, but to compensate for their absence. Where time and opportunities for exposure are seriously limited, instructional aims are most plausibly furthered by planned approaches involving, among other elements, careful selection and prioritizing, proactive syllabus design, and concentrated engagement with a limited range of high-priority language elements, so as to establish a core linguistic repertoire which can be deployed easily and confidently. Such an approach will inevitably be far from 'natural' in some respects: indeed, substantial contrivance will be needed, both in materials design and in teaching methodology, to ensure that key material is encountered often enough and processed thoroughly enough to become part of the learners' competence.

5.2 The case for a grammar syllabus

There will thus necessarily be a role, in most instructional contexts, for the outlawed grammar syllabus. Holistic focus on form is valuable once learners are ready to integrate the language elements they know into realistic communicative exchanges, but this will often need to be preceded by discrete presentation and practice: one cannot learn a dozen new forms at the same time. It is therefore useful to have a list of structural features which learners need to control and which are known from experience to need focused teaching; it is also useful to put them in a reasonable order of priority. Sequencing is probably less of a problem than is often suggested. Despite R. Ellis's accusation that published grammar practice materials 'present and practice grammatical structures in accordance with notions of difficulty that have been passed down from one generation of writers to another without bothering about whether these notions have any psycholinguistic basis' (2002: 163), traditional structure grading is informed by pedagogic experience and expertise: future research is unlikely, for example, to stop us teaching present tenses before subjunctives. The need for a grammar syllabus does not, of course, imply that it should occupy the bulk of the teaching programme, as has sometimes been the case in the past (though not nearly so often as is claimed in the TBI literature). A grammar syllabus alone is no more suitable as an overall organizing principle for language teaching than is a lexical syllabus, a functional-notional syllabus, a syllabus of tasks or any other single strand of the complex fabric of language forms and use.

The question of level—rarely mentioned in the literature—is highly relevant in this context (Bruton 2002b: 287). Despite the suggestions of J. Willis (1996: Ch 8) and R. Ellis (2002: 22–23) that grammar is unnecessary for beginners, many teachers take the opposite view: that beginners urgently need a simple grammatical repertoire. Learners can hardly make the 'occasional shift in attention to linguistic code features' recommended by Long and Robinson (1998: 23) if they know so little basic grammar that they cannot produce discourse to shift from. At lower levels, too, the argument commonly advanced against a traditional structural syllabus—that structures are taught in isolation from communicative need—loses its force. The most basic structures are needed all the time as learners struggle to talk about themselves, their surroundings and their experiences; a well-planned traditional structural syllabus is therefore, very precisely, an expression of a needs analysis. As learners progress, the grammar syllabus becomes more remedial and reactive, and communicative tasks can take a more important role: 'it is a well-established principle of syllabus design that the unit of organization should change in the course of the language-teaching operation' (Johnson 1996: 168).

5.3 Teachers and TBI

In the light of these considerations, it is not surprising that, as several researchers note (e.g. Skehan 1998: 94; Ellis 2003: 320), many teachers and learners seem unwilling to adopt TBI. Skehan, commenting on such attitudes, complains (1998) that: '… a conservative [teaching] profession, out of touch with language acquisition studies, has for many years simply transmitted essentially the same view of how teaching should be organized, and what teachers should be like', preferring proactive syllabus-based teaching because it favours 'teacher control', 'accountability' and 'emphasis on product'. No doubt Skehan's strictures are partly justified: the world's language teachers may not generally be achieving very good results, perhaps they do tend to conservatism, and probably many of them could benefit from greater familiarity with language acquisition studies. However, typical 3hpw teachers are likely also to be sufficiently aware of the constraints inherent in their situation to be sceptical of the value of state-of-the-art methods, whether or not these appear to be validated by language acquisition research, which seem to them clearly inappropriate to the circumstances in which they work.

5.4 Polarization or integration?

> Perhaps Spada's ... conclusion that form-based and meaning-based approaches need not be in opposition to each other but can operate synergistically is the most realistic current judgment.
> (Wesche and Skehan 2002: 220)

Rather than being regarded as a replacement for 'traditional' approaches, task-centred work is surely best seen as one of many diverse resources that can support effective teaching in the world's classrooms. Languages present different types of learning problem; learners differ; instructional contexts vary. In the conspicuous absence of proof to the contrary, it seems plausible that the best strategy for most teaching situations is not to limit oneself to one type of activity, 'starting with independent communication tasks and attempting to extend their application to the maximum' (Bruton 2002b: 287), but to draw on all the resources and techniques available. In such an approach, tasks of various kinds will take their place as components of 'task-supported' instructional programmes (R. Ellis 2003: 27), alongside a variety of other procedures which will range from the most 'natural' to the most 'unreal', traditional and allegedly 'discredited', from the most learner-centred to the most teacher-centred, as complementary components of a multi-faceted syllabus (Cook 2000: 170–173; Swan and Walter 1990: vi–viii).

How the balance is struck, in a particular case, between pre-planned input–output work and more naturalistic activities will depend on several factors, including the time available and the learners' level. But excessive reliance on one or other kind of approach can only lead teachers to unproductive extremes, where language is taught and practised but not carried over into spontaneous production (probably the weakest aspect of traditional approaches), or where the language that is most needed is not all reliably supplied and taught (which I have argued is the weakest aspect of TBI). As Widdowson puts it:

> the belief underlying the [traditional] approach is that competence is primary, and performance will emerge as a by-product. The TBI belief is the reverse: get performance right and competence will, with some prompting, take care of itself.
> (Widdowson 2003: 128).

Clearly, both competence and performance need to be addressed in their own terms: neither follows straightforwardly from the other in second-language learning. Only by integrating form- and meaning-centred approaches, I suggest, can teachers maximize their chances of successfully teaching all those aspects of language that learners most need to master, and thus meeting the 'central challenge for language teaching ... to develop learners' communicative language ability through pedagogic intervention' (Bygate 2001: 23). Any teaching philosophy which deliberately excludes one of these complementary elements in favour of the other has arguably forfeited its right to be taken seriously.

6 Conclusion; reflections and implications

> [T]he basic assumption of Task-Based Language Teaching—that it provides for a more effective basis for teaching than other language teaching approaches—remains in the domain of ideology rather than fact.
> (Richards and Rodgers 2001: 241)

The claim that TBI is a superior teaching approach, solidly based on the findings of current theory and research, cannot be sustained. The hypotheses frequently associated with TBI, to the effect that second-language acquisition happens exclusively as a result of 'noticing' during communicative activity, and is constrained by inflexible developmental sequences, are supported neither by convincing theoretical argument nor by empirical evidence, and are contradicted by common language-learning experience. The model of acquisition relates almost exclusively to the development of interlanguage grammar. Assertions that basing instruction on proactive syllabuses has no theoretical justification ignore the fact that language learning can be classed at least partly as a form of skill learning. The claim that 'traditional' approaches have failed is not well founded, and frequently involves misrepresentation of the approaches in question. The naturalistic communication-driven pedagogy characteristic of TBI has serious limitations, especially as regards the systematic teaching of new linguistic material. Its exclusive use is particularly unsuitable for exposure-poor contexts where time is limited—that is to say, for most of the world's language learners. No reports of successful long-term classroom implementation are available.

The recent promotion of TBI at the expense of other approaches reflects a recurrent dynamic in our discipline. Since the fall of the tower of Babel, language-teaching theory and practice have swung backwards and forwards in attempts to reconcile the polar opposites of form versus use, knowledge versus skill, control versus freedom, artifice versus nature. Dissatisfaction with the results we are obtaining (which, second-language learning being what it is, will always be relatively unsatisfactory) leads us regularly to reject existing practices in favour of more promising-looking alternatives, announcing yet another 'paradigm shift' as we do so. Unfortunately such changes of focus are characteristically subtractive as well as additive, outlawing central aspects of previous approaches as they focus on the key concerns of the new one (Cook 2001: 8; Swan 1985: 86). We therefore spend much of our time working with one hand or the other tied behind our backs.

Hypotheses are the driving force of scientific progress: they generate research agendas, channel creativity and catalyse discovery. But hypotheses are double-edged, especially perhaps in disciplines such as ours which are not anchored by a strong empirical base. The theory supporting a fashionable new language-teaching approach easily transmutes into ideology. Models of acquisition are then no longer provisional conceptualizations, helpful in organizing our knowledge but subject to continual testing and revision; they become their own justification. Speculation passes for proved fact, so that it is possible for unvalidated theoretical orthodoxies to become established and to exercise enormous influence on the teaching profession, prescribing and proscribing instructional practice on the basis of nothing better than acts of faith. In living memory, such legislation by hypothesis has required language teachers at different times to ignore the learners' mother tongue; to base teaching on contrasts between the mother tongue and the second language; to avoid showing beginners the written word; to establish habits by drilling; to refuse to explain grammar; to explain grammar but avoid drilling; to rely exclusively on comprehensible input; to minimize opportunities for error; to regard errors as constructive; not to ask questions to which the teachers know the answers; to use simplified material; to avoid using simplified material; and so on.

Approaches which fit the theory of the day, however questionable, may be felt to need no further support, as when R. Ellis (2002: 32), arguing for procedures which include postponing grammar teaching to intermediate level, says 'These proposals are theoretically based and, as such, provide a solid foundation for the teaching of grammar'. At the same time, widely-used and effective activities may be condemned because they conflict with current doctrine. In the present intellectual microclimate it is actually possible, without the absurdity being apparent, to criticize language teachers for concerning themselves with language. Robinson (2001: 292) criticizes 'language-based approaches' because, unlike task-based approaches, they often involve practice that is 'focused on functionally and linguistically simplified tasks and dialogues encouraging recognition, and repetition of forms targeted for explanation in an earlier presentation phase'. But without the tinted spectacles imposed by the theory, the procedures in question actually look perfectly reasonable. Would one condemn a piano teacher on the grounds that her lessons were 'music-based' and included work on scales and simple studies? It has also become conventional to tell teachers not to behave like teachers. D. Willis, in the passage cited earlier (2003: 167), criticizes the use of materials and activities which give learners the message 'Your teacher is the guide and mentor, who will show you what to learn and how to learn it. Listen to your teacher and do as you are told. Then you will learn.' Teaching can certainly be too form-focused and too teacher-centred; but if we have reached a point where language teachers are supposed neither to teach nor to concern themselves with language, it is perhaps time for a change of direction.

The issues discussed here are far from being purely academic: their implications reach into the real world and affect millions of learners and their teachers. Each year, large numbers of overseas students follow post-graduate courses in TESOL and applied linguistics at universities in English-speaking countries. Many of these people are academic high-fliers, sent to familiarize themselves with cutting-edge theory before returning home to careers in which they may come to exercise substantial influence on educational policy. Most of them will ultimately be working in contexts where time and resources for language teaching are limited, and where planned approaches incorporating careful prioritizing, proactive syllabus design, and concentrated work leading to the mastery of a limited range of high-priority language elements, are likely to offer the best chance of success. In the nature of things, however, such visiting students can easily become extremely committed to the theories and models to which they are exposed during what, for many of them, will be an important and deeply formative educational experience. If these theories and models are seriously inappropriate to the teaching situations to which the students will be returning, immense harm may be done.

Note

1 For convenience I am using the term 'second language' to refer to any non-native language which is studied either in or outside the country where it is spoken.

9
Chunks in the classroom: let's not go overboard

(Reproduced by permission of *The Teacher Trainer*, where it first appeared in Volume 20 Number 3, pages 5–6.)

Two concerns led me to write this article. I felt there was a danger that the new-toy effect might encourage disproportionate attention to formulaic language (important though it is) in the classroom. And I was also worried about the apparent belief of some scholars that learners should be aiming to approach a native-speaker command of this kind of language.

Formulaic language

Formulaic language ('chunks') has attracted increasing attention among researchers and teachers in recent years, as the growth of large electronic corpora has made it easier to tabulate the recurrent combinations that words enter into. Such combinations include, for instance:

- fixed phrases (idiomatic or not) such as *break even, this morning, out of work*
- collocations (the preferences that some words have for particular partners) such as *blazing row* (more natural than *burning row*) or *slightly different* (more natural than *mildly different*)
- situationally-bound preferred formulae such as *Sorry to keep you waiting* (more natural than *Sorry I made you wait*)
- frames such as *If I were you, I'd ... , Perhaps we could ...* or *I thought I'd ...*

Researchers differ in their analysis and classification of formulaic language, and the storage and processing models they propose—see Wray (2002) for a clear and comprehensive survey. It is, however, generally agreed that these chunks behave more like individual words than like separately constructed sequences. *Unemployed* and *out of work*, for instance, both consist of three morphemes. If the first is handled mentally as a unit for comprehension and production, rather than being analysed into or built up from its constituents every time it is processed, it seems reasonable to suppose that its multi-word synonym may be treated similarly, even if we happen to write this with spaces between the three components.

Languages clearly contain very large numbers of such items: one often-quoted estimate suggests that English may have hundreds of thousands. If this seems implausible, think how many common fixed expressions are built around one meaning of the noun work: *at work, work in progress, go to work, a day's work, man's/woman's work, take pride in one's work, part-time work, shift work, the world of work, nice work, carry out work, in the course of one's work, out of work, build on somebody's work, work permit, take work home, equal pay for equal work, the work of a moment, look for work, all my own work* ... It seems possible, in fact, that languages may have preferred formulaic sequences for virtually every recurrent situation that their speakers commonly refer to.

Language of this kind is notoriously challenging for learners. A knowledge of grammar and vocabulary alone will not indicate that *slightly different* is preferred to *mildly different*, or that *Can I look round* is a more normal thing to say in a shop than *May I see what you have?*—such things have to be learnt as extras.

Paradoxically, therefore, what looks easiest may be hardest. To construct a novel utterance like *There's a dead rat on the top shelf behind Granny's football boots*, a learner only needs to know the words and structures involved, but such knowledge will not help him or her to produce a common phrase like *Can I look round?*—if the expression isn't known as a whole, it can't be invented. Since chunks constitute a large proportion of spoken and written text—studies put forward figures ranging between 37.5% and 80% for different genres—it seems sensible to give them a central role in our teaching, and we are often urged to do so. Four reasons are commonly advanced.

'Chunks save processing time'

The brain has vast storage capacity, and memorisation and recall are cheap in terms of mental resources. For a foreign learner, as for a native speaker, it is obviously more efficient to retrieve *If I were you* as a unit than to go through the process of generating the sequence from scratch in accordance with the rules for unreal conditionals. Using chunks means that processing time and effort are freed up and made available for other tasks.

'You can learn grammar for free'

Children learn their mother-tongue grammar by unconsciously observing and abstracting the regularities underlying the sequences they hear. Many of these sequences are recurrent and formulaic (*Who's a good baby, then?*; *'s time for your bath*; *If your father was here now*; *One more spoonful*; *All gone*), and children's internalisation of such elements plays a central role in acquisition. It seems logical that second language learners, too, should be able to take a similar route, abstracting the grammar of a language from exposure to an adequate stock of memorised formulae. Lewis (1993) suggests for instance that, instead of learning the *will*-future as a generalised structure, students might focus on its use in a series of 'archetypical utterances', such as *I'll give you a ring, I'll be in touch, I'll see what I can do, I'll be back in a minute.*

'You can produce grammar for free'

Formulaic 'frames' bring their grammar with them. Take for example a sentence like *I thought I'd start by just giving you some typical examples of the sort of thing I want to focus on*. This consists almost entirely of frames and fixed expressions:
- *I thought I'd* + infinitive
- *start by ...ing*
- *give you* + noun phrase
- *typical example of* + noun phrase
- *the sort of thing* + (*that*)-clause
- *I want to* + infinitive
- *focus on*.

So, given a knowledge of the component frames and expressions, the sentence can be produced with minimal computation—hardly any reference to general grammatical rules is required.

'A mastery of formulaic language is desirable/necessary if learners are to approach a native-speaker command of the language'

Even students who have an advanced knowledge of English grammar and vocabulary may be far from native-speaker-like in their use of the language. What lets them down is likely to be their imperfect mastery of formulaic language, especially collocation and situationally-bound language. This seems, therefore, an obvious area for pedagogic intervention. '... formulaic sequences have been targeted in second language teaching because they seem to hold the key to native-like idiomaticity' (Wray 2000: 479).

How good are these reasons?

Persuasive though these arguments are, they need to be looked at critically.
- Storage may be cheap in terms of mental resources, but putting material into store is extremely time-consuming. Learning quantities of formulaic sequences may exact a high price in exchange for the time eventually saved.
- The question of whether classroom learners are able to generalise from formulaic sequences without explicit instruction has scarcely been investigated. It seems likely that (as with first-language learning), a vast amount of exposure would be necessary for adult learners to derive all types of grammatical structure efficiently from lexis by the analysis of holistically-learned chunks; and this amount of exposure is not available in

instructional situations. As Granger (1998: 158) puts it 'It would ... be a foolhardy gamble to believe that it is enough to expose L2 learners to prefabs and the grammar will take care of itself'.
- Much of the language we produce is formulaic, certainly; but the rest has to be assembled in accordance with the grammatical patterns of the language, many of which are too abstract to be easily generated by making small adjustments to memorised expressions or frames. If these patterns are not known, communication beyond the phrasebook level is not possible—as Scott Thornbury once memorably put it, language becomes 'all chunks but no pineapple'. Grammar hasn't gone away because we have rediscovered lexis.
- Most importantly, the notion that foreign learners should aspire to a 'native-speaker command' of phraseology, or anything similar, requires very careful examination.

The native-speaker target

Discussion of the acquisition of formulaic language often assumes something approaching a native-speaker target:

> It appears that the ability to manipulate such clusters is a sign of true native speaker competence and is a useful indicator of degrees of proficiency across the boundary between non-native and native competence.
> (Howarth 1998a: 38)

> It is impossible to perform at a level acceptable to native users, in writing or in speech, without controlling an appropriate range of multiword units.
> (Cowie 1992: 11)

Such sweeping pronouncements are, however, of little value in the absence of clear quantified definitions (which we do not have) of such notions as 'a level acceptable to native users' and 'an appropriate range of multiword units.' No doubt certain lexical chunks need to be mastered for certain kinds of pragmatic competence; but we need to know which chunks, for what purposes. Certainly, a mastery of relevant formulaic and other language is necessary for effective professional or academic work, as ESP and EAP teachers are well aware.

> Both undergraduates and postgraduates serve a kind of apprenticeship in their chosen discipline, gradually familiarising themselves not only with the knowledge and skills of their field, but also with the language of that field, so that they become capable of expressing their ideas in the form that is expected. As they do this, their use of formulaic sequences enables them, for example, to express technical ideas economically, to signal stages in their discourse and to display the necessary level of formality.

The absence of such features may result in a student's writing being judged as inadequate.
(Jones and Haywood 2004: 273)

Assimilating the necessary formulaic inventory of a particular professional group is not, however, the same thing as acquiring a generalised native-speaker-like command of multi-word lexical expressions. The first is necessary and achievable, the second is neither, and to require such a command of non-native students is unrealistic and damaging. The size of the formulaic lexicon makes it totally impracticable to take native-speaker phraseological competence, or anything approaching it, as a realistic target for second-language learners. (Memorising 10 formulaic items a day, a learner would take nearly 30 years to achieve a native-speaker command of, say, 100,000 formulaic items.)

Consciousness-raising and strategies

One response to the practical impossibility of teaching native-speaker-like formulaic competence is to recommend equipping learners with a conscious awareness of the learning task they face, as suggested by Howarth (1998b: 186), or with strategies which will 'enable them to acquire the knowledge needed to use formulaic sequences accurately and appropriately in their own work' (Jones and Haywood 2004: 277).

It is of course helpful to advise students to pay attention to and memorise instances of formulaic language (to the extent that they do not already do so). However, since formulaic expressions have to be learnt individually, like other kinds of lexis, it is not immediately clear how the enormous learning problem can be addressed, and native-speaker competence approached, by either consciousness-raising or the deployment of ill-defined strategies. Transferring the problem from the teacher to the learner in this way does little to solve it.

Realism and prioritising

Given these problems, our only realistic course, as more pedagogically oriented writers such as Willis (1990) or Lewis (1993) point out, is to accept our limitations and to prioritise. Most non-native speakers must therefore settle for the acquisition of a variety characterised by a relatively restricted inventory of high-priority formulaic sequences, a correspondingly high proportion of non-formulaic grammatically generated material, and an imperfect mastery of collocational and selectional restrictions. This may seem disappointing, but there is nothing we can do about it—languages are difficult and cannot generally be learnt perfectly. Failure to recognise this may lead teachers to neglect important aspects of language teaching, in order to devote excessive time to a hopeless attempt to teach a comprehensive command of formulaic language—like someone trying to empty the sea with a teaspoon.

10

English teaching in the nineteen-sixties and seventies

(Originally published in 'Forty Years of Language Teaching' in *Language Teaching* 40, 2006.)

In 2006 the editor of Language Teaching decided to survey 40 years of language teaching by rounding up scholars of various ages and asking them to give brief sketches of the periods they were most familiar with. The following article is my far from scholarly contribution to this pleasant initiative.

From the mid-60s to the late 70s I was an untrained EFL teacher, working first in Oxford and then in Paris. What follows is therefore necessarily more of an 'underview' than an overview—the period as seen by someone who, in between preparation, teaching and marking, was trying to educate himself professionally and to keep track of the changing winds of theoretical fashion.

At first everything was very simple. Our 'theory' was a vague post-direct-method orientation (we were experts at explanation without translation: any EFL teacher could mime 'mortgage repayment' or 'epistemology' at the drop of a hat). Beginners' textbooks recounted the exciting experiences of two young foreigners visiting London. At higher levels we did grammar, pronunciation, dictation and conversation, taught 'situational' language, 'went through' texts and asked 'comprehension' questions. We set and corrected homework. It was well known that this was how you taught English. Our students got better, which proved that it worked—although they did go on making lots of mistakes. The full-timers, who spent their days in class with other foreigners, didn't learn as fast as the part-timers, who worked with English people in Oxford. Perhaps this should have told us something.

Structuralism and audiolingualism reached us belatedly and complicated matters. It appeared that language was a set of habits; a second language was another set of habits; mistakes came from old habits interfering with new ones; the solution was 'overlearning' through repeated structure drills. This was best done in one of the new language 'laboratories' (a wonderful term that made us all feel like scientists). The resulting lessons combined ineffectiveness and boredom, qualities that today's teaching generally manages to keep separate.

120   *Thinking about Language Teaching*

I read what I could find on language and methodology. The journals *ELT* and *Language Learning* were helpful, as were books by Palmer (1925), Kruisinga (1932), Weinreich (1953), Hornby (1954), Lado (1957), Billows (1961), Gimson (1962) and Quirk (1968). Some writers, like Halliday, MacIntosh and Strevens (1964), were difficult, but I supposed that if couldn't understand a professional book it must be my fault. The Association of Recognised English Language Schools ran useful weekend teachers' courses. Membership of ATEFL (later IATEFL) and BAAL, both founded in 1967, also broadened my horizons. As I worked out a personal synthesis of traditional approaches and recent developments, I came to feel that I knew pretty well how to teach languages. Things were no longer simple, but they were still manageable.

Then everything suddenly got MUCH more complicated, as researchers started coming up with new theoretical and methodological bases for language teaching. These were, in alphabetical order: analytic syllabuses, authentic materials, communication in the classroom, communicative competence, discourse analysis, discovery, drama, ESP, functions, groupwork, humanistic teaching, information gap, interlanguage, learner control, needs analysis, notions, pairwork, problem solving, process-not-product, projects, role play, self-access, simulations, skills, strategies and the threshold level.

It was an exhilarating time: the air was full of discovery. In Paris, where I was now working, the British Council's inspirational English Language Officer, Alan Maley, brought over all the big names. For 50 francs you could attend, for example, a weekend workshop on discourse analysis by Coulthard and Brazil, with free coffee thrown in. At last I got my professional training.

Attitudes to the new ideas were often more enthusiastic than critical. Needs analysis generated great excitement. You established what your learner needed to do with English, punched in the code for the relevant language functions, pressed a button, and the machine cranked out the appropriate language specifications. Or would do, after a little more research. Taxonomies mushroomed: the 'skill' of reading was now 19 subskills (Munby 1978), all of which you were supposed to teach on the assumption that learning a new language took one back to cognitive zero. Everybody talked about language *use*, citing Hymes (1971: 278): 'There are rules of use without which the rules of grammar would be useless'. For many, newer was axiomatically better. People promoted, with enormous conviction, novel methodologies which they would not have tolerated themselves for five minutes from teachers of driving, skiing or the trumpet.

Books for teachers proliferated; in my memory, they have become one impenetrable tome called 'The communicative teaching of language as communication in the communicative classroom'. Our job, we discovered, was no longer to teach English, but to train learners in the interactive interpretive and expressive skills and strategies required for negotiating meaning and assigning contextually-determined values in real time to elements of the linguistic code, while attending not only to the detailed surface features of discourse but also to the pragmatic communicative semiotic macro-context.

I now decided that if I couldn't understand a professional book, perhaps it wasn't my fault after all.

Paris is never a hostile environment to a prophet with a message, and fringe religions such as Silent Way, Suggestopaedia and Counselling Learning flourished, especially in the private sector. Some merged imperceptibly into DIY New Age psychotherapy, so that you could simultaneously learn a language, remodel your personality and find true happiness. It was a bewildering time for teachers. Some embraced one faith and stuck to it. Many adopted a confused eclecticism, feeling that if you threw enough kinds of mud, some would stick. Others (including many state school teachers) went on doing what they were doing before, but called it 'communicative' if anybody was listening.

In retrospect, I have a sense of an opportunity missed. Our handling of the new insights and research findings was often exaggerated and naive; none the less, we had made enormous progress. Our knowledge of both formal and functional aspects of language, our growing understanding of acquisitional processes, and our vastly improved methodology and materials, provided all the necessary ingredients for a balanced and effective model of instructed second-language learning. In practice, however, we probably threw away on the swings most of what we had gained on the roundabouts. The new interest in learner-centred, naturalistic, activity-based learning was allowed to fill the horizon, so that teaching language was all too easily replaced by doing things with it. All these years later, I believe we are still paying the price.

11

Teaching grammar—does grammar teaching work?

(Originally published in *Modern English Teacher* 15/2, 2006.)

For the practising teachers to whom this article was addressed, the teaching of grammar can be something of a conceptual maze, full of confusing questions relating to problems of selection and methodology. This article was an attempt to offer some simple guidelines which might help teachers to navigate the complex terrain.

> The researches of many commentators have already thrown much darkness on this subject, and it is probable that, if they continue, we shall soon know nothing at all about it.
> (Mark Twain)
>
> I'm no longer sure that what is important is more important than what is not.
> (Wisława Szymborska)
>
> Litel misteak is not mestak.
> (Inscription found on school blackboard circa 1975)

Why do people worry so much about grammar teaching?

Despite all the work that has been done on first- and second-language acquisition, we know surprisingly little about how languages are learnt, and even less about how they can best be taught. Theories come and go, assertions are plentiful, facts are in short supply. This is nowhere more true than in the area of grammar. The trouble with teaching grammar is that we are never quite sure whether it works or not: its effects are uncertain and hard to assess. If we teach rules, sometimes students manage to apply them and sometimes they don't. Practice may have some effect, but carry-over to spontaneous production is often disappointing. If students speak more correctly as time goes by, is this because of our teaching, or would they have got better anyway? Research on methodology is inconclusive, and has not shown detectable, lasting and wide-ranging effects for implicit versus explicit instruction, for inductive versus deductive learning, or for separated-out study of structure versus incidental focus on form during communicative activity. Understandably, teachers are unsure how much importance they should give to grammar, what grammar they should teach, and how they should teach it. Language-teaching fashions consequently oscillate from one extreme, where grammar is given star billing, to the other, where it is backgrounded or completely ignored.

Should we teach grammar at all?

Currently, the theoretical pendulum is near the 'backgrounding' end of the swing. In recent decades grammar teaching has been called into question for several reasons. These include:
- A resurgence of the long-standing disillusionment with the results of heavily grammar-oriented approaches: 'He can recite long lists of irregular verbs but can't ask for a cup of coffee'.
- The associated rise of more 'communicative' meaning-centred approaches involving situational, functional, notional or task-based syllabuses, and a consequent shift of focus away from grammar.
- The view, associated particularly with Stephen Krashen, that 'learning' (the conscious assimilation of information about language structure) cannot lead to 'acquisition' (the development of the unconscious ability to produce the relevant structures spontaneously).
- The post-Krashen view that, while conscious attention to language form may after all be necessary, this will only lead to acquisition if it coincides with communicative use of language, so that the separate study of grammar, decoupled from communication, is ineffective.
- The development of large electronic corpora, leading to an explosion of interest in lexis, an increased understanding of the lexis–grammar interface, and a feeling in some teachers' minds that all of grammar therefore reduces to vocabulary: 'We don't do grammar any more. We follow the lexical approach'. (One should perhaps beware of anything called 'The ... approach' or 'The ... method'—not because of what it does, but because of what it stops one doing.)

There has been something of a split in teachers' reactions worldwide to these developments. Many non-native speaking teachers have gone on teaching grammar very much as before, not always for clearly thought-out reasons. Native-speaking teachers, on the other hand, have often been influenced more strongly by recent Applied Linguistic theory. (To be cynical, some native-speaking teachers have found the downgrading of grammar extremely convenient. The Direct Method and its descendants absolved them of the need to learn anything about the grammar of their students' languages; now they don't need to learn about the grammar of their own language either.)

The need to teach grammar

In this article I shall take the position that, in general, grammar does need to be taught to foreign-language learners. I shall not defend this view in detail, but briefly:
- Languages have structural features that are complicated and hard to learn. For learners to master them, adequate experience, understanding and use of these features are necessary. Where time is limited and learners have little out-of-class exposure (as in most language-teaching situations the world over), this can only be brought about with the help of pedagogic intervention: explicit teaching and systematic practice informed by a syllabus of known problems. (For detailed discussion, see Swan 2005.)
- Grammar has not gone away because we have rediscovered lexis. In English, relative clauses follow their nouns; prepositions can come at the ends of clauses; adverbs cannot generally be put between a verb and its object; there are two 'present' tenses which are used in different situations. These are not facts about words—they are facts, which many students need to learn, about general linguistic categories. It is true that some wide-ranging structural generalisations have lexical components—English question formation can be presented as if it was a fact about the verb 'do', or perfective aspect as if it was a fact about 'have'. However, this merely amounts to some rather unconstructive relabelling, and tells us nothing new that will help in teaching these difficult structural points. And while children arguably learn the grammar of their mother tongues by starting with lexical 'chunks' which are later analysed and generalised from, there is no good evidence that this is a generally viable strategy in second-language learning.

So I shall assume, without further argument, that we need to teach grammar. If this is so, what exactly should we teach, how much priority should we give it, and how should we teach it?

There is grammar and grammar

If we are unsure whether grammar teaching works, it may be partly because the question is too general. The word 'grammar' covers very many different kinds of things, not all of which are equally teachable or learnable. As Jan Hulstijn puts it in an important article (1995), 'not all grammar rules are equal'. Let's look at three examples.
- To make a *yes/no* question in Mandarin Chinese, put *ma* at the end of the corresponding statement.
- To make a question in English, put the auxiliary verb before the subject. If there is no auxiliary, introduce the dummy auxiliary *do*, and proceed as before (remembering that *do* has a distinct 3rd-person singular present form *does*). But don't do any of this if the question has as its subject an interrogative expression such as *who* or *what*—in this case, the structure is that of a statement.

- When using a Russian noun, be sure to give it the right ending. A singular Russian noun can have up to six different endings depending on its grammatical role (e.g. subject, direct or indirect object, possessor, object of one or other preposition). Not all nouns take the same set of endings: the forms for a given noun depend on which of three grammatical classes ('genders') and several subclasses it belongs to. Further, many nouns have irregular forms which deviate from these patterns.

It is clearly pointless to generalise about whether conscious learning of a grammatical feature can lead to accurate spontaneous use, without taking into account the complexity of the feature and the amount of processing necessary for its accurate and appropriate production. The rule for Chinese question formation is easy, and can probably be picked up with little or no formal teaching. English question formation is more difficult, and is likely to be learnt more quickly and accurately with the help of systematic teaching and practice. Russian noun inflections are a learners' nightmare, and conscious learning and practice of these forms may well not enable students to get them right.

Fortunately, English does not have the kind of morphological complexity which makes Russian so difficult. It does, however, have other areas of grammar where it is difficult or impossible to provide learners with rules which are both accurate enough to provide a basis for making correct structural choices, and simple enough to be remembered, internalised, and acted on. Such areas include, for instance, the expression of the future (*will*, *going to* or present progressive?), many aspects of article usage, the three options for noun compounding (compare *table leg, John's leg, leg of lamb*), or tense/aspect problems such as the use of the present perfect. While some learners may achieve mastery of these points through long exposure, explicit teaching will have limited success.

Prioritising: comprehensibility and acceptability

Leaving aside those points that can be picked up without teaching, and those that cannot reliably be taught or learnt, we are still left with far more grammar than we can ever fit into any teaching programme. How are we to decide what to concentrate on and what to drop?

In general terms, there are only two good reasons for teaching a point of grammar. One is to do with *comprehensibility*: if we teach the point successfully, learners will make themselves understood better, or will understand better, than if we don't. Unfortunately we can't measure the functional load of a structure—the extent to which getting it wrong, or using it inappropriately, will hinder communication. Context contributes to meaning in unpredictable ways, so that a mistake which causes communication to break down on Tuesday might pass unnoticed on Wednesday. However, we can make informed guesses. We can be reasonably sure, for instance, that 3rd-person *'s* rarely contributes to comprehensibility; it is a linguistic fossil, irrelevant to the mechanisms of modern English. On the other hand, the active/passive distinction is obviously more significant: if somebody says *'John told about the meeting' instead of 'John was told ...', the wrong meaning is signalled, and context will not necessarily disambiguate.

It would be nice if we could take comprehensibility as our only criterion. Unfortunately, many learners are under pressure to achieve a higher level of accuracy than is needed for effective communication. Students may have to satisfy examiners; and even in these 'communicative' times, examinations often impose criteria that have little to do with effective language use. Someone who makes frequent small mistakes may also be unacceptable to a potential employer: defective grammar could reflect badly on the organisation in question. Speakers of a foreign language want native-speaking interlocutors to accept them on equal terms; but someone whose language is grammatically deviant may be regarded, unfairly, as uneducated or even unintelligent. And learners themselves may seek high standards of accuracy, feeling—as they have a perfect right to—that they want their command of a language to come close enough to native-speaker performance to satisfy their own personal aspirations.

So comprehensibility may clash with *acceptability*, making it difficult to decide what to teach and what not to. None the less, it is helpful to keep these two criteria in mind. And if we feel—as we often may—that a point of grammar is not only difficult to teach, but contributes little in either area (the present perfect, for example?), then we should not hesitate to give it low priority or drop it altogether.

Other criteria

Two other rather obvious criteria are the *scope* of a rule, and the *frequency* of the relevant item. The rules defining the structure and use of the English future perfect, for instance, have very wide scope—nearly all verbs have future perfect forms—but they apply to a very infrequent structure. On the other hand, the rule specifying the plural of *child* has extremely narrow scope—only one noun now forms its plural in that way—but the word is very frequent. Balancing scope against frequency, we will probably decide to teach *children*—if we feel that the comprehensibility/acceptability factors are important enough—but not to worry about the future perfect. In another case we might make the opposite choice, giving scope priority over frequency.

Another criterion is *relevance*: the grammar that we teach should relate to learners' problems with English. This is self-evident to non-native teachers. An Italian teacher knows very well what aspects of English are difficult for Italian learners, and what points need no attention because they can be picked up, or transferred from the mother tongue. Native speakers teaching abroad have to find these things out. Without knowing something about how their learners' language works, they are in danger of teaching unnecessary points and overlooking others which are important. Courses and grammar-practice books published for a global market need to be used critically and selectively for this reason. Speakers of Arabic, German, French, Turkish and Japanese all have different kinds of problem with English relative clauses: one-size-fits-all materials cannot take facts of this kind into account. Where a teacher is working with multinational classes, there is obviously a limit to the extent to which he or she can personalise grammar instruction so as to do justice to L1-specific problems. However, knowledge about such problems is an essential part of the toolkit of an EFL teacher. Fortunately information about how particular languages work, and the problems their speakers encounter when they approach English, is nowadays not hard to get hold of.

Teaching too much grammar

Thinking about comprehensibility, acceptability, scope, frequency and relevance, then, can help us to prioritise effectively, selecting for attention those items which are likely to be most useful to our students. Failure to prioritise can cause valuable time to be wasted on relatively unimportant grammar points; in extreme cases teachers may effectively be teaching grammar instead of English. There are all sorts of reasons for this. Teachers may do grammar simply because it's in the textbook. (The celebrated mountaineer George Mallory explained his obsession with Everest with the words 'Because it's there'. This may be a good reason for trying to climb a mountain, but it is a thoroughly bad reason for uncritically teaching a point of grammar.) And then, grammar is (or at any rate seems) reasonably tidy and systematic, compared with, say, the jungle of vocabulary or the swamp of skills teaching. Grammar is testable—and there is a pleasantly symmetrical satisfaction in teaching things that can be tested and then testing what you've taught. Grammar rules provide a (largely illusory) sense of security, standing out as signposts in the complicated landscape of language learning. For some teachers, grammar has a quasi-symbolic character-building role: it was an important part of the educational discipline that turned them into the splendid people that they now are, and they want their learners to enjoy the same benefits. And—occasionally—one finds teachers who like grammar because, more than anything else in language, it sets them apart from their learners, giving them the prestige and power that come with superior knowledge. In these computer-literate times, teachers almost certainly have students who know vocabulary that they don't. And non-native teachers may well have students with a better pronunciation than theirs. But the teacher is the only person in the classroom who knows what the past perfect progressive passive is. Stick to grammar and you stay on top.

Misguided perfectionism

A common reason—and the worst—for doing too much grammar is a kind of misguided perfectionism. Teachers naturally want to set high standards for themselves and their learners. This is in itself admirable, but it can easily transmute into error-phobia. Non-native teachers are often seriously distressed by the fact that they themselves sometimes make mistakes, feeling that this is a sign of failure to master their subject. Their anxiety may be projected onto their teaching, leading to a perfectionist concern for accuracy that is nothing short of disastrous. Teachers who treat learners' mistakes as weeds to be ruthlessly rooted out, who pick up every error and allow nothing to pass uncorrected, do an immense amount of harm. If students can never get to the end of a sentence without a correction, they understandably become reluctant to produce sentences at all—why should they keep trying when everything they say is wrong? And so they end up in a condition that a German teacher I was talking to described as 'fehlerfreies Schweigen'—error-free silence. They make no mistakes, because they say nothing.

Teachers with this attitude can find themselves trapped in a battle of wills, where students continue to make unimportant mistakes (because they know perfectly well that they are unimportant), while the teachers continue to correct them, repeatedly re-teaching the points and setting remedial exercises. It can be hard for teachers when students refuse to learn what they teach—it seems like an affront to their professionalism, a mark of failure—but it is worth asking who is right: the teacher who thinks a small structural point matters or the student who thinks it doesn't.

Small children aside, people who learn foreign languages do not usually achieve native-speaker accuracy, and this includes teachers. To pretend the contrary is unrealistic, counterproductive and damaging. There is a marvellously comforting remark about the impossibility of achieving perfection in parenting, attributed both to Bruno Bettelheim and D. W. Winnecott: 'A good enough parent is good enough'. The same is true of language teaching: high standards are important, but a good enough teacher is good enough, and good enough English is good enough. Realising and accepting this can relieve teachers of a great deal of unnecessary guilt and anxiety, and prevent them from wasting valuable time doing remedial work on small points of grammar. There are more important things to do.

How should we teach grammar?

Once we have decided what to teach, how do we teach it? An enormous amount has been written about the methodology of teaching grammar. Much of this is useful; unfortunately there is also an awful lot of nonsense around. Dogmatic prescriptions and proscriptions abound ('Stop doing that—it's wrong. As a result of recent research, we now know …'). However, 'grammar' is many different things which are best taught and learnt in very different ways. Learners and teaching situations also vary widely; an approach which works well for one kind of student in Britain or the US may be totally inappropriate for someone else studying English for three hours a week in his or her own country. Level is crucial: the more learners know, the more effectively grammar work can be integrated into other more communicative activities; the lower their level, the more likely they are to benefit from separated-out syllabus-based explanations and practice. We should reject nothing on doctrinaire grounds: deductive teaching through explanations and examples, inductive discovery activities, rule-learning, peer-teaching, decontextualised practice, communicative practice, incidental 'focus on form' during communicative tasks, teacher correction and recasts, grammar games, corpus analysis, learning rules and examples by heart—all of these and many other traditional and non-traditional activities have their place, depending on the point being taught, the learner and the context.

Explanations

The purpose of grammar explanations is not simply to describe structural features; it is to build bridges from the learners' present knowledge to the knowledge we want them to have. If we are going to, so to speak, take learners from A to B in this way, we need to look carefully at both ends of the bridge. Where is A? What do the learners know about a point already, by virtue of either its similarity with a mother-tongue structure or of their previous experience? Where is B? It can't be too far away from A, or the bridge will collapse. Given too much information, learners won't assimilate it. Explanations don't have to give the whole truth: they must be true enough to be useful, but also short, simple, and clear enough to be taken in, remembered and acted on. It should also go without saying (but unfortunately doesn't always) that explanations should be in the mother tongue if possible. The old dogma that the mother tongue should never be used in language teaching has not been taken seriously by linguists for decades. And, as far as grammar is concerned, it defies common sense. (Suppose you were starting to learn, say, Mongolian. Would you want your grammar explanations in Mongolian?)

Examples

When I started teaching, textbook examples were often extremely unrealistic. One I remember is 'Birds fly high'—particularly bizarre because it was presented for transformation into the past. (When would you say 'Birds flew high'? After the comet struck and the atmosphere was skimmed off?) Such examples are still found occasionally—I was recently shown an exercise on irregular plurals which contained the remarkable statements 'The oxen are stepping on my feet' and 'Those people have lost their teeth'. Nowadays, however, the pendulum has swung the other way, and the flavour of the month is authenticity. Some scholars, indeed, say that we should present no examples which have not been spoken or written during authentic communication. This sounds good, but a quick look at a corpus can dampen one's enthusiasm. A typical corpus example of *fly* with a third-person plural subject is 'He says DC10 aircraft fly out of Europe every day to distribute flowers all around the world in what is an extremely valuable industry'—scarcely an improvement on 'Birds fly high'. Corpus examples are generally hard to interpret taken out of the context that gives them their authenticity, and are full of nuisance vocabulary that distracts attention from the relevant grammar point. What we need, surely, is not corpus authenticity but classroom authenticity: not 'real' examples, but realistic examples which serve our pedagogic purposes.

Exercises

The communicative approach has brought us a greatly enriched repertoire of exercise-types, enabling learners to practise grammar while saying real and interesting things to each other. The communicative emphasis on pair-work and group-work is particularly beneficial: if students speak one at a time, nobody gets enough practice to master a grammatical feature. However, contemporary theory has given many teachers a bad conscience about doing anything that is not 'communicative'. If students practise past tenses by telling each other their life stories, this is GOOD; to revise irregular verbs by filling in gaps in sentences is BAD. I am all for life stories, and gap-filling is pretty unexciting, but here as elsewhere we can benefit from some common sense. Students often need to get used to building a structure, or to contextualising it appropriately, before they are ready to use it more freely. In this respect, undemanding 'mechanical' exercises which enable students to think about one thing at a time have obvious value.

Will it work?

A common objection to systematic grammar teaching is that what is learnt may not carry over into spontaneous use. Students learn rules, and get their grammar right during practice, but they still make mistakes when they are speaking or writing more freely. 'Declarative knowledge isn't the same as procedural knowledge,' we are repeatedly told; 'Practice doesn't make perfect'—as if these were reasons for not providing declarative knowledge or doing practice. Well, of course practice doesn't make perfect—nothing does. Carry-over from rule-learning and controlled practice, through semi-controlled work, to correct spontaneous use, is very difficult to achieve—that is one reason why languages are hard to teach. The fact that a procedure doesn't guarantee success is not, however, a reason for abandoning it. Generations of teachers have felt that explicit syllabus-based grammar teaching and practice can help students along the rocky road towards reasonably correct spontaneous production, and the insights that the teaching profession has accumulated and passed on always need to be taken seriously. Planting seeds may not guarantee that they will grow; but not planting them is scarcely a superior strategy.

12

Two out of three ain't enough: the essential ingredients of a language course

(Abridged from an article originally published in *IATEFL Conference Selections*, 2006.)

In 1967, as a young teacher much in need of professional guidance, I attended the first ATEFL conference, to my considerable benefit. In 2006, older if not necessarily wiser, I was privileged to deliver the opening plenary at the 40th conference of what had long since become IATEFL. Not surprisingly, the occasions were very different in character. The 1967 conference covered a very limited range of topics. We discussed methodology and the pros and cons of structure drilling and language labs; ways of improving testing; how to design teaching programmes for different contexts (especially immigrant education); and the training of EFL teachers. At the 40th Conference we were able to choose from presentations dealing with a vast range of concerns, some of which a 1967 audience might have found baffling. (Prefabs—isn't that a kind of house? ELF—like in Lord of the Rings? *Critical Discourse Analysis—What???) Trying to put myself back into the head of a young teacher attending his or her first conference, I was struck by the complexity of what was now on offer, and the difficulty such a teacher might have in seeing the overall shape of the conceptual landscape. The talk, from which this article is abridged, was intended to offer a simple analysis of the necessary components of a language teaching programme.*

It's all very complicated

Looking over the programme at the beginning of an IATEFL conference, one can easily experience two rather contradictory reactions. First of all, sheer gratitude. Such an occasion offers us a remarkable opportunity to meet colleagues, exchange ideas and extend our professional knowledge. Annual conferences don't arrange themselves, and we owe a considerable debt to the many people whose work, past and present, has made this kind of event possible.

A second, equally valid, reaction is bewilderment. Titles of sessions on this year's programme included references to the following topics, among many others:

anxiety, CALL, classroom research, collaborative learning, consciousness-raising, corpus, critical discourse analysis, critical reading, cultural awareness, developing teacher reflection, ELF, innovation management, interactivity, intercultural competence, internet, IT, kinaesthetic learners, learner differences, learner independence, learner preferences, learner training, learner's self-concept, metaphor, motivation, multiple intelligences, negotiated interaction, new technologies, pragmatics, prefabs, professional development, reflective practice, scaffolding, strategy training, teacher's role ...

(And if I told you that there was a seminar on 'multiple kinaesthetic interactive classroom discourse strategy development', you might have to think for a moment before you could be quite sure I was making it up.) It is easy to see how a young teacher, attending IATEFL for the first time, can feel daunted and discouraged: 'If I need to know about all this in order to be a good English teacher, how am I ever going to manage it?'

When I started in ELT, you had to know how to teach grammar, pronunciation, vocabulary and the 'four skills'. We have come a very long way since then, and this is all to the good; but there really is an awful lot to know about. The landscape has become extremely complicated, and we don't seem to have much in the way of maps—it is not nearly as easy as it used to be to see where we are going and how to get there. Does this matter? Perhaps not. Should we, in the spirit of the age, avoid getting hung up on product, and decide that it is the process which is important—so that it is enough to choose roads that look interesting, and go where they take us? To travel hopefully, Stevenson said, is a better thing than to arrive. This is certainly the attitude of more than one influential scholar in the field. However, I believe that the view is profoundly mistaken. The world is full of language learners who travel hopefully without arriving, and these learners are not generally pleased. Language learning and teaching cost time, effort and money, and it is reasonable to expect a product—a knowledge of a language—as a result. A language course should, therefore, contain the essential elements which will make this result possible. What are these elements? The topics listed above may all contribute usefully to more effective learning and teaching, but they are not in themselves constitutive of a language course. We need to know what are the fundamental components that actually make language teaching work.

Language teaching takes place, of course, in a vast variety of contexts, and there are very great differences between these. One thing that is common to all situations, though, is that teaching and learning can fail—things can go wrong. Essentially, this can happen for three reasons. One is that teachers and learners may simply be working under impossible circumstances: there may be far too little time for effective teaching, or classes may be dominated by undisciplined students who are determined not to learn. A second reason for failure is that teachers may just not be doing things right: the methodology may be so inappropriate, or the quality of the teaching so poor, that no significant learning is possible. Thirdly—and this is what I want to focus on—teachers may not be doing the right things.

What are these right things? In what follows, I shall offer a suggested answer to this question—a map, so to speak, showing what I think are the main roads through the complicated language-teaching terrain. I must stress that this is a personal view, not based on empirical research, and scarcely to be dignified with the name of 'theory'. It does, however, derive from many years of practical involvement in, and thought about, language teaching.

Three elements

Language learners need **extensive input**. Children learning their mother tongues are immersed in a bath of language, some of it roughly attuned to their level of development, much of it not. Without this element, it is unlikely that they would succeed in acquiring language. Second-language learners, similarly, must have extensive input—they need to be exposed to quantities of spoken and written language, authentic or not too tidied up, for their unconscious acquisition processes to work on.

Equally, learners need **intensive input**—small samples of language which can be assimilated, memorised, analysed unconsciously, and/or used as templates for future production. Children instinctively seek this kind of input, and their caretakers instinctively provide it, in the form of nursery rhymes, songs and stories, which—children insist—must always be repeated in exactly the same words. Daily routines also provide children with intensive samples of language—the little scripts that are repeated at mealtimes, bathtime, bedtime and so on. Adult second-language learners are no different in principle: they too need intensive engagement with small samples of language which they can internalise, process, make their own and use as bases for their own production. (For a fascinating discussion of this element of language acquisition and use, see Cook (2000).)

A third kind of input is what one might call **analysed**: information about the workings of particular aspects of the language, presented implicitly or explicitly. As far as first-language acquisition is concerned, this is perhaps of less importance: children naturally pick up grammar and pronunciation without being told anything about the workings of the very complex systems involved, and corrective feedback generally has little effect. (On the other hand, children are very conscious of their need for explanations of vocabulary—English-speaking children learn something like eight new words a day—and they very often ask for explicit information about words: 'What's a ...?'; 'What's that?'; 'What does ... mean?'.) While the value of analysed input to adult second-language learners has become controversial, it seems likely that it is helpful or necessary for at least some aspects of language. Since adult learners are past the critical period when a perfect command of a language can be acquired naturally and unconsciously, and since instructed second-language learners have only a fraction of the input that is available to child first-language learners, the deliberate teaching of regularities helps to compensate for the inadequacy of naturalistic exposure.

Input, of course, is only half the story. By and large, people seem to learn best what they use most. Children produce quantities of extensive output, activating what they have taken in by, in many cases, chattering non-stop. They also recycle the intensive input they have received, repeating their stories, nursery rhymes and so on, and speaking their lines in the recurrent daily scripts of childhood life. Some children, at least, also seem to produce certain kinds of analysed output, rehearsing and trying out variations on structures that they have been exposed to, like more formal language learners doing 'pattern practice' (Weir 1970).

Adults, of course, also need opportunities to produce all three kinds of output. They must have the chance to engage in extensive, 'free' speech and writing; they must be able to do controlled practice in which they recycle the intensive input that they have more or less internalised (and thus complete the process of internalisation); and they need to practise the analysed patterns and language items that have been presented to them, so that they have some chance of carrying them over into spontaneous fluent production.

A properly-balanced language-teaching programme, then, has three ingredients—extensive, intensive and analysed—at both input and output stages. All three ingredients are important. A song written by Jim Steinman and performed by Meatloaf has the chorus:

I want you
I need you
But there ain't no way I'm ever going to love you.
Now don't be sad
'Cause two out of three ain't bad.

Leaving aside the question of whether the addressee is comfortable with this reduced offering, one thing is certain: in language teaching, two out of three ain't enough.

A balanced programme			
input	extensive	intensive	analysed
	books, magazines, etc speech	spoken or written texts studied in detail material learnt by heart	rules, examples, lists
output	extensive	intensive	analysed
	free writing free speaking	controlled speaking or writing reusing learnt material	exercises

Gaps in courses

It is instructive to look at some typical language teaching approaches (discussed here in rather stereotypical versions) to see how well they satisfy this principle. Nearly always, something is missing.

One formula, traditional but still very common in various guises round the world, is a course-type that relies heavily on teacher-fronted text study, often coursebook-based (textbooks, as the name implies, tend to be disturbingly text-heavy). This approach is strong on 'intensive' input (though I would suggest that this is often pseudo-intensive); analysed input also typically gets good coverage, at least as regards grammar; extensive input is usually weak or completely lacking. As far as intensive output is concerned, the input from text study is not generally recycled very efficiently—often, all that the learners do with it is to answer a few so-called 'comprehension' questions. Analysed output is common, in the form of grammar exercises. There is often little or no extensive output.

Although we like to feel that we have moved on from the methods of a century or so ago, there are actually close structural resemblances between a modern text-heavy course and a grammar-translation approach (though the methodology is somewhat different). Similarly, the audiolingual approach that was popular a few decades ago, revolutionary though it was felt to be, differed mainly in the type of text that was used (spoken rather than written), and in the methodology of grammar teaching; the balance of ingredients was not very different. Revolutions do not always change the underlying structure of things very much.

Heavily 'communicative' courses do have a rather different kind of structure, but again, there are problems of coverage and balance. Typically, they are much stronger than more 'traditional' course types on output. On the other hand, there may be little extensive input, and far less analysed input or output than in 'traditional' courses—this element may be limited to studying and practising the language of particular communicative functions ('apologising', 'eliciting personal information', 'inviting', 'enquiring about timetables' and so on).

Some approaches—what one might call the Atkins Diets of language teaching—simply leave out most of the ingredients. One extreme case is the kind of course (if it was ever put into practice) recommended by scholars such as Stephen Krashen a couple of decades ago. The basic principle was that 'comprehensible input' was all that was needed for successful acquisition. If this was provided, output would take care of itself. 'Theoretically, speaking and writing are not essential to acquisition. One can acquire 'competence' in a second language, or a first language, without ever producing it' (Krashen 1981: 107–8). Furthermore, analysed input such as grammar rules was said to be useless, since (it was claimed) it had no effect on acquisition, and would not carry over into spontaneous production. While the 'input is all' line of thought was greatly consoling to teachers who had trouble getting output from their learners (they no longer needed to try), it can scarcely have benefited the students of any teachers who took it seriously.

At the other extreme, what one might call the hard-core task-based approach, recommended by some contemporary researchers, puts almost all the emphasis on extensive output, to which everything else is subordinated.

Balance

While a normal language course must, I believe, contain all three elements, they do not of course need to occur in equal proportions: the appropriate balance will depend on the learners' level, their purposes and their learning context. In particular, if students are learning a language in the country where it is spoken, or if other parts of their education are in the target language, extensive input and perhaps output may be taken care of outside the language course. And analysed input and output are likely to be less appropriate or necessary for younger learners. But in general terms, in my view, these criteria apply; so that if students fail to learn, it may simply be because their course is not doing all the right things. It is therefore, worth checking over the menu that our materials, activities and syllabuses are offering to our students. Do the ingredients—text-study, grammar, dictation, comprehension, communicative tasks or whatever—add up to a balanced diet, or are essential elements missing? As in other areas of life, it is important to look not only at what we are doing, but at what we are not doing.

Why the gaps?

If a language course lacks some of the essential ingredients, this may be for several possible reasons. One is purely practical: in many teaching situations round the world, it can be hard to provide extensive input. There isn't time in class for students to do extensive reading; it may not be possible to get them to do it out of class; good extensive listening materials may be in short supply; a non-native-speaking teacher may not feel confident in his or her ability to compensate for this by talking freely to the class. Fortunately, the internet is making it much easier for learners to obtain interesting and motivating forms of exposure to authentic input, and this is likely to improve language-learning worldwide.

A second reason may be cultural. In countries where the educational tradition favours authoritarian teacher-fronted presentation and a traditional transmission model of education, there is likely to be a strong emphasis on input and a correspondingly reduced emphasis on learner output. And if public self-expression is discouraged, as it is in some cultures, it may be particularly hard to get students to recycle input material creatively in personalised communicative activities. Equally, in strongly rule-governed societies, the rule-based part of language—grammar—tends to be highly valued and to play a dominant role, taking away time from other important components.

Theoretical fashions can also push language teaching towards extreme positions where important components are sidelined or dropped altogether. Contemporary theory is in fact fairly hostile to the kind of intensive input–output work discussed above. The theoretical preference today is emphatically for learner-centred models, with extensive communicative output being highly valued. Intensive output, deliberately reusing what has been taught, is condemned as being unoriginal, not properly communicative, mere 'regurgitation' of other people's language. But teacher-controlled input–output work has a key place in language teaching, alongside other types of activity. You cannot teach by eliciting what is not there, and the best way of making sure that new language is acquired is, very precisely, to give learners other people's language (as we have to—they can't make the language up for themselves) and to help them to make it their own as they use it for personal and creative purposes.

Changes in theoretical or pedagogic fashion often come about because of disillusionment: our teaching doesn't seem to be getting very good results, and the temptation is to drop what we are doing and look for alternatives. But this may not bring about any net gain. If we are doing too much formal input and not enough communicative output, the solution is to balance things up, not to move to a position where we are doing too much communicative output and not enough formal input. This is to act like a man who, feeling cold, puts on a sweater and then takes his trousers off. We need to face the sobering fact that language teaching won't usually get very good results. Languages are hard to learn, and there is never enough time to teach them properly. In particular, the depressing gulf between successful controlled classroom practice and correct spontaneous use—the carry-over problem—will always to some extent be with us. But we can at least optimise our work, so as to get the best results we can under the circumstances. This means, among other things, making sure that our courses have all the key ingredients. We need in particular to beware of miracle solutions, and of packages with labels like 'The X Approach' or 'The Y Method'. Such approaches are nearly always subtractive as well as additive, putting a great deal of emphasis on one or other ingredient of language teaching while neglecting others.

Conclusion

I began by claiming that our professional landscape has become very complex, offering a bewildering variety of features for our attention. I have suggested that there are, however, main roads through this complicated terrain. If we keep to these roads most of the time, we will be better placed to make useful side trips to benefit from the many interesting and instructive features that can be found along the way, without getting totally distracted and disoriented as we do so. In this way, we can perhaps not only travel hopefully, but also arrive.

13

History is not what happened: the case of contrastive analysis
A follow-up to Claire Kramsch's review of *Linguistics across Cultures*

(Originally published in *International Journal of Applied Linguistics* 17/3, 2007.)

I have always been interested in cross-language influence, and in my early years of teaching I was greatly helped by the work of contrastive analysts such as Fries, Lado, and Weinreich. The criticisms their work received from later scholars seemed to me unnecessarily hostile and largely unjustified. The Classic Book Reviews series in International Journal of Applied Linguistics provided an opening for this brief article, which offered a defence of Lado in particular.

Reading Claire Kramsch's excellent 'classic book review' (2007) of Lado's *Linguistics across Cultures* (1957) in the previous issue of this journal, I was reminded not only of how valuable I found the work of the Contrastive Analysis (CA) school when I was first teaching, but of how disgracefully misrepresented this work has been by succeeding generations. What follows is a brief attempt to set the record straight.

When the intellectual wind changed in the 1970s with the move towards cognitive and nativist models of language acquisition, CA, which had been a powerful force in the study of second language learning, was rapidly and comprehensively discredited. A key element in the discrediting was the claim that Lado and his colleagues were guilty of a very elementary mistake. This was their alleged attribution of all or most of second language learners' problems to the direct influence of the first language, as might seem to be implied by Lado at the beginning of *Linguistics across Cultures*.

> Those elements (of a foreign language) that are similar to [the student's] native language will be simple, and those elements that are different will be difficult. The teacher who has made a comparison of the foreign language with the native language of his students will know better what the real learning problems are and can better provide for teaching them. (Lado 1957: 2)

'Overprediction'

The indictment was in fact two-fold. The first charge was that CA overpredicted learners' problems. As recapitulated by Odlin:

> The claims made by Lado and Fries about the predictive power of contrastive analysis ... faced serious challenges by the 1970s ... Some differences between languages do not always lead to significant learning difficulties.
> (Odlin 1989: 17)

Odlin goes on to point out that while Spanish has two verbs, *saber* and *conocer*, corresponding to *know*, this creates problems for English learners of Spanish but not for Spanish learners of English. Lightbown and Spada, illustrating the same objection to the CA position, cite the fact that pronoun objects are problematic for English-speaking learners of French, but that the converse is not the case, although

> [A] traditional version of the [Contrastive Analysis Hypothesis] would predict that, where differences exist, errors would be bi-directional, that is, for example, French speakers learning English and English speakers learning French would make errors on parallel linguistic features.
> (Lightbown and Spada 1999: 73)

In the face of these criticisms, the reader is tempted to shake his or her head in pity at the naivety of the contrastive analysts' views. Clearly they were onto something; but to assume that all language differences cause difficulty regardless of their nature and the direction of learning—really!

Linguistics across Cultures is a small book; it takes a couple of hours to read. In the course of those two hours, it becomes disturbingly clear that Lado did not in fact hold the view of cross-language influence attributed to him by the scholars cited above, and that the criticism is almost completely without foundation. Despite the book's rather nebulous opening identification of 'difference' with 'difficulty' on page 2, neither Lado nor other contrastive analysts predicted that errors resulting from language difference would necessarily be 'bi-directional'. *Linguistics across Cultures* actually deals with a number of one-directional learner problems of exactly the kind instanced by the critics: for example, the fact that English noun modification is harder for Chinese speakers than Chinese noun modification is for English speakers, or that, while the English *beat/bit* contrast is hard for Japanese speakers, English learners do not find the Japanese single-phoneme equivalent difficult (p. 61). It was indeed a commonplace of CA that learning difficulties can be one-way. Weinreich (1963), for instance, looking at cross-language influence in populations rather than individuals, goes into admirable detail about the asymmetrical effects, in contact situations, of distinctions in one language which are not parallelled in another.

'Underprediction'

So much for the accusation of overprediction. The second charge traditionally levelled against Lado and other contrastive analysts was the converse: that CA failed to account for a substantial number of errors which language learners do in fact make.

> An even more serious challenge to the validity of contrastive analyses is the occurrence of errors that do not appear to be due to native language influence.
> (Odlin 1989: 17)

> For several decades, linguists and teachers assumed that most second language learners' errors resulted from differences between the first and second languages. … Studies show … at most 20% of the [grammatical errors] adults make can be traced to crossover from the first language. Learners' first languages are no longer believed to interfere with their attempts to learn second language grammar, and language teachers no longer need to create special grammar lessons for students from each language background.
> (Dulay et al. 1982: 5)

Leaving aside Dulay et al.'s dubious statistics, and their bizarre claim that up to 20% of errors are not worth teachers' attention, the real point here is that, once again, the criticism is simply untrue. It appears to rest on a failure to read past page 2 of *Linguistics across Cultures*, where Lado talks about language difference, and to assume without further investigation that he must have been talking exclusively about the transfer of specific features from L1 to L2. (Note the covert sidestep from 'differences' to 'crossover' in the second citation above.) In fact, Lado gives ample consideration to learning difficulties which involve L2 elements with no L1 equivalent, and which cannot therefore be due to direct L1 'influence' or 'crossover': he discusses for instance problems English-speakers have with the learning of lexical tone (p. 45) and grammatical gender (p. 64).

Difference and transfer

The failure to see that not all difference-based errors involve transfer is not confined to the critics of CA. It is surprisingly common in discussions of learner language to find errors divided into two watertight classes: 'interlingual errors' (due to L1 interference), and 'intralingual errors' (attributable to complexities in L2, and supposedly having nothing to do with L1–L2 differences). This leads to a recurrent self-inflicted conundrum in cases where the intrinsic 'intralingual' difficulty of an L2 feature is magnified by the 'interlingual' absence of a parallel feature in L1: does one then talk about 'transfer' or not?

> As Kellerman (1987) has pointed out, researchers tend to reflect their theoretical biases in what they interpret as transfer effects. He notes that Arabski (1979) made the somewhat surprising assertion that the 974 article errors in his Polish-English corpus were not transfer errors on the grounds that, because Polish does not have articles, there is nothing to transfer. Clearly, though, the absence of a structural feature in the L1 may have as much impact on the L2 as the presence of a different feature.
> (Ellis 1994: 311–312)

This was not a confusion shared by the contrastive analysts. Unlike their critics, they were perfectly well aware that the effects of language difference on learning are not limited to the transfer of L1 features to L2. In principle, of course, the first language can do three things for a learner: it can help, hinder, or simply stand aside. In the behaviourist language of the period:

> A student may have some habitual responses which are contrary to the responses required for a new skill which he is trying to master (negative) or which are similar to the new responses (positive), or which have no relation to them (zero).
> (Bowen and Stockwell 1965)

Both of the traditional charges against CA, then, are unfounded. Lado and his colleagues did not say what their critics say they did: that all language differences necessarily result in learning difficulty; and they did say what their critics say they did not: that some errors are not due to first-language interference.

Why?

What happened? Why were the views of the contrastive analysts so grossly misrepresented by mainstream scholars of the following generation (though there were distinguished exceptions), and why are they still misrepresented? One factor, as Kramsch points out, was certainly the association of CA with behaviourism, which by the 1970s was subjected to a degree of vilification more normally associated with undesirable political attitudes, with candidates for academic posts no doubt being routinely asked 'Are you, or have you ever been, a behaviourist?' This was not a climate conducive to a careful reading and balanced consideration of the CA literature. In addition, however, some of the most vociferous 1970s and 1980s critics of CA, such as Dulay, Burt and Krashen in their widely read book *Language Two* (1982), had a very clear intellectual agenda which was deeply hostile to CA. They were concerned to show, in accordance with the new orthodoxy of the time, that all language development was driven by unconscious mechanisms whose operation was similar, if not identical, for both L1 and L2, involving inter alia the acquisition of specific morphological and syntactic features in a relatively predetermined sequence. The belief that specific L1–L2 differences were an important determinant of the content and sequencing of language learning was not at all compatible with this view, and needed to be discredited. While one is reluctant to attribute deliberate bias to scholars, it does seem that many of the critics of CA may have been more concerned to scan works such as *Linguistics across Cultures* for ammunition to suit their polemic purposes than to look objectively at what was actually there.

The result

The discrediting was certainly extremely effective. As a result largely of the criticisms of that generation of critics, Lado and his colleagues have virtually sunk without trace below the intellectual horizon. Although important work continues to be done on cross-language influence, this is no longer widely regarded as being part of mainstream linguistics. Gregg (1995) goes so far as to tell us firmly that '… contrastive analysis, error analysis, etc., are not simply unrelated to linguistic theory in particular, they are dead meat in general'. Howatt's history of English language teaching (2004) has very little to say about the contrastive analysts. Where accounts of CA are given in present-day reference works, these tend to be black-boxed repetitions of earlier misrepresentations, rather than descriptions derived from the original sources.

> … the Contrastive Analysis Hypothesis … claims that difficulties in language learning derive from the differences between the new language and the learner's first language, that errors in these areas of difference derive from first language interference and that these errors can be predicted and remedied by the use of CA.
> (Johnson and Johnson 1998: 85)

(Note the sidestep, once again, from 'difference' to 'interference'.)

Kramsch's review of *Linguistics across Cultures* is a welcome move towards the rehabilitation and vindication of an eminent scholar whose work was important and formative, and whose reputation has been particularly badly served by his successors. It is also, unfortunately, a timely reminder of the sad fact that, in our discipline as perhaps in many others, history is not what happened: it is what people say happened.

14

Grammar, meaning and pragmatics: sorting out the muddle

(Originally published online in *TESL-EJ* 11/2, September 2007.)

In the first of my 1985 articles on the Communicative Approach, I devoted some space to criticizing the idea that 'rules of use' should form a central part of the input to language teaching. A quarter of a century later, the idea is still around; I continue to feel that, plausible though it may sound, it actually makes little sense. This article addressed the issue once again, arguing the point in some detail.

Two kinds of meaning

Since the early days of the Communicative Approach, language teachers have been told that they have to pay attention to two kinds of meaning: the 'semantic' meanings of words and structures which can be found in dictionaries and grammars, and the 'pragmatic' values which these linguistic elements take on when they are used in communication. In an influential paper published in the early 1970s (Hymes, 1971), the sociolinguist Dell Hymes put forward the view that 'communicative competence' involves knowing not only dictionary/grammar meaning, but also the rules which determine the appropriacy or otherwise of utterances in context. This line of thought was welcomed for several reasons. Language teachers at the time were dissatisfied, as language teachers usually are, with their learners' inability to convert their knowledge of linguistic forms into successful language use, and the idea that they could solve the problem by teaching something called 'communicative competence' was an attractive one. The construct offered an engaging alternative to the purely formal type of language competence investigated by Chomskyan linguistics. It chimed well with the concerns of many applied linguists, who were then turning their attention from language on the page to language between people—discourse analysis was the new syntax. It added some intellectual kudos to applied linguistics by forging a link with the work of linguistic philosophers such as Searle and Austin, who were also looking, broadly speaking, at what people do with language. And, quite simply, it fitted in with the 'spirit of the age', which was deeply concerned with interpersonal dynamics. So

Hymes' pronouncement that there are 'rules of use without which the rules of grammar would be useless' (1971: 278) became something of a mantra for the applied linguists of the time.

> One of the major reasons for questioning the adequacy of grammatical syllabuses lies in the fact that even when we have described the grammatical (and lexical) meaning of a sentence, we have not accounted for the way it is used as an utterance ... Since those things that are not conveyed by the grammar are also understood, they too must be governed by 'rules' which are known to both speaker and hearer. People who speak the same language share not so much a grammatical competence as a communicative competence. Looked at in foreign language teaching terms, this means that the learner has to learn rules of communication as well as rules of grammar.
> (Wilkins 1976: 10–11)

Despite the difficulty of clarifying what exactly might be meant by teaching 'rules of use' or 'rules of communication' (see Swan 1985 for discussion), the notion that teachers and learners need to concern themselves with two levels of meaning has remained prominent in pedagogic thought and writing. Celce-Murcia and Larsen-Freeman, in a widely used course on pedagogic grammar, explain that 'Grammatical structures not only have a morphosyntactic form, they are also used to express meaning (semantics) in context-appropriate use (pragmatics)' (1999: 4). Ellis (2005), discussing the need for learners to focus on meaning, similarly distinguishes two senses of the term: semantic and pragmatic. Doughty and Williams, discussing the rationale for the task-based teaching of structure, say:

> [W]e recognize that the term meaning, which is often equated only with its lexical component, in fact subsumes lexical, semantic and pragmatic meaning. To be more accurate, we note that focus on form includes forms, meaning and function (or use) ... We suggest that the degree of effectiveness ... of focus on form ultimately depends on the level of integration of the learner's attention to all three aspects of form, meaning and function in the TL.
> (Doughty and Williams 1998: 244–5)

Problems with the 'two levels of meaning' notion

The idea that we should be teaching two kinds of meaning is so familiar that we can easily fail to see how problematic it actually is. Stated in general terms, the claim does indeed seem quite plausible. We know very well that the exact significance of an utterance in communication can be different from the apparent meanings of the words and structures involved. *What do you think you're doing?* is probably not a simple enquiry about the hearer's mental processes. *I thought we might go out for a drink* refers to the present, not the past. Problems arise, however, when we try to focus on what exactly is meant, in practice, by saying that in general the structures of a language have both semantic and pragmatic meanings, and that these can be taught. Larsen-Freeman, while encouraging teachers to deal with both 'meaning and use' in grammar (2003: 35–42), concedes that for some structures the two can be difficult to tease apart. They certainly can. Plural morphology encodes reference to more than one entity: is this meaning or use? Whichever it is, where is the other? The English future perfect refers to anteriority in the future; if this is meaning, what is the use of the tense? The modal *must* can express both certainty and obligation; but if one of these is meaning and the other use, which is which? Some grammatical elements, indeed, do not seem to have any kind of meaning. Attributive adjectives normally precede nouns in English and follow them in French, but it is hard to assign any semantic value to this structural fact. English quantifiers are followed by *of* before another determiner (*some of those people*), but not before a bare noun (*some people*); again, it seems unrealistic to ask what this 'means'. And what is the 'meaning' of gender agreement in French, or of the verb-second rule in German?

Why?

If the idea that grammatical structures intrinsically have two distinguishable kinds of meaning, 'semantic' and 'pragmatic', is fundamentally flawed (as I think it is), why has it persisted for so long? I believe that this has a good deal to do with a widespread and continuing confusion about what exactly is meant by 'pragmatic'. Although the term 'pragmatics', relating loosely to the study of 'how we do things with language', is pervasive in discussions of language teaching, it can be very hard to pin down exactly what people mean by it, or how it relates to syntax, lexis and semantics. Essentially, I think that this is because the term actually has two very different kinds of reference which are often tangled up one with the other. Let's call these 'Pragmatics A' and 'Pragmatics B'.

Pragmatics A: what is not encoded

When we encode an utterance, our hearer or reader can use dictionary/grammar knowledge to decode it to the point of establishing its meaning in a kind of general-purpose sense. But (as we are constantly reminded) the dictionary/grammar meaning of any utterance underdetermines its meaning in context: its 'value', or the role it plays in the ongoing communication. To understand a sentence like *Your driver will be here in half an hour*, a hearer needs to feed a good deal of extra information into the utterance: the fact that in this instance the variable *your* refers to the hearer him/herself; the identity of the driver in question; the location of *here*; and the time frame within which *in half an hour* has to be calculated. None of this information is encoded in the grammar and semantics of the sentence itself. The sentence *I still haven't forgiven her for the thing about the hedgehog and the music*

stand depends for its interpretation on shared knowledge, which is in no way expressed by the language forms used. Correct interpretations of utterances can indeed take us a very long way away from their surface encodings. In specific situations the following sentences, for example, might be used to convey the messages shown in brackets (or other very different ones), and be successfully understood as doing so.
- *Your coat's on the floor.* ('Pick up your coat.')
- *Jane's got her exams on Friday.* ('I can't come to lunch.')
- *Let's not have a repetition of last time.* ('Don't get drunk and start flirting with Melissa.')
- *It's Wednesday.* ('Put the trash out.')

The linguistic discipline known as pragmatics (what I am here calling 'Pragmatics A') takes this kind of problem as its principal subject matter. Textbooks on pragmatics (e.g. Levinson, 1983; Yule, 1996; Horn & Ward, 2004) concern themselves centrally with the principles used by speakers/writers and hearers/readers to bridge the gap between code meaning and context-determined meaning. Such works typically discuss, among other things:
- the way context, shared knowledge, and familiarity with conventional schemata, routines and genres all contribute to meaning, and are taken into account in framing and interpreting utterances.
- the 'co-operative principle' underlying successful communication, whereby speakers and writers normally avoid saying too much or too little, give true information, say what is relevant, and aim at clarity of expression (the maxims of quantity, quality, relation and manner identified by the philosopher Grice).
- 'implicature'—the ways in which the flouting of these maxims can be interpreted (e.g. damning with faint praise, showing off, exaggeration for emphasis, irony, metaphor).

By definition, Pragmatics A is concerned primarily with what is not encoded, and its analytical categories are applicable to every act of communication: there is surely no sentence which has an absolute universal value totally independent of the personal and situational context in which it is uttered.

Pragmatics B: what is encoded

When language teachers talk about 'pragmatics', however, they are not generally thinking about the branch of linguistics discussed above, or the topics that this is mainly concerned with. By virtue of being efficient communicators in their mother tongues, students already know how to relate code to context so as to determine the communicative intention of a given utterance, and the strategies and principles involved are to a great extent universal and language-independent. Certainly, there are some culture-specific differences—for example, one culture may value silence, indirectness or the overt expression of respect more than another. But by and large, Pragmatics A,

Grammar, meaning and pragmatics: sorting out the muddle 147

dealing as it does with what is not encoded, is outside the scope of the language classroom.

'Pragmatics', for language teachers, is to do with what is encoded. Languages do not leave their speakers to grapple unaided with the problem of bridging the gap between the dictionary/grammar meanings of utterances and their precise value in certain kinds of communicative context. All languages provide ways of reducing the problem by labelling, in general terms, the typical communicative roles that utterances can take on. So we can encode linguistically the fact that we are making a request, or expressing doubt, or adding information, or showing respect, or making an objection, or exaggerating. It is these language-specific features—what I am calling 'Pragmatics B'—that are of direct concern to language teachers. Pragmatics B deals with questions like the following:

- How are common speech acts encoded in the target language? How does one make requests, express respect, invite, interrupt, etc?
- Are there cross-language differences in the distribution of speech acts? Does L2 mark a logical contrast overtly while L1 leaves it to be interpreted from the context? Does L1, unlike L2, have an answer form that indicates that the speaker has asked a stupid question? Does one language go overboard for respect while the other only makes a few gestures in that direction? Do speakers necessarily have to use politeness markers in one of the languages, but not the other, when asking a question; or is there a default interrogative structure which will do unless one needs to be especially polite (as in English)?
- What are the false friends? Does a negative question work for making requests in L1 but not in L2? Does the equivalent of *Have you eaten?* mean 'Have you eaten?', or does it mean 'How are you?' or something else? Is the equivalent of *Please* used in L2, but not in L1, when offering something or replying to thanks?

Pragmatics B is not easy to delineate clearly. The kind of topics listed above are often grouped in a general way under the heading 'doing things with language'. But where does one draw the line? If making requests, issuing invitations and enquiring about health are 'doing things with language', then so presumably are defining things, predicting the weather and talking about computers. Another common definition of pragmatics in language teaching characterizes it as being concerned with 'the choices that users of a particular language make when using the forms of the language in communication' (Celce-Murcia and Larsen-Freeman 1999: 4–5). But of course all use of language involves choices: we do not use the same words to talk about cars as to talk about flowers, or the same structures to refer to the past as we do to refer to the future.

Whatever the problems of definition, though, language teachers and pedagogic writers find it convenient in practice to use the term 'pragmatics' mainly with reference to two specific areas where the roles that utterances can take on are perhaps especially in need of linguistic labelling. These are:

1 The construction of spoken exchanges, where interpersonal aspects of communication involving respect, face etc. are often key issues, so that languages tend to have quite complex ways of framing utterances to ensure that speakers' intentions are not misinterpreted.
2 The construction of written text, where failure to interpret the flow of argument may cause misunderstanding, and where the use of devices such as structuring conventions, anaphoric elements and discourse markers can facilitate interpretation.

This, then, is the domain of Pragmatics B: not (as with Pragmatics A) the whole of a linguistic system, but the subset of linguistic structures which encode the particular types of meaning just referred to.

The confusion

The common claim that all structures have two kinds of meaning, both of which we need to teach, seems to derive from a simple confusion between these two different versions of 'pragmatics'. Certainly, we can agree that all utterances have not only dictionary/grammar meanings but also separate context-determined values in use (Pragmatics A). However, we cannot legitimately import this generalisation into a discussion of pragmatic encodings (Pragmatics B). Context-determined values are features of utterances; they are not encoded in the structures used to create these utterances, and do not therefore give rise to structure-specific 'rules of use' which can be taught. English passives, for example, can be used to imply agency without stating it directly, and this can be exploited for the pragmatic purpose of making veiled criticisms. But, as Batstone points out, we cannot relate this insight very closely to specific contexts. While the sentence *The windows haven't been cleaned for months* may be uttered with the intention of causing embarrassment or hurt, 'it would appear odd to assert that the passive can be used to cause embarrassment or hurt in domestic disputes concerning the cleaning of windows' (1994: 14).

A crucial issue is that, as pointed out above, those pragmatic encodings which can be taught (and which are therefore relatively context-independent) are not by any means found in all the elements of a language. Pragmatics B, unlike Pragmatics A, has limited and partial scope. This is easy to see with lexis. While some words and expressions encode centrally pragmatic functions (for example *Please, Dear Sir* or *Feel free*), others encode no pragmatics at all (for example *dishwasher, marinate* or *in time*). Yet others have both pragmatic and non-pragmatic functions: *this* can be used not only to indicate physical or temporal proximity, but also to clarify the linking of items in text; *certainly*, as well as conveying definiteness, can label a concessive move in an argument (*Certainly, she did some good work at the beginning. But ...*). The situation is exactly the same for grammatical structures. Imperatives perform a variety of pragmatic functions, labelling their associated utterances as being for example commands, requests, or invitations. In contrast, plural morphology in English nouns has no pragmatic significance: its function is purely semantic. Plural morphology in French pronouns and verbs, on the other hand, can encode either semantic meaning (reference to more than one thing or person), or pragmatic meaning (where using the second-person plural to address a single person expresses respect by metaphorically aggrandising the addressee).

If not all structures can be exploited for purposes that we might reasonably call pragmatic, there are certainly many structures which can be, as research by construction grammarians and others is making increasingly clear—see for example Goldberg (1995), Celce-Murcia and Larsen-Freeman (1999), Green (2004), Kay (2004). Even where structures do have more than one kind of potential function, however, the distinction between 'meaning' and 'use', or 'semantic' and 'pragmatic' meaning seems somewhat artificial, and it is not always easy to operationalize. As pointed out earlier, the two main senses of English *must* do not seem to fit neatly into the two slots. For another example, take the past tenses in the following sentences:

1 I **saw** Oliver yesterday.
2 Only 18? I thought you **were** older.
3 If I **had** time I'd do a lot more reading.
4 I think it's time we **went** home.
5 If you **had** a moment, I wouldn't mind a bit of help.
6 How much **did** you want to spend?

We can if we wish describe the tense in 1) as having a 'literal meaning', referring as it does simply to past time, and the tense in 6) as involving a 'pragmatic use' of the past form for polite distancing. But what about the others? It seems difficult to assign the various intertwined nuances of time reference, hypotheticality, and interpersonal indirectness to one or other category. In the case of such polyvalent items, it would be simpler, surely, to abandon the notion of a two-part division between 'meaning' and 'use', and simply say that the structures have several different functions.

Conclusion

Looking at the conceptualization of pragmatics in language teaching that developed during the communicative revolution of the 1970s and that is still very much with us, I cannot help feeling that, in the words of the old cliché, what was true wasn't new and what was new wasn't true. It has always been considered important for students to learn how the language they are studying encodes the most important pragmatic functions, even if the heavily structure-based pre-communicative language courses of forty years ago were not always very good at teaching these systematically. The interest of the last few decades in various dimensions of 'language in use' has certainly expanded our knowledge of how languages work, and our concern to approximate real-life language use in the classroom has greatly improved our teaching methodology. However, it is irritating to be told, as one often is, that the pragmatic dimension of language, 'language in use' or 'grammar as choice', is a recent discovery, unknown before the advent of the communicative approach, or even (as is sometimes implied in contemporary academic and pedagogic writing) neglected before the researches of the author and his or her colleagues.

> Most grammars have focused on structure, describing the form and (sometimes) meaning of grammatical constructions out of context. They have not described how forms and meanings are actually used in spoken and written discourse.
> (Biber et al 2002: 2)

(Note the interesting suggestion that in the bad old days we did not teach even semantic meaning most of the time, concealing from our students the potentially inflammatory information that plural nouns refer to more than one entity, that past tenses are prototypically used to refer to past time, and that forms like *older* and *more beautiful* express comparison.)

Here is Gurrey, writing about language teaching in the mid-fifties:

> … it is comparatively easy to memorize grammatical forms, but difficult to master the usage of those forms. And it is of no value at all to know all the Tense forms of a Verb, unless one knows also which Tense to use. It is more useful to know when to say "Have you finished that letter?" and when to say "Did you finish that letter?" than to know the Principal Parts of the Verb "to finish".
> (Gurrey 1955: 71)

Billows, writing a few years later about how a teacher might approach the simple present tense, gives an impressively long list of the various kinds of reference that the tense can have in communication (1961: 166–7). If it is felt that this is not exactly 'pragmatics', then consider the language functions covered in lessons 1–8 of a typical structure-based course of the 1960s (Candlin 1968). They include: greeting, enquiring about health, leave-taking, thanking, expressing regret, eliciting and giving information, offering, requesting goods and services, proffering, self-identification, asking for more precise information, confirming what has been said, exhortation, identifying and naming, agreeing to carry out instructions, and enquiring about plans.

And here is the very first lesson of another popular English course of the 1960s (Alexander, 1967):

MAN:	Excuse me.
WOMAN:	Yes?
MAN:	Is this your handbag?
WOMAN:	Pardon?
MAN:	Is this your handbag?
WOMAN:	Yes, it is. Thank you very much.

(Text accompanied by illustrations of a woman leaving her handbag on a train.)

It would be hard to find a better demonstration of how to integrate the teaching of structure and pragmatic use at beginners' level.

As a glance at any history of language-teaching (e.g. Howatt and Widdowson 2004) will show, 'language in use' has been taught, well or badly, since languages were first studied. The recent construct of a distinct 'communicative competence', separate from ordinary language knowledge and skills, that can be taught by focusing on how all the forms of a language 'are actually used in spoken and written discourse', is in my view a chimera, based on a confused understanding of what is meant by 'pragmatics'. It is certainly important to make sure that students understand the various ways—pragmatic or not—in which the principal structures of a language can be used, and that they become proficient in these uses. But to approach this goal by encouraging teachers to try to identify and teach as separate items the 'meaning' and 'use' of all grammatical structures is in my view to send them on a wild goose chase.

15
Talking sense about learning strategies

(Originally published in *RELC Journal* 39/2, 2008.)

This article arose out of dissatisfaction with a conference whose main topic was learning strategies. Although many of the contributions to the conference were interesting and valuable, I felt that there was a good deal of confusion surrounding both the notion of strategy and its relevance to language learning and teaching. What follows was partly an attempt to clarify my own ideas on the subject.

Introduction

Learning a foreign language is difficult, complicated and time-consuming. Any procedure that might make it a little easier, faster or more successful therefore needs to be taken seriously. Hence the explosion of interest in learning strategies over the last three decades or so, and the presence of titles such as Oxford (1990), O'Malley and Chamot (1990) and Macaro (2001) on teacher trainees' reading lists.

However, as with many other key concepts in our field (e.g. *skill*, *pragmatics*, *task*, *process*), there are substantial problems of definition, scope and applicability (Macaro 2006). How can we best delimit the notion of 'strategy' so that it will serve our purposes? What are the criteria for deciding that a strategy can usefully be taught? Is it helpful to classify strategies; and if so, into what categories should we divide them?

Defining strategies

Perhaps a good starting point is to look at how the word 'strategy' is deployed in ordinary usage. A key element is that of problem-solving. A strategy is not simply what you do to obtain a result; rather, it is the way you choose to deal with questions that arise on the way to obtaining that result. For instance, if your purpose is to go to work in the morning, getting up is not what one would normally call a 'strategy'; it is just what you have to do if you are going to get to work at all. But if you have problems getting to work on time, the notion of strategy becomes relevant. Should you take the car, leaving early to miss rush hour; or go by bike and dodge the traffic; or go by rail and hope that the trains are running normally? To take another example: if you are going away on holiday, packing is not a strategy—it is a normal part of holiday travel. But there are all sorts of strategies for packing, depending on the circumstances, the packer's fussiness and his/her individual preferences. Fold all your clothes carefully and put them in with the biggest at the bottom; just throw things in as they come to hand; make a list; rely on your memory; do your packing the night before you travel; get up early and do it just before you leave; get your partner to do it; and so on.

Inherent in this everyday idea of strategy is that of alternatives. A strategy is one of several possible ways of solving a problem: the way that you think will work best, or that you are most comfortable with. Surprisingly, however, in discussions of language-learning strategies the choice-of-solution element is not always prominent. It does not occur even by implication in four of the five definitions cited by Macaro in his book on the subject (2001: 17). It seems to me, however, that this criterion is crucial for language learning as for other activities; without it, the notion of 'strategy' becomes too heterogeneous and all-inclusive to be useful. In a recent paper (Griffiths 2007) on teachers' and students' perceptions of strategies, the author includes the following in the list of 32 'strategies' that she selects for examination:

- spending time studying English
- learning from the teacher
- doing homework
- revising regularly
- using a dictionary
- learning from mistakes
- studying English grammar
- consciously learning new vocabulary

But it is hard to see these as approaches that learners might choose to follow (or not) after weighing the alternatives. What would such alternatives be? Not spending time studying English? Not learning from the teacher? Not learning from mistakes? Not studying vocabulary or grammar? Apart perhaps from one or two small tribes living in the more remote mountain fastnesses of second language acquisition theory, people involved in language instruction surely take it for granted that learning from the teacher, revising, studying vocabulary and so on are necessary parts of the business. The same goes for activities such as practising and paying attention (Oxford 1990: 19, 20). But then it is not, I think, useful to call these things 'strategies'. If everything that one does in order to learn a language is brought under the umbrella of 'strategy', there is nothing that is not a strategy, and the concept becomes vacuous.

If we limit learning strategies to types of behaviour that learners can choose or not to engage in, as seems reasonable, then we must surely exclude mental processes that are automatic and cannot be 'switched off'. Macaro (2001: 21) argues for a conscious–unconscious continuum in the analysis of strategies, and this may well be reasonable in the light of his view that strategies can be automatized. However, it is hard to see how an intrinsically unconscious procedure (such as some types of inferencing) can usefully be included in a pedagogic programme. A number of the items included in Oxford's strategy lists and in her associated questionnaire for investigating strategy use, the 'Strategy Inventory for Language Learning' (1990), seem to me to be susceptible to this criticism. For example, one of her strategies (1990: 295) is, while engaged in conversation, to try to guess what one's interlocutor will say next. It seems highly likely, however, that this is a normal and automatic part of the mental processing of spoken interchanges, not under conscious control, or subject to teaching or learning. Another of Oxford's strategies, listed also by O'Malley and Chamot (1990: 45), is deductive reasoning. As an imaginary example of successful use of the strategy Oxford offers the following:

> Julio, who is learning English, hears his friend say, "Would you like to go to the library with me at five o'clock?" Julio correctly understands that he is being asked a question to which he must respond, because he recognizes that part of the verb comes before the subject (a general rule he has learned).
> (Oxford 1990: 82)

But identifying a sentence as interrogative, in a language of which one knows the basic grammar, is a relatively automatic business. Whatever processing is involved in Julio's recognizing that he is being asked a question, and in his appreciation that the question requires an answer, it is hard to see a case for saying that he is deliberately operating a strategy of 'deductive reasoning', any more than deductive reasoning is involved in his identification of the word 'library' as the name of a place where books are kept.

Selecting strategies for teaching

For pedagogic purposes, then, I suggest that strategies need to be problem-oriented and subject to conscious selection from a range of alternatives. They also need, obviously, to involve procedures that not all learners would automatically engage in without teaching. One might wonder for instance whether Oxford's 'Pascual', presented as an example of a student engaging in 'scanning', really owes his effective behaviour as a traveller to strategy training:

> Waiting in the Köln train station, Pascual (a learner of German) is worried about his late train, and therefore he listens closely for an announcement of its estimated arrival time and scans the schedule board periodically.
> (Oxford 1990: 81)

Strategies also need to be effective; or—given the poverty of empirical evidence in this respect (Macaro 2006)—they should at least offer solutions that look plausible. It is hard, for example, to imagine a Chinese student of English getting very far with strategies such as coining words or switching to the mother tongue (Macaro 2001: 201; Oxford 1990: 295); nor does 'avoiding communication' (Oxford 1990: 48) seem obviously to qualify as an effective language-learning strategy.

Most importantly, perhaps, as Rees-Miller stresses (1993: 681, cited in Macaro 2006: 322), specific strategies need to be defined in terms which make it clear what exactly one is talking about. Simply suggesting that a learner 'use the English words I know in different ways' or 'try to find out how to be a better learner of English' (Oxford 1990: 295) is likely to result in bafflement rather than improved learning. Again, it may well make sense to encourage a strategy of 'trying to think in English' (Griffiths 2007: 96), but if so, we need at least to decide just what this means. Arguably, much thinking is not verbal. Some is, certainly; but just what kinds of thinking? For the instruction to be useful, the focus needs to be narrowed to something the learner can get hold of. For instance: 'Mentally explain to somebody in English how to cook something', or 'Mentally draft a letter to your partner in English'. Similarly, it does not seem very constructive to encourage a strategy of trying 'to talk like native English speakers' (Oxford 1990: 295) without further specification. Students might well wish to do exactly this; but they must be told how to get closer to doing it, not just told to do it. What exactly are they being instructed to imitate—intonation, rhythm, articulatory setting, specific sounds …? The whole lot all at once? Surely not.

Oxford's book includes a number of activities designed to get teachers thinking about learning strategies and relating their use to concrete situations. This is a welcome feature, but here again there are places where the focus seems somewhat unclear:

> ON TOUR: You are an Australian tourist in Greece. You have never been here before, and your study of Greek has been limited to skimming the Berlitz phrasebook. You managed to find your hotel with the help of a taxi driver. You went out for a walk on your own and got lost. Nobody around you seems to speak English. Your task is to find out where you are and get back to your hotel before it gets dark. You have two hours to do this. You are getting a little worried! Which language learning strategies do you need to use?
> (Oxford 1990: 32)

Language learning strategies? I think I've failed.

Reading skills

The issues discussed above surface strikingly in discussions of strategies for improving 'reading skills'. This area is something of a conceptual morass, and it is often quite unclear precisely what effect a given teaching approach can realistically be expected to produce. Much of the teaching of reading skills is predicated on the assumption that learners do not already possess them: that a student who understands the grammar and vocabulary of a foreign-language text needs to learn something else in addition in order to 'comprehend' what he or she is reading. Hence the standard battery of exercises designed to train students in 'skimming', 'scanning', 'predicting', 'inferring' and so forth, that one finds in textbook after textbook. But this needs to be questioned. Certainly, there are learners who are poor readers in their mother tongue, and who for one reason or another need to acquire enhanced reading skills in another language. However, such students are something of a special case. I think a reasonable default position is that most literate foreign-language learners simply need to be able to access the processing skills that they are already able to deploy in other areas: for instance, when reading mother-tongue texts; and that accessing these skills is largely a function of increased proficiency. On this view, 'comprehension' difficulty, where it is not simply caused by unfamiliar language, is likely to result from temporary processing overload, with too much of working memory taken up with low-level decoding and not enough left available for the higher-level mental structure-building which underlies effective text comprehension. With increased experience of the foreign language, decoding becomes more automatic and the learner is better able to access his or her higher-level processing skills. (See Walter 2007 for detailed discussion.) If this is the case, it can be argued that much of the work that is done in classrooms in order to 'teach' reading skills or strategies is more or less a waste of time.

One of the standard 'reading skills' lessons involves trying to train students to guess the meanings of unknown words that they encounter while reading. Recommended strategies include decomposing compound words ('*de–compose–ing*'), looking for cognates ('encounter = *incontrare*'), looking for clues in the context ('John was angry, so *he growled* may mean that he made an angry noise'), and various others (see for example O'Malley and Chamot 1990: 178–9; Oxford 1990: 90–94; Macaro 2001: 190). The question is: what exactly is the purpose of all this? Certainly not to help students to learn vocabulary—this kind of guessing is a compensatory strategy, not a learning strategy. If you want to learn what a new word actually means, reference to a dictionary or an informant is far more efficient and reliable than guesswork. In a study by Parry (1991), students were able to guess the meaning of unknown words in text only about 50% of the time.

To help students to understand texts better, then? Perhaps—but the ultimate purpose of language teaching is to give students the language they need in order to read texts, not to teach them to manage as well as they can without that language. Research has shown that for efficient reading, skilled readers need to be able to recognize rapidly 95% or more of the words in a text (Grabe & Stoller 2002: 186). And in any case, if a student is seriously held up while reading by a difficult word, looking the word up beats guessing; words that cause less trouble can be skipped. (Now there is a useful strategy.)

A practical example may help to clarify the issues, while enabling us at the same time to put ourselves in the same position as an intermediate language learner. Readers are invited to look through the following text (Garioch 1980: 33) and examine their approach to understanding it. It is written in Lallans, a literary Lowland Scottish dialect of which readers are likely, by virtue of their knowledge of standard English, to have intermediate-level comprehension. In the text Robert Garioch offers an original view of Sisyphus, the character in Greek mythology who was condemned by the gods to spend eternity pushing a large boulder up a mountain, only to find that every time he got it to the top it rolled down again.

> SISYPHUS
> *Bumpity doun in the corrie gaed whuddran the pitiless whun stane.*
> *Sisyphus, pechan and sweitan, disjaskit, forfeuchan and broun'd-aff,*
> *sat on the heather a hanlawhile, houpan the Boss didna spy him,*
> *seein the terms of his contract includit nae mention of tea-breaks,*
> *syne at the muckle big scunnersom boulder he trauchlit aince mair.*
> *Ach! hou kenspeckle it was, that he ken'd ilka spreckle and blotch on't.*
> *Heavin awa at its wecht, he manhaunnlit the bruitt up the brae-face,*
> *takkan the easiest gait he had fand in a fudder of dour years,*
> *haudan awa frae the craigs had affrichtit him maist in his youth-heid,*
> *feelin his years aa the same, he gaed cannily, tenty of slipped discs.*
> *Eftir an hour and a quarter he warslit his wey to the brae's heid,*
> *hystit his boulder richt up on the tap of the cairn—and it stude there!*
> *streikit his length on the chuckie-stanes, houpan the Boss wadna spy him,*
> *had a wee look at the scenery, feenisht a pie and a cheese-piece.*
> *Whit was he thinking about, that he just gied the boulder a wee shove?*
> *Bumpity doun in the corrie gaed whuddran the pitiless whun stane,*
> *Sisyphus dodderan eftir it, shair of his cheque at the month's end.*
> (Garioch 1980: 33)

First of all, let us consider what stands between the average reader and a complete understanding of the text. Not 'reading skills', surely? Few readers will have exclaimed, on reaching the end of the poem, 'Oh, dear! I wish I was better at skimming/predicting/inferring/ ...' The problem is of course vocabulary, as it generally is for intermediate language learners grappling with difficult texts. About a third of the words in *Sisyphus* do not occur in standard English. On the plus side, however, readers will have quickly spotted that many of these (about half of the difficult words) are cognates, similar to standard English words but spelt differently—for example *doun, stane, seein*. Identification of cognates is certainly a useful strategy for learners who speak the few languages that are closely related to English, and worth teaching to such of those learners (probably a minority) who do not operate the strategy automatically. Cognates are however not always easy to identify: perhaps not all readers will have spotted that *manhaunlit* the *bruitt* corresponds to 'man-handled the brute'. And students need of course to bear in mind that cognates are often misleading, especially as between English and Romance languages.

(Even in the present example there is at least one false cognate: a *cheese-piece* is a cheese sandwich, not a piece of cheese.)

If we discount the cognates, there are still over twenty difficult words in the poem. How far can we get towards understanding these by applying the standard 'guessing unknown words' strategies? Not very far, I think. A few words or expressions can be decomposed into parts at least one of which is familiar. A *hanlawhile* (given the context) must have something to do with 'a while'; *fricht* in *affrichtit* looks like 'fright', so the word probably means 'frightened'; *youth-head* is probably just 'youth'; *chuckie-stanes* will be some kind of stones. For the other twenty or so words, the only recourse is to look at the context and guess. If you have identified *sweitan* as 'sweating', then *pechan* perhaps means 'puffing' or 'gasping'; *disjaskit* and *forfeuchan* may also refer to uncomfortable physical or mental states. It is not that hard to deduce that *takkan the easiest gait he had fand in a fudder of dour years* means something like 'taking the easiest route he had found in a lot (?)/long period (?) of hard (?)/sad (?) years'. And so on. However, we need to remember that this kind of speculation, even when successful, is a one-way process: our belief that *gait* means something like 'route', for instance, came from the text in the first place, so adds nothing further to our overall understanding: taking information from the text does not put additional information back into it. It would have made no difference, in fact, if the word *gait* had not been there, and the line had read 'takkan the easiest —— he had fand ...'.

Readers probably finished the exercise with a reasonable understanding of Garioch's wonderful poem. (And for those who would like to get closer to the exact meaning, there is a rough translation into standard English at the end of this paper.) But—to repeat my earlier point—I would argue that this understanding arises mainly from readers' possession of normal reading skills, rather than from any training they might have received in the kind of strategies that it is conventional to teach to foreign-language learners (most of whom also have normal reading skills). And the exercise should also have made it clear, if this was necessary, that strategies for 'guessing unknown words' have very limited effectiveness. It is worth asking, in fact, under what circumstances language learners really find themselves needing to understand, as well as they can, unknown words in a difficult text, without having recourse to a dictionary. Mainly, perhaps, in language examinations, and in the classroom during lessons where they are being prepared for such examinations. Is it possible, then, that the whole 'guessing unknown words' business is nothing more than a solution to an artificial and self-inflicted problem; simply another example of the way we can be forced to spend valuable teaching time training students to jump through the hoops that our examinations set up for them?

Classifying strategies

Categorizing and labelling are perhaps the most fundamental of all intellectual strategies: they are our basis for understanding and managing our infinitely complex world. However, category systems can take on a life of their own, with the danger that they may obscure the real nature of the phenomena that we are classifying. This can, I think, be the case in discussions of learning strategies. Taxonomies such as O'Malley and Chamot's (1990: 46) or Oxford's (1990: 14–22) are quite elaborate, distinguishing several general types of strategy—in Oxford's case 'memory', 'cognitive', 'compensation', 'metacognitive', 'affective' and 'social'—each with numerous subcategories. Oxford's categorization in particular, with its several levels of subdivision, is somewhat daunting, and it is hard to share her belief that teachers and students can internalize and work from the scheme (1990: 24–25). There are inevitable problems of classification and overlap between categories, as Oxford herself recognizes (1990: 16–17). And it is not in fact always easy to see the rationale underlying the classifications. Oxford's 'cognitive strategies' (1990: 19), for example, fall into four oddly disparate groups: A 'Practicing', B 'Receiving and sending messages', C 'Analysing and reasoning' and D 'Creating structure for input and output'. Group B has two subdivisions: 1 'Getting the idea quickly', and 2 'Using resources for receiving and sending messages'. This style of categorization seems to owe more to brainstorming than to a reasoned analysis of the processes involved.

Macaro (2001: 24) adopts a rather different classification system involving a number of related continua (e.g. cognitive–metacognitive/social/affective; subconscious–conscious; direct–indirect). This is also quite elaborate, but Macaro in fact questions whether, for pedagogic purposes at least, it is actually important to come up with a 'definitive and clear classification'.

It certainly seems possible that, for teachers and learners, it would be more transparent and useful to list strategies by target, rather than on the basis of mental processes which risk being ill-defined and impressionistically subcategorized. So that instead of schemes like 'cognitive strategies' → 'practising' → 'recognizing and using formulas and patterns' (Oxford 1990: 44), with the subsequent problem of relating these procedures to specific aspects of learning or skills use, one's strategy inventory might simply read: 'ways of memorizing vocabulary', 'ways of internalizing difficult grammar rules', 'ways of becoming better at perceiving weak forms or vowel contrasts', 'ways of getting information from dictionaries', and so on. Such an approach, by pinning discussion down to specifics, might also put a brake on the enormous proliferation of strategies that is a disturbing feature of some of the literature.

Conclusion: the value and limitations of strategy training

Despite the generally critical tone of this paper, and the concerns raised by many scholars and well summarized by Macaro (2006), I do not of course wish to question the value of a judicious concern with well-defined learning strategies. Sensitizing students to the role of strategies and giving them training in their use is obviously a constructive thing to do, provided such strategies are genuinely teachable, clearly targeted and plausibly effective. In particular, training in the 'metacognitive strategies' that can help students to organize and assess their learning is widely recognized as contributing to success in all fields of study. And while recent work may not have added as much to the traditional strategy inventory as some writers might suggest, it is certainly helpful for language teachers to be provided with accessible accounts of the different ways in which their students can be helped (or can help themselves) to learn. To the extent that research provides reliable information about the effectiveness or otherwise of specific strategy use and training, this too is valuable.

Valuable approaches to language teaching can, however, be counter-productive if taken to extremes. This has happened often enough in the history of our discipline—one thinks of structure drilling and the language lab, the banning of the mother tongue, the exclusive use of functional/notional syllabuses, the insistence that all student activity be 'communicative', or the rush to bring corpora into the classroom. Strategy training, too, can cause trouble if it is given too much importance. Encouraging students to try out a limited range of well-focused approaches to specific learning problems is one thing; swamping them with multifarious and complex inventories of ill-defined strategies is quite another. And given the current vogue for self-directed learning, and the evangelistic tone of some of the writing in the field, there is a further danger that training in strategy use may be seen by inexperienced teachers as a replacement for traditional teacher-directed learning. Nobody would dispute the value, up to a point, of learner independence. But learners are not necessarily themselves the best judges of what learning strategies are appropriate for them. We have all known students who believed the key to success in language learning was simply to learn grammar rules by heart. ... Learner independence needs to be guided. And of course teaching strategies does not remove the need to teach language. It is of limited value, for instance, to train students to handle aural comprehension difficulties by deploying broad-spectrum 'listening skills' (scanning, asking for repetition or whatever), if they are not also trained to overcome the specific phonological problems, such as difficulty in perceiving weak forms, vowel contrasts or complex consonant clusters, which cause the aural comprehension difficulties in the first place. ... Well-designed strategy training is undoubtedly very valuable in its place, but it is simply one of the many resources available to language teachers. It must not be allowed to fill the horizon.

Robert Garioch's *Sisyphus*: a literal translation into standard English

Bumpity down in the gully went thundering the pitiless boulder.
Sisyphus, panting and sweating, worn out, exhausted and fed up
sat on the heather for a short while, hoping the Boss didn't spy him,
seeing the terms of his contract included no mention of tea-breaks,

*then at the great big horrible boulder he struggled once more.
Oh, how familiar it was, that he knew every glint and blotch on it.
Heaving away at its weight, he manhandled the brute up the hillside,
taking the easiest route he had found in a burden of hard years,
keeping away from the crags that had frightened him most in his youth,
feeling his years all the same, he went cautiously, careful of slipped discs.
After an hour and a quarter he wrestled his way to the hilltop,
hoisted his boulder right up on the top of the cairn—and it stayed there!
stretched his length on the pebbles, hoping the Boss wouldn't spy him,
had a little look at the scenery, finished a pie and a cheese sandwich.
What was he thinking about, that he just gave the boulder a little shove?
Bumpity down in the gully went thundering the pitiless boulder,
Sisyphus doddering after it, sure of his cheque at the month's end.*

16
We do need methods

(Originally published in *RELC Journal* 39/2, 2008.)

This, like one or two more pedagogically oriented articles, was concerned with the rather obvious notion that language itself must be at the centre of language teaching. In a draft of another paper written for a prestigious academic journal, I made an appeal at one point to common sense, but was told firmly by the editor that I must remove this, since common sense has no academic standing. (As I had sometimes suspected.) In this article I managed to get away with it.

Method, methods, postmethod
Introduction: definitions

Learning languages is a notoriously complex business, involving the mastery of several different kinds of knowledge and skill. Over the years, language teachers have developed numerous ways of imparting these various aspects of language competence, drawing on research, individual exploration, and the accumulated wisdom of the profession. Since learning and competence are difficult to measure, there is inevitably substantial room for differing opinions about the value of one or other method of achieving a particular goal.

Such opinions range from the general to the particular. Some claims seem intended to apply to all of the multifarious activities that constitute language instruction: 'The mother-tongue must never be used in foreign-language teaching'; 'Learning can only be effective if it involves genuine communication'; 'Comprehensible input provides all that is necessary for effective acquisition'. Others relate to more specific aspects of a language teacher's work; for instance the belief that learners need training in reading skills; or that linguistic regularities are best learnt inductively; or that new lexis must always be contextualized; or that teaching phoneme discrimination by the use of minimal pairs helps to improve pronunciation; or that recasts are (or are not) more effective than explicit correction.

Methodological views have been categorized in differing ways by scholars from Anthony (1963) to Richards and Rodgers (2001: 18–34). There is consequently some terminological confusion both in the professional literature and in more general usage as to what it is and is not appropriate to call a 'method', and how or whether 'method' is to be distinguished from 'approach'. While it can be helpful to distinguish levels of generality, attempts to establish watertight categories suffer from the usual problem of trying to draw lines on a continuum. In what follows, I shall bypass the problem, using these terms in accordance with normal informal practice without attempting rigorous definitions or distinctions.

The so-called 'postmethod' condition

Discussion of methodology is currently further complicated by the frequently-heard claim that language teaching has moved into a 'postmethod' era (e.g. Brown 2002; Kumaravadivelu 2006). Up till fairly recently, the story goes, there have been successive and often contradictory views about how best to teach languages. These have tended to harden into relatively systematic sets of precepts or 'methods', often going into considerable detail about the optimum design of syllabuses, materials and activity types. Such methods have not delivered what they promised, due largely to the limited views of language, teaching and learning which they embodied. Methods are, we are told, top-down and prescriptive. Their efficacy cannot be demonstrated as they are not testable against each other. The role of the individual teacher is minimized. Methods fail to address the broader contexts of language teaching.

> By concentrating excessively on method, we have ignored several other factors that govern classroom processes and practices—factors such as teacher cognition, learner perception, societal needs, cultural contexts, political exigencies, economic imperatives… .
> (Kumaravadivelu 2006: 165)

Autonomy, self-fulfilment and personal development are precluded by an outcome/objectives approach (Finney 2002: 72). Methods, indeed, may carry (undesirable) sociopolitical agendas (Brown 2002: 10; Finney 2002: 71).

Now, however, it is claimed, we are freeing ourselves from the constraints of one or other method, and are able to adopt a more open and promising approach to language teaching which can take into account all of the factors—linguistic, psychological and sociological—that shape our activity and that of our learners. Kumaravadivelu (2006: 201) lists ten 'macrostrategies' which characterize postmethod language teaching, and from which teachers can generate situation-specific need-based microstrategies or teaching techniques. They are:

1 Maximize learning opportunities
2 Facilitate negotiated interaction
3 Minimize perceptual mismatches
4 Activate intuitive heuristics
5 Foster language awareness

6 Contextualize linguistic input
7 Integrate language skills
8 Promote learner autonomy
9 Ensure social relevance
10 Raise cultural consciousness.

How method-bound has language teaching really been?

Large-scale methodological views which embody, so to speak, a whole instructional philosophy may certainly impose directions and constraints at a level of considerable detail, so that the whole business of language teaching can be seen as taking on the colour of this or that 'approach'. The old 'Direct Method' requirement that all language teaching should be mediated through the target language caused generations of teachers to go through contortions to avoid translation, and to forbid their students to use bilingual dictionaries (as some still do, discredited though the belief now is). Some teachers and course designers who followed hard-core varieties of the audiolingual approach tried to make as many aspects of their teaching as possible conform to the behaviourist principles of 'mimicry-memorization' and 'overlearning' through drilling. The fringe methods which became popular in the 1970s, such as Suggestopaedia, Counselling Learning or Silent Way, sometimes required an almost religious type of observance from their devotees. Similarly, some versions of the 'communicative approach' have severely discouraged specific teaching activities which are seen as not mirroring 'real-life' communication: for example, asking students questions to which the teacher already knows the answer, or practising grammar through decontextualized sentence-level drills.

However, I suspect that the 'postmethod' account of language teaching history, whereby monolithic approaches have generally and comprehensively dictated the shape of courses, materials and teaching techniques, may be somewhat over-simplified. It is debatable how far such approaches usually constrain everything that is done. The term 'grammar-translation', for instance, which is commonly used as a derogatory label for a certain way of teaching languages, really only characterizes one aspect of classroom activity: dealing with morphology and syntax by teaching explicit rules and making students practise them by translating phrases or sentences. Whatever the drawbacks or inadequacies of this kind of approach, it does not necessarily spill over into other aspects of language learning such as reading or writing practice. This probably goes for any other 'named' method, audiolingual, communicative or whatever: as is often clear when one looks at the relevant coursebooks, the philosophical umbrella may in practice cover a good deal of eclecticism. Our familiar view of the succession of approaches that has seemed to characterize the last hundred years or so is perhaps therefore in part a convenient myth. Possibly a more realistic view would be that some parts of some methods have dictated, through syllabus, materials and test design, what some teachers have done, and continue to do, in some parts of their teaching. The successive rejection of one method by another may thus amount, in practice, to the replacement of what does not quite happen by something else that does not quite happen either.

How postmethod is the postmethod condition?

A brief look at the characterizations of 'postmethod' teaching cited above is enough to show, as Bell (2003) makes abundantly clear, that we have not in fact moved into the broad sunlit uplands of a new era, unconstrained by the limiting perspectives of one or other method or approach. Postmethod thinking is not at all methodologically neutral. On the contrary, like its predecessors, it can carry a heavy weight of sociopolitical and educational-philosophical baggage. Kumaravadivelu's ten 'macrostrategies' legislate in favour of negotiated interaction, learner autonomy, intuitive heuristics, social relevance and the raising of cultural consciousness. On the other hand, they have nothing at all to say about, for example, the selection of high-priority linguistic input, the organization of input material into progressive syllabuses, the role of systematic practice in learning, the value of memorization, the need for teachers to have a detailed explicit knowledge of the grammar, phonology and lexis of the languages they are teaching, or many other things that might be regarded by some teachers as centrally important for language teaching.

It is not my purpose here to argue pointlessly for one perspective as against another: both are obviously relevant to our work. In language teaching and learning, there is an eternal and inevitable pendulum-swing backwards and forwards between form and meaning, control and freedom, imitation and expression, knowledge and skill, learning and using. But clearly the 'postmethod condition', as described in the citations above, is well towards the meaning-freedom-expression-communication end. In this, it is simply another offshoot of the 'communicative approach' of the last thirty years which it is promoted as supplanting, with the same strengths and weaknesses, and with the same empirically unsupported methodological value-judgements and dichotomies (Swan 1985a, 1985b, 2005). In so far as it is distinguished from other versions of the communicative approach, it is so principally by virtue of its greater focus on socio-political-cultural concerns.

Despite the fine words, then, we are not in anything so grand as a 'postmethod condition'. What we are in, I would suggest, is a complex centrifugal muddle.

The centrifugal muddle
Doing things and teaching things

In order to teach the forms of the target language, the conventions for their use, and the receptive and productive skills necessary for their effective retrieval and deployment, teachers need interesting and engaging presentation and practice activities. As students learn more language, more general fluency-practice activities also take on increasing importance. Unfortunately, this increased focus on doing things can bring with it a correspondingly reduced focus on the specific knowledge and skills which learners need to acquire and consolidate by means of the activities. Unconsciously, teachers can be drawn into a centrifugal dynamic whereby they move further and further away from the linguistic centre, activities become paramount, and the language the activities are supposed to teach is lost sight of. Doing things is easier, and more fun, than teaching things. Activities such as getting students to prepare a mock radio programme, to give each other lectures on their academic specialities, or to discuss something that is in the news, can seem to be their own justification, with no requirement that there be an identifiable linguistic payoff for the time and energy invested.

Spoken or written texts, in this mind-set, may no longer be seen as vehicles for teaching and consolidating high-priority new language, or promoting receptive fluency. They can simply become a given, there because they are there, to be 'gone through' because that is what language students do, along with answering 'comprehension questions' of uncertain value.

> We do not believe that it is necessary for students to understand or translate every word of a reading or listening text. If students complete the task we set—answering a certain number of questions, marking a given number of sentences true or false—we feel that they have read or listened successfully.
> (Bowler and Parminter 2002: 59)

The key question, of course, is not whether students 'have read or listened successfully', but what, if anything, they have learnt in the process. Teachers' journals often contain articles on ways of using texts, as if the text was primary and uses had to be found for it. But this is like approaching household repairs by picking up a hammer and wondering what one can do with it, rather than starting by assessing what needs doing and then considering what tools are most appropriate. There seems in fact to be a widespread act of faith that any kind of engagement with texts is bound to teach language. This is by no means necessarily the case.

The communicative bias

The centrifugal dynamic has been greatly encouraged in recent decades by theoretical views according to which instructed language learning should attempt to simulate the conditions of 'natural' acquisition, and distance itself from the traditional form-focused teacher-dominated classroom.[1] If exposure to comprehensible input is all that is required for effective language acquisition (Krashen 1981: 107–8), or if communicative tasks incorporating incidental focus on form provide more or less everything that learners need

(Long and Robinson 1998), then appropriate activities become the central element in language teaching; language itself is no longer at the centre, and 'language-based' teaching methods are misguided (Robinson 2001: 292). Activity-related concepts that are universally approved of and automatically assented to in this framework—the applied linguistic equivalents of democracy and motherhood—include 'learner-centred', 'meaning-based', 'holistic', 'discourse', 'discovery', 'process', 'interaction', 'negotiation' and 'strategy'. On the other side of the communicative fence, concepts related to 'bad' pedagogic attitudes felt to be discredited and undesirable include 'teacher-dominated', 'form-based', 'discrete', 'sentence-level', 'transmission model', 'product', 'memorization', 'repetition' and 'drill'.

Systematic syllabus-based grammar teaching is naturally disfavoured by this approach; pronunciation has also been elbowed out. Behaviourist-oriented language teaching often incorporated early and systematic study of the phoneme distinctions and suprasegmental features of the target language. Perhaps because it is difficult to make phonological features 'communicative' in any very interesting sense, this kind of work has now largely disappeared. Similarly, communicative approaches to teaching 'listening comprehension', from Blundell and Stokes (1981) to Ellis (2003), typically focus on getting students to extract meaning from texts, rather than on training them to become better at perceiving and decoding the phonetic features—for example difficult consonant clusters, voicing or vowel rounding—that may be making it difficult for them to access the meaning in the first place (Ur 1984; Field 1998).

Large numbers of language teachers, particularly those whose training has been influenced by currently fashionable applied linguistic theory, now take the communicative natural acquisition bias for granted.

> In the 21st century, it is not necessary to defend the premise that learning a foreign language should be based on a communicative approach which prioritizes meaning over the form in which this meaning is communicated.
> (Irún-Chavarria 2005: 20)

But of course it is necessary to defend this premise—and equally necessary to contest it, along with others like it. It is by no means obvious why 'meaning' should be prioritized over 'form' (whatever that means exactly); or, for example, why learner-directed process should necessarily take precedence over teacher-directed product. Assertions about 'communicative' teaching of the kind under discussion are not generally based on empirical evidence as to the efficacy of the teaching approaches they promote (Sheen 1993, 1994, 2002; Swan 2005). Such approaches are ideological in nature: they belong to the category which Richards (2002: 21–23) characterizes as based on 'theory-philosophy conceptions', views of what ought to work or what is right, what stands to reason, what is self-evident, or what is believed to be psychologically or sociologically desirable.

Other biases

The centrifugal dynamic is, I believe, fuelled by several additional biases, both academic and practical, which can encourage a focus on activity in classrooms in preference to the study of language itself.

The innovation imperative Young applied linguists naturally want to carry out original research, publish articles, make their mark and climb the professional ladder. It is certainly possible to do this while investigating the teaching and acquisition of language forms and their uses, and a good deal of distinguished work takes place in this area. But there is perhaps more glory in coming up with exciting findings drawn from a new and unexplored area of research, remote from the central and perhaps intractable-seeming problems that so many researchers have already worked on.

The ESL bias A further bias may arise from the fact that many of those applied linguists whose views contribute to language teaching theory have typically gained their classroom experience either in second-language situations, where learners have rich exposure to the target language outside the classroom, or at university level in other environments. In both of these situations, learners may benefit from teaching programmes with a heavy emphasis on guided communicative activities, and a correspondingly reduced emphasis on the systematic study of language forms. Unconsciously, writers on language teaching theory can easily extend generalizations which are valid for the situations they are most familiar with to others where these principles are less applicable.

The nature of English The applied linguistic research and theorizing which form the basis of current thinking and practice relate overwhelmingly to the teaching and learning of English. Now English, as it happens, is a morphologically light language. Although the grammar presents beginners with some syntactic and semantic problems, a good deal of the structure can be picked up easily from exposure and practice. Beginners in English are, then, not faced with a very heavy formal learning load, and can move quickly towards a working knowledge of the language. It is interesting to speculate what current language-teaching theory would look like if the reference language were, say, Russian. Russian has a formidable array of inflectional grammar, with nouns, verbs, adjectives and pronouns all having a wide range of only partly predictable endings signalling grammatical relations. A beginning or elementary student of Russian has to pay a great deal of attention to these forms if he or she wants a moderate level of grammatical accuracy, they cannot easily be picked up from simple exposure to the limited input available to most students, and there is a powerful case for learning tables of inflections by heart. It is not at all certain that the centrifugal drift from form to activity, or the act of faith whereby forms are taken to be learnable largely by simply using language, would be possible if Russian were the focus of language teaching theory to the extent that English is.

Native speaking teachers and grammar At a more practical level, a bias away from grammar can arise in the common situation where native speakers of English are involved in teacher training or course design. Such teachers are less likely to have studied the details of English grammar during their training than their non-native speaking counterparts, and some may therefore feel sufficiently insecure about their knowledge to favour approaches which avoid explicit grammar study.

The expanding periphery

I do not of course wish to suggest that theorists, researchers and practitioners no longer have any concern at all with the 'linguistic centre'. Applied linguistics journals commonly publish articles reporting research on the teaching of at least some aspects of language form; at the more practical end of the scale, teachers' magazines such as *Modern English Teacher* and *English Teaching Professional* devote considerable space to discussing grammar, vocabulary and pronunciation. None the less, it seems clear that there is a real and substantial swing towards a concern, both theoretical and practical, with matters that are ancillary or peripheral to language teaching itself. These include learner characteristics and perceptions, societal needs, cultural contexts, economic imperatives, autonomy, teacher cognition, self-fulfilment and personal development.

> While confidence in specific methods has declined, interest in individual learner differences, such as motivation, aptitude, family background, has noticeably increased … If what I do in class depends mainly on who I am as a person, then I must develop myself as much as I can if I wish to improve as a teacher.
> (Sowden 2007: 304–308)

At the first annual conference of what is now the International Association of Teachers of English as a Foreign Language (then ATEFL) in 1967, participants discussed the following topics:
- teaching methodology
- the pros and cons of structure drilling and language labs
- ways of improving testing
- how to design teaching programmes for different contexts (especially immigrant education)
- the training of EFL teachers.

At the 40th IATEFL conference in 2006, the titles of talks listed in the programme included references to:

> *anxiety, CALL, classroom research, collaborative learning, consciousness-raising, critical discourse analysis, critical reading, cultural awareness, developing teacher reflection, innovation management, interactivity, intercultural competence, internet, IT, kinaesthetic learners, learner*

differences, learner independence, learner preferences, learner training, learner's self-concept, metaphor, motivation, multiple intelligences, negotiated interaction, new technologies, pragmatics, professional development, reflective practice, scaffolding, strategy training, teacher's role.

Among this proliferation of non-central concerns, there are no doubt matters that do require attention. Language teaching is not just teaching language, as Richards and Renandya remind us in their list (2002: 2) of 'Key issues that shape the design and delivery of [English] language teaching':

- understanding learners and their roles, rights, needs, motivations, strategies, and the processes they employ in second language learning
- understanding the nature of language teaching and learning and the roles teachers, teaching methods and teaching materials play in facilitating successful learning
- understanding how English functions in the lives of learners, the way the English language works, the particular difficulties it poses for second language learners, and how learners can best achieve their goals in learning English
- understanding how schools, classrooms, communities, and the language teaching profession can best support the teaching and learning of English.

However, a balance is needed between ancillary concerns and the central language teaching priorities that they are ancillary to. In the limit, communicative or postmethod philosophy can actually seem to be in danger of losing contact with language teaching altogether and replacing it by other things. Allwright (2003: 114) makes the remarkable statement that according to the principles of 'exploratory practice' we should 'above our concern for instructional efficiency, prioritize the quality of life in the language classroom'. And Ellis, arguing for a full-scale task-based approach to language teaching, says that the blurring of the distinction between syllabus and methodology is an 'attractive feature' of task-based work, and that a central tenet of the approach is arguably the idea that 'no attempt is made to specify what learners will learn, only how they will learn' (2003: 30–31).

There is not very much time for language teaching in most instructional situations, and peripheral matters cannot be allowed to divert scarce resources from the teaching of what is more central. Prioritization is important; so (to invoke a non-academic concept) is common sense. The quality of life in the language classroom is not insignificant, but it is certainly not more important than instructional efficiency. To make a virtue of not specifying at all what learners will learn is a very strange approach to the teaching of language, music, mathematics, history or anything else. What a normal teacher does in class surely depends even more on what he/she is teaching than on his or her state of personal development. Language teaching is not only teaching language, but that is its central business. The complexity underlying this deceptively simple-sounding fact is no excuse for substituting ill-directed activity, excessive concern with peripheral topics, or complacent references to a 'postmethod condition' for hard thinking about what to teach and how it can best be taught: that is to say, for decisions about method.

Language teaching and the need for methods
'I don't know how to say *he had.*'

Macaro (2001: 146) describes a study in which English-speaking secondary school learners of French were being trained in strategy use. At one point in the study one of the children, who was trying to draft a letter to an imaginary French contact, was clearly too overwhelmed by the task to make constructive use of the strategies that might have helped her, failing for instance to attend to part-of-speech information in her dictionary. In any case, strategies did not seem to be her most important gap: at one point in her ordeal she confessed that could not remember how to say in French *he had*. Now it may well be important and cost-effective to teach selected learning and communication strategies, and there is certainly no reason why a researcher should not investigate their use in whatever situation he or she chooses. But if a pupil who has been learning French for over three years does not know the equivalent of *he had*, there is something wrong, and strategy use is peripheral to the problem. Without knowing more about the individual case, it is impossible to know exactly what was the source of the child's difficulty. But a reasonable hypothesis, in the light of Macaro's transcripts and what one knows about the approach to foreign language teaching popular in many British schools, is that the girl's class had done a good deal of work on chunk-learning and 'scripts' (describing one's family, home or pets, recounting one's holidays, discussing one's plans for the future, writing an introductory letter to a penfriend, etc.), but had done relatively little work on fundamental grammar. That is to say, the teaching is likely to have used one and the same kind of activity both for fostering fluent use of what was known, and for building up basic knowledge. Not surprisingly, the method worked better for one than the other.

The main problem with large-scale language teaching approaches ('methods' in the wider sense) is not, it seems to me, that they fail to take into account the complex nature of society, culture, human psychology or interpersonal relations. It is that they do not take into account the complexity of language itself. Discussion of methods can only be really constructive if given a tighter focus, looking at separate aspects of language and asking for each 'how can this best be taught?' Just as one can talk about good and bad ways of putting a hinge on a door, organizing a tennis tournament or training a sheepdog, one can talk about good and bad ways of teaching German technical vocabulary, demonstrating Chinese tones, introducing English question formation to beginners, organizing role play in groups, planning a three-week intensive Spanish course for tourist guides, or indeed teaching the French for *he had*. Language is very many different things, very many different types of activity are involved in learning and teaching it, and considerations of method are relevant to all of these. Teachers, where they are not too influenced by theoretical fashion, are of course generally well aware of this; few teachers seem persuaded that methods are dead (Thornbury 1998; Block 2001; Bell 2007).

The components of language instruction

Any course of language instruction must provide the learner with an appropriate knowledge and skills base. This necessarily means addressing four problems:

- *selection and presentation*: The language elements that learners most need must be identified and made available for learning.
- *establishment of a knowledge base*: The forms and use of these elements must be fixed in learners' long-term memory.
- *development of recall and deployment*: New material, once learnt, must become efficiently retrievable for comprehension or production. Where language use involves not only recall but also computation (for example applying a morphological or syntactic rule, matching a grammatical form to a meaning or situation), learners must acquire the ability to perform the operations required with reasonable accuracy in real time.
- *course architecture*: The syllabus components—the different language elements and skills selected for teaching—need to be fitted together into a coherent smoothly-functioning package: a course. This must link different elements together efficiently and economically, while exploiting the interpersonal dynamics of the instructional situation to the best advantage, and allowing for adaptation and variation in the light of individual differences and local conditions.

In each of these areas, questions of method arise at various scales. How can we best select material for learning, by identifying both the highest-priority forms, and the most important functions, notions and skills for which appropriate forms must be taught? (These are not the same question; they are two different questions with complementary answers: see Swan 1985b: 79.) For each language element that we have identified, what is the most appropriate presentation vehicle, and how can this element best be fixed in long-term memory and made efficiently retrievable and available for fluent use? What principles are relevant to linking items of vocabulary, grammar and pronunciation into packages (lessons) and deciding what kinds of activity will at the same time teach these items and practise more general skills? How can we provide adequate opportunity for realistic communicative practice of the different kinds of thing that have been learnt? Does a given skill need to be taught, or will learners access it naturally in due course by virtue of already being able to deploy it in their mother tongues (Walter 2007)? What can best be learnt through extensive reading or listening, what through intensive input, and what through analysed (form-focused) input? What is most usefully presented or practised in a whole-class format, what is better handled through group work, and what lends itself best to individual study? Do learners have easy access to extensive input, and if not, how do we provide it? What can be learnt outside the instructional situation, and by what routes? What cannot? What can be learnt through discovery and what is more efficiently taught by more directive methods?

For the central formal aspects of language, questions of method may need to be considered virtually on an item-specific basis. Definition, paraphrase, contextualization, illustration, mime and translation are all viable vocabulary-teaching strategies; but they would not all be equally effective for teaching each of the lexical items *thanks, elephant, solution, curly, in principle, mortgage, jump, hang on* and *gearbox*. The same applies to grammar. How you can best teach a point—and indeed whether you need to teach it, or can teach it—depends very much on what you are teaching. Japanese question formation? The position of French object pronouns? Spanish tense use? English noun compounding? Russian noun morphology? In Hulstijn's words (1995): 'Not all grammar rules are equal'.

'Method' is an obstacle to methods

Questions of this kind, then, cannot be answered by reference to the kind of sweeping generalization that often dictates methodological stances, and such generalizations can in fact seriously hamper what we are doing. 'Method' can get in the way of methods. Of course, we need to pay attention to what theory and research have to tell us about learning, language acquisition, social behaviour and so on. But from an ideological point of view, language-teaching methodology is, and must be allowed to be, neutral. If we wish to decide whether language laboratory-type pattern repetition will help Mandarin speakers to master English conditional structures, we cannot settle the question by appealing to current views on behaviourism; we must try it and see what happens. The same goes for such activities as practising French rounded vowels in front of a mirror, committing to memory a table of Polish case-endings, learning a bilingual vocabulary list, translating a foreign text into one's own language and back, filling gaps in sentences or mining a corpus for authentic usage examples. These may or may not be useful things to do, but the issue cannot be decided on the basis of their conformity with current views about, for instance, the importance for learning of interaction and meaningful communication. Such views may well be relevant to some aspects of language teaching and learning; for other aspects, they are not necessarily any more applicable than they are to teaching learner drivers to reverse into parking spaces, training novice skiers to execute snow-plough turns, or showing mathematics students how to solve simultaneous equations. Interaction with other learners in a controlled role-play task may be an excellent way of increasing one's fluent command of a particular range of speech functions, and an extremely inefficient way of mastering the grammar of relative clauses. The same goes for learner-directed work or 'learning to learn': these approaches work for some things and not for others. Sentence-level grammar practice (to take one of the activities instanced above) is condemned by many scholars on the grounds that it isolates structural elements from their use in 'discourse': the larger-scale structuring of language for effective communication (see for example Celce-Murcia 2007). But discourse is not some kind of absolute value to which homage must always be paid. Some grammar is discourse-oriented (for example Italian word order); much of it is not (for example the use of a dative case after the German equivalent of *to help*, or the syntax of English questions). And in general, the fact that grammatical knowledge needs to be integrated into fluent communicative production does not mean that there is no place for less meaning-focused teaching activities. 'What we need is an appropriate balance between exercises that help learners come to grips with grammatical forms, and tasks for exploring the use of those forms to communicate effectively' (Nunan 1998: 109).

This rejection of ideological stances is not just a matter of principle. In many areas it has solid empirical justification. Despite the standard condemnation of 'traditional' approaches in much academic writing about second language acquisition, there is persuasive evidence, as Sheen reminds us (1993, 1994, 2002), for the superiority of 'traditional' against 'communicative' approaches for some aspects of language teaching. Consciously repeating learnt material in practice activities is condemned for instance by Robinson (2001: 291) and Skehan (1998: 123), who calls it 'regurgitating'. But as Tomasello (2003: 66) points out, we have good research evidence for the importance of repetitive and scripted exchanges for mother-tongue vocabulary learning, and it is at least highly plausible (Cook 2000; Swan 2006) that such activities play an equally essential part in L2 learning. Similarly, translation has been shown to aid vocabulary learning (Ramachandran and Rahim 2004; Folse 2004), despite its general rejection as a teaching technique by successive methodological doctrines.

Syllabus content and design: the theory–practice gap

The methodological area where contemporary theorists and practitioners diverge most, it seems to me, is that defined by the first and fourth of the problems listed [on page 172 of this article]: the selection of language elements for teaching, and their integration into courses.

Since languages are vast, and time for learning them is usually very limited, the principled selection of input material is crucial. An hour spent learning low-priority words, structures, pronunciation features or skills is an hour that is not available for other more urgent matters. At different times in the last hundred years or so, language teaching theory has therefore concerned itself with one or other aspect of selection. Word frequency, grammatical structures, pronunciation, situational language, speech functions and their exponents, skills, strategies and discourse structure have all received considerable attention. Unfortunately, focus on one element has often entailed lack of concern for others. My first German textbook (a reprint of a very old course) made a reasonable job of sequencing the structures of the language, but vocabulary selection was subordinated to the exigencies of a plot-line based on German mythology: one of the first nouns I learnt was *der Greif*: 'the gryphon'. Vocabulary selection based on frequency counts came in later, to the considerable benefit of language teaching, as did a rather short-lived concern with the systematic teaching of phonology. Communicative approaches to syllabus design brought language functions into focus at the expense of language forms: Munby's exhaustive work on needs analysis (1978) does not have an index entry for 'grammar'. Systematic vocabulary selection has been given a renewed boost in recent years with the explosion of corpus-based research: Willis (1990: vi) stresses that satisfactory lexical coverage in language teaching can only be ensured with the aid of a frequency-informed lexical syllabus. Currently, however, as ever, there appears to be little concern by theorists in general to survey synoptically the various areas where selection might be relevant. Indeed, much recent academic writing on instructed language acquisition simply has nothing to say about the principles involved in the pedagogical selection of central language elements of any kind. Brown's list of 12 principles on which 'viable current approaches to language teaching are based' (2002: 12–13) says nothing whatever about the selection of material. An interesting exception to the general pattern is Ellis (2006: 87–88), who offers detailed, if incomplete, criteria for the selection of grammar points for teaching, while however making the bizarre claim that course-book writers and the authors of grammar practice materials are unaware of these criteria and 'try to teach the whole of the grammar'.

The present relative lack of concern, at an academic level, for selection criteria is accompanied by a similar failure to address the overall design of teaching programmes. While there has been a good deal of discussion of syllabus types over the last two or three decades, this has rarely extended to the consideration of what I have called course architecture. This is, however, a crucial matter. When language elements have been chosen for presentation and practice, they are not usually presented in an isolated fashion one by one; it is generally considered desirable to integrate them. So, for instance, a course writer might 1) create, edit or reproduce a reading text—let us say a narrative, while 2) ensuring that it contained both high-priority vocabulary and selected structures—for instance past progressives, and/or descriptive and defining noun phrase structures, and at the same time 3) building in work on a pronunciation point—the weak pronunciation of *was/were* would fit in well here. Learners would study the text, work on the elements presented in it by means of various types of controlled and free practice activity, and perhaps finish the input–output cycle by using the new language to write a similar kind of narrative themselves. A typical mainstream language course for use in class is built up, as everyone knows, of successive units of this kind together with testing and revision material, commonly packaged into a student's book, teacher's book, workbook and set of recordings. Producing such material—interweaving different syllabus components into the complex architecture of a language course—is a highly skilled activity to which a number of theoretical issues are relevant. In other words, there must be such a thing as a theory of language course construction. It is, however, hard to locate such a theory: discussion in this area is not common in the applied linguistics literature. While there are certainly exceptions (e.g. Tomlinson 2003, Cook 2008, Johnson 2008), it does seem as if the design principles of language courses are not a matter for widespread academic attention. A typical paper on the role of materials in the language classroom (Crawford 2002), for instance, makes no mention at all of the textbook as a selection and presentation vehicle.

There are millions of language learners in the world. Most of these learners follow syllabuses that are instantiated in courses. The courses are created by experienced professionals who typically spend years at the job, and who build on a developing tradition established by their predecessors over centuries. And yet it seems as if these thousands of creative practitioners, perhaps because they do not often contribute to learned journals, are effectively invisible in the academic world—although names such as Alexander, O'Neill, Abbs, Freebairn or Soars have probably become known to more people worldwide, with good reason, than those of almost any contemporary novelist. There is an excellent collection of important papers on cognition and second language instruction (Robinson (ed) 2001) in which many of the authors, in the nature of things, touch on language syllabus design. The bibliography at the end of the book contains 1025 references; writers cited include two evolutionary biologists and two philosophers of science. Six of the 1025 references are to work by language-teaching practitioners; none of the six is a course designer. It is true that the papers are at a theoretical level some distance removed from the classroom. But it would be odd to find a collection of essays on, say, the neurophysiological basis for learning and playing the piano, which a) recommended new approaches, and b) did not mention a single practising pianist. Are the principles underlying the work of practising course designers really not worth the attention of those scholars who specialize in the theory of instructed language acquisition?

Home-made materials

The perennial lack of concern for the work of course designers is reinforced by a widespread contemporary belief that language courses can be produced on a 'do it yourself' basis. Allwright (1981) criticizes published materials for making decisions that, in his view, could be made by the teacher and/or students; the idea that syllabuses should be negotiated between teachers and learners is a commonplace of communicative and postmethod thinking; it is clear from internet discussion forums such as the TESL-L list that many teachers feel that they can provide better courses for their students than are available between the covers of published textbooks.

It is certainly true that, where students have limited and closely defined needs (for example for fluency practice or special-purpose vocabulary), hard-working and gifted teachers may be able to provide materials or activities which are better attuned to their students than any externally produced course can hope to be. However, in the more typical situation where students need a general course which will teach them all the highest-priority elements of a new language, matters are very different. To put together a cost-effective full-scale language course with adequate coverage, a materials writer needs a great deal of specialist linguistic and pedagogic knowledge, together with access to reliable inventories, graded by frequency and usefulness, of vocabulary items, structures, functions and notions (and their exponents), situational language, discourse features, and any number of other things. The work of selecting language elements for teaching and incorporating them into appropriate presentation material, described above, is enormously time-consuming, and can take up to two years' full-time work for one level of a course. The notion that a teacher, or a teacher and students acting in concert, can somehow substitute for this in their spare time, is quite unrealistic. Course production is a specialist activity drawing on quite different skills from those that are required for teaching. To expect the average working teacher, however gifted, to write a viable general language course is like expecting the first violinist to compose the whole of the orchestra's repertoire in his or her evenings off.

The future

How can we expect language-teaching methodology to develop in the future? Obviously all that we can sensibly say is that we don't know. Two things, however, seem to me to be reasonably certain. One is that we will make progress. Just as we have made very considerable improvements over the last half century, we can expect to make further advances as we benefit from technological innovations, and as we find out more about language and how it is learnt. Textbook-based classroom learning is likely to be at least partly superseded by far more flexible and varied approaches to the delivery and practice of the elements of a foreign language, to our considerable benefit. What also seems certain, however, is that progress, though real, will never be spectacular. Foreign languages are very hard for most people to learn well after childhood, and they will continue to be hard. There are no miracle methods waiting to be discovered.

Progress is likely to be faster if we are able to remove some of the obstacles that we have allowed to stand in our way. Repeatedly disillusioned by our failure to bring students close to a native-speaker level of accuracy, we have been all too ready to throw out the methods we have been using, like a bewildered dictatorship executing its minister of agriculture because of the collapse of yet another unworkable five-year plan. In replacing old methods by new ones, we have often allowed new and promising-looking macrostrategical stances to dictate our acceptance or rejection of micromethods, whose value should in fact be judged solely by their efficacy. And in recent years we have allowed our interest in learner-centred, naturalistic, activity-based learning to fill much of the horizon, so that teaching language has all too easily been replaced by doing things with it.

I believe that quite substantial progress in most language teaching environments would be possible immediately, simply by making more intelligent use of all the resources we have at our disposal. It seems to me that our knowledge of both formal and functional aspects of language, our growing understanding of acquisitional processes, and the vast range of methodology and materials that we have developed over the last century or so, provide all the necessary ingredients for a balanced and effective model of instructed second-language learning. What we need, perhaps, is therefore not so much to find new methods, as to take stock of the existing ones and integrate them into more ideologically neutral and comprehensive approaches.

Conclusion: a plea for common sense

Common sense is an unreliable faculty with no scientific standing. There are, however, times when it can usefully be appealed to. In the face of some of the more extravagant methodological views which are currently in the air, we need perhaps to bring our feet back into contact with the ground. I have always felt that language teaching theorists would do well to consider how they would respond themselves to the kind of methodology that they recommend. Speaking purely for myself, if I imagine (to take one common type of language-learning context among many) that I have just enrolled in a London school for a beginners' course in, say, Hungarian:

- I do not wish to negotiate with the teacher in order to decide what aspects of a language about which I know little it is or is not useful for me to learn. If I hire a guide to take me up Mont Blanc, I do not expect him or her to consult me about the route.
- I do not want to be taught reading skills. I have reading skills. What I want is some Hungarian to deploy them on.
- I do not want to work out Hungarian grammar for myself. Trying to establish the regularities underlying examples of usage is difficult and time-consuming, with no guarantee of success, even in one's first language. I know: this is one of the things I do for a living.
- Nor do I want to learn Hungarian grammar by 'negotiating meaning' with other beginners.
- I am not receptive to the idea that I can pick up complexities such as the Hungarian definite and indefinite tense inflection system by incidental focus on form during communicative activity. My previous language learning experience suggests that this is unlikely.
- I do not want to be deprived of information about the grammar until I reach intermediate level, as advised for example by Ellis (2002: 32).

- I do not want to learn by working on texts and activities that the teacher has devised in his/her spare time. These might well reflect my interests and those of the other students to perfection, but the chance of their also providing well-planned coverage of high-priority Hungarian forms and their functions is remote.
- I do not want concern with my 'identity'. If the teacher remembers my name, keeps track of my progress and has some sense of my strengths and weaknesses as a learner and a linguist, that will do very well.
- If I want self-fulfilment, I will not go to a language classroom; I can think of much better places. Nor do I want my personality developed. For better or worse, my personality is probably about as developed as it is going to be. In any case, if I thought improvement was possible, I would go to a specialist in these matters, not to a language teacher. I don't ask a hairdresser to fix my central heating.

In short, I do not wish to be told that I should be happy to substitute process for product. Product is exactly what I want: a working knowledge of Hungarian, delivered in a focused and cost-effective way by the methods most appropriate to provide it.

Note

1 I feel impelled to point out, if only in a spirit of mischief, that the two strands of this ideological stance run in opposite directions. If instructed language learning is to be a socially egalitarian, learner-directed matter, liberated from the authority of the traditional directive teacher figure, then it cannot also proceed according to the principles of 'natural' first language acquisition, since first language learners (babies) are in a situation that is anything but egalitarian and authority-free. You can have one or the other; not both.

17

Using texts constructively

(Originally published in two parts on the British Council's *Teaching English* Website, January 2011.)

This article repeated an analysis of the structure of language learning which was offered in an earlier article (Article 12: 'Two out of three ain't enough: the essential ingredients of a language course'), and discussed the relevance of this analysis to the effective use of texts.

1 What are texts for?

Text use may seem a dull topic in comparison with all the exciting matters that [other guest writers have dealt with recently]. However, language learning is, after all, learning language, not just doing fun things with it. And texts—by which I mean the relatively short spoken and written passages that come in textbooks and other teaching materials—can, if they are used properly, play an important part in the learning process.

Three kinds of input

Let's start by looking at the overall structure of language learning. It is useful to identify three kinds of useful input: *extensive*, *intensive* and *analysed*. Children learning their mother tongues receive massive **extensive input** from the cloud of language that surrounds them, some of it roughly attuned to their level of development, much of it not. They also receive substantial **intensive input**—small samples of language such as nursery rhymes, stories, songs, the daily mealtime and bedtime scripts, and so on, which are repeated, assimilated, memorised, probably unconsciously analysed, and/or used as templates for future production. And children receive **analysed input**: explicit information about language. Although they are not generally told very much about grammar and pronunciation, they constantly demand explanations of vocabulary: 'What's a …?'; 'What's that?'; 'What does … mean?'

Second-language learners are no different in principle from small children in these respects. They, too, need **extensive input**—exposure to quantities of spoken and written language, authentic or not too tidied up, for their unconscious acquisition processes to work on. (For evidence for the effectiveness of extensive reading, see for example Day and Bamford 1998, or Alan Maley's survey of the research in his December 2009 guest article.) Equally, learners need **intensive** engagement with small samples of language which they can internalise, process, make their own and use as bases for their own production (Cook 2000). And since most instructed second-language learners have only a fraction of the input that is available to child first-language learners, the deliberate teaching of grammatical as well as lexical regularities—**analysed input**—helps to compensate for the inadequacy of naturalistic exposure for at least some aspects of language.

Three kinds of output

Input is only half the story. People generally seem to learn best what they use most. Children produce quantities of extensive output, chattering away as they activate what they have taken in. They also recycle the intensive input they have received, repeating their stories, nursery rhymes and so on, and speaking their lines in the recurrent daily scripts of childhood life. And some children, at least, seem to produce certain kinds of analysed output, naming things or rehearsing and trying out variations on structures that they have been exposed to, like more formal language learners doing 'pattern practice' (Weir 1970).

Adults, too, need opportunities to produce all three kinds of output. They must have the chance to engage in extensive, 'free' speech and writing; they must be able to systematically recycle the intensive input that they have more or less internalised (and thus complete the process of internalisation); and they need to practise the analysed patterns and language items that have been presented to them, so that they have some chance of carrying them over into spontaneous fluent production.

A properly-balanced language-teaching programme, then, will have these three ingredients—extensive, intensive and analysed—at both input and output stages. While all the ingredients are important, the proportions in a given teaching programme will naturally vary according to the learners' needs, their level, and the availability of each element both in and out of class.

What can texts do?

So where do textbook texts—relatively short continuous pieces of spoken or written language—come into all this? Clearly they can contribute in various ways to the three-part process outlined above. They can provide material for practice in receptive skills, and thus facilitate access to extensive input. They can act as springboards for discussion, role play, or other kinds of extensive output work. They can support analysed input by contextualising new language items. A further role—and a very important one—is to provide the intensive input that all learners need: short samples of appropriately selected language which are carefully attended to and partly internalised, and which can then serve as a basis for controlled production.

What do texts usually do?

Unfortunately, this aspect of text use is often neglected or ineffectively put into practice. A language-teaching text may simply be seen as something to be 'gone through' in one way or another, without any clear definition of the outcomes envisaged. (Text-work is an awfully convenient way of filling up a language lesson, and teachers often feel that any text-based activity is bound to be beneficial. This is not necessarily the case.) One approach to 'going through' is the traditional pseudo-intensive lesson where the teacher uses a text as the basis for a kind of free-association fireworks display. He or she comments on one word, expression or structure after another, elicits synonyms and antonyms, pursues ideas sparked off by the text, perhaps gets the students to read aloud or translate bits, and so on and so on. Meanwhile the students write down hundreds of pieces of information in those overfilled notebooks that someone once memorably called 'word cemeteries'. When the end of the 'lesson' is approaching, students may answer some so-called 'comprehension questions'. (As Mario Rinvolucri asked in his November 2008 guest article, what exactly are these for? If you have spent an hour working on a text with your class and still need to find out whether they understand it, perhaps there's something wrong.) Students then go away to write a homework on a topic distantly related (or even not at all related) to that of the text. This kind of activity tends to fall between two stools: the text is too short to contribute much to learners' extensive experience of language, but the work done on it is not really intensive either. At the end of the cycle the students have been given much too much input, have engaged with it too superficially to assimilate much of it, and have used (and therefore consolidated) little or none of it. They have been taught—inefficiently—one lot of language, and then asked to produce a substantially different lot.

Another approach which has been fashionable in recent decades is to use a written text to teach 'reading skills'. The text is typically accompanied by a battery of exercises which require students to predict, skim, scan, identify main ideas, match topics to paragraphs, sort out shuffled texts, and so on. There is an implicit assumption that even perfectly competent mother-tongue readers actually need to learn to process text all over again in a new language. For a critique of this view, see Walter and Swan 2008. Here again, students may spend substantial time working through a text without any very identifiable payoff in terms of increased language knowledge or genuine skills development.

While texts can undoubtedly be valuable in various ways, I believe they are best used with a clear purpose in mind, and a reasonable certainty that they will help to achieve this purpose. In [Section 2] I will focus on the intensive input–output cycle referred to above, which I believe is centrally important, and I will consider ways in which texts can be exploited efficiently to support this aspect of language learning.

2 Intensive input–output work

The need for intensive input–output work

I [argued in Section 1] that *intensive* input–output work is crucial for cost-effective language teaching and learning. This is particularly the case in learning situations where extensive input, and opportunities for extensive output, are limited. In these situations, intensive language activity has to carry more of the instructional burden. (If learners encounter fewer examples of high-priority words and structures, each example needs to make more of an impact.) Well-planned text-use can contribute importantly to this aspect of language learning. Ideally:

1. Students engage in depth with a short sample of spoken or written language. They work hard enough on this text to make some of the language their own: words, expressions and structures stick in their minds; perhaps whole stretches of the text are even memorised (as when a dialogue is learnt by heart).
2. Then their acquisition of the new input is consolidated by controlled but creative output work related to the text—by using what they have learnt to express their own ideas, they fix it in their memories and make it available for future use.

Possible approaches

The key here is to create effective links between input and output, so that new language is recycled and consolidated. It is not really very difficult to bring this about: there are all sorts of possible approaches. Here is one way of using a text intensively with a lower-level class.

- Take a story or other text of perhaps 200 words, not too difficult, which contains some useful language.
- Tell it or read it to the class, explaining anything that seriously hinders comprehension.
- Get the class to tell you anything that they can remember of the text.
- Repeat it and see how much more they can recall.
- Hand out the text/get them to open their books.
- Go through the text explaining and answering questions where necessary, but concentrating mainly on a relatively small number (perhaps 8–12) of useful words, formulaic expressions, collocations or structural points which the students don't yet have an active command of.
- Tell them to note and learn these points.
- Ask them to choose for themselves a few other words or expressions to learn.

- Get them to close their books or put away the text, and ask recall questions (NOT 'comprehension questions'), designed specifically to get them to say or write the words and expressions picked out for learning.

Finally, set a written exercise in which they are expected to use most of the new material, but in their own way (this is crucial). For instance, ask them to tell the story they have studied in the form of a letter written by one of the characters in it; or to write about a similar incident from their own experience.

There are enormous numbers of other ways of achieving this level of close engagement with input material, followed by creative output using what has been learnt. Texts can be 'fed in' through dictation, storyboard-type activities, or by various other routes. Students can work on a dialogue, and then script and perform (or improvise) new dialogues on a similar theme. One class I heard about hijacked the whole of their boring textbook, rewriting the stories and dialogues with added elements (a pregnancy, an explosion, an arrest, a lottery win, alien invaders, …) so as to make them more interesting, and thus using what they had learnt in highly original and motivating ways. What is essential is that close engagement with texts should allow students, little by little, to build up a repertoire of key lexis and structures that they have made their own by working on them intensively and reusing them in this way. Compared with the typical 'superficial text study–comprehension questions–free writing' cycle, the crucial difference is that learners do more with less, so that they really do learn, remember and are able to use what they take in, instead of forgetting most of it before the lesson is over.

Overcoming problems

In operating an effective input–output cycle, some obstacles may need to be overcome. One may be cultural. In countries where the educational tradition favours authoritarian teacher-fronted presentation and a traditional transmission model of education, there is likely to be a strong emphasis on input and a correspondingly reduced emphasis on learner output. And if public self-expression is discouraged, as it is in some cultures, students may need encouragement (and an explanation of the rationale of the approach), before they are ready to recycle input material creatively in personalised communicative activities, particularly in oral work.

A second obstacle is theoretical fashion. A good deal of contemporary applied linguistic theory is fairly hostile to the kind of intensive input–output work discussed above. There is a widespread preference for learner-centred work, with extensive spontaneous communicative output being highly valued. Intensive output, deliberately reusing what has been taught, is often condemned as being unoriginal, not properly communicative, mere 'regurgitation' of other people's language. This is all very well if one is working with students who have already learnt a great deal of language, and whose main need is to activate it through task-based fluency practice. But most language students need to learn more language, not simply to get better at using what they know. And for such students, teacher-controlled input–output work has a key role alongside other types of activity. You cannot teach by eliciting what is not there, and the best way of making sure that new language is acquired for later extensive use is, very precisely, to give learners other people's language (as we have to—they can't make the language up for themselves) and to enable them to make it their own as they use it for personal and creative purposes. In helping to achieve this, properly-focused text use can play an important part.

18
Grammar

(Originally published in J. Simpson (ed.): *The Routledge Handbook of Applied Linguistics*. London: Routledge, 2011.)

The main purpose of this article was to examine the role of grammatical investigation in applied linguistics as a whole—not simply in language teaching. Consequently, it has a more objective slant than the other papers in this collection, though opinions do surface in the sections on language education.

Introduction

This article deals with grammar in the narrower sense; that is to say, it refers not to all linguistic systems, but specifically to syntax and morphology. Narrow or not, this is a vast subject, relevant to very many topics which come under the heading of 'applied linguistics'. I have shaped what follows partly in order to avoid excessive overlap with other chapters in this volume[1] and have therefore said relatively little about some matters which are dealt with in detail elsewhere. I begin by discussing briefly what grammar is, why languages need it and how they use it. This is followed by a word on the remarkable proliferation of grammatical models in present-day linguistic theory, and a note on the relationship, such as it is, between these models and applications of linguistics. I then look briefly at applied linguistics at its most ambitious: the period when it was believed that investigating the nature of language would inform us about the world; and at later offshoots of this line of thought. A short note on the language–mind–brain relationship is followed by two more extensive sections, on grammar in mother tongue education and foreign language teaching respectively.

What is grammar?

Not all meanings can be conveyed by simply stringing words together in an unstructured way. For one thing, unsupported vocabulary cannot specify the direction of causal and other relationships. Putting together the words *man*, *dog* and *bite*, or *floorboards*, *water* and *under*, for instance, leaves important questions unanswered. A second limitation is to do with modality: no string of words on its own can indicate whether it is intended as a statement, a question, an expression of uncertainty, a negation or some other type of communication. And finally, words are mostly labels for classes of things, qualities, processes and so on, whereas we most often talk about particular members of these classes. So, in order to construct references to particulars, we need to group words: while the words *my*, *old* and *dog*, for example, taken separately, can each refer to millions of entities, the phrase *my old dog* pins down one specific individual. In more complex communications, grouping may not be transparent, so that we need ways of showing what goes with what.

Languages solve these problems essentially by the devices that we call 'syntax' and 'morphology', supplementing purely lexical information by establishing ordering and movement conventions, changing the forms of words, and using function words (like English *may* or *not*). These devices—grammar—make it possible to distinguish for example *dog bites man* from *man bites dog* or (the Latin equivalents) *canis hominem mordet* from *canem homo mordet*. They permit the expression of modality, distinguishing for instance *floorboards are under water* from *are floorboards under water*, *floorboards may be under water* and *floorboards are not under water*. And they facilitate grouping, showing where necessary which words go together (*small man bites big dog* as against *big man bites small dog*).

Simple in principle, grammar generates considerable complexity in practice. Given a way of grouping words, you can group groups of words, and group groups of groups of words, and so on upwards. Grammatical mechanisms also give rise to, and operate differentially on, distinct word classes. And ordering and movement conventions can be applied in complicated ways to whole assemblies of language. In addition, once grammar is in place it turns out to be useful for many purposes beyond those identified above. The world's languages put time relations, number distinctions, evidentiality, social relationships and any number of other meanings into their grammars—notions that can be handled by vocabulary, but for which grammar seems to be a convenient vehicle. All of this is somewhat analogous to the elaboration that characterizes computer programmes, so simple in their basic mechanism—sequences of 0 and 1—and so complex and multi-functional in their applications.

The conventional syntax–morphology distinction—like that between grammar and lexis—is not always clear-cut, and varies somewhat in scope from one language to another. Also, languages seem to balance off their use of the different devices to a certain extent, with some relying largely on morphology while others put a heavier load on syntax. There is an old belief that all languages are pretty well equally complex, with simplicity in one area being counterbalanced by complexity in another. There is, however, no good evidence for this, and it may be that some languages just are simpler than others. Certainly there are languages in which morphology, in particular, reaches baroque levels of complication—gender-marking in the West African language Fula (McWhorter 2001: 188–9) is a striking example. However that may be, some aspects of complexity seem to be limited in all languages in the interests of processing efficiency, so as to facilitate production and comprehension (Hawkins 2004).

Models of grammar: a bewildering variety

Grammarians attempt to establish categories of linguistic elements and operations which can capture accurately and economically the nature of particular languages. They may also wish to go further, setting up theoretical models at a level of abstraction which will accommodate the multifarious structural features of all possible human languages, and thus illuminate the nature of language in general. In addition, some linguists are concerned to show how the structure of language enables children to perform the astonishing feat of learning their mother tongues. Because the grammatical systems of languages are so complex, and differ so greatly, there is room for substantial disagreement about what kind of generalized model can best account for the facts. It is in fact remarkable how much controversy there is about the analysis of a phenomenon, language, for which we have so much data—at least as much as many physical scientists have for the subjects of their investigations. A glance at the index of a linguistics encyclopaedia will direct the reader to a daunting range of different 'grammars': transformational, phrase structure, dependency, word, functional, systemic, construction, cognitive and dozens of others. (For accounts of some of these, see the chapters on generative linguistics, systemic–functional linguistics and cognitive linguistics in this volume.)

These differences partly reflect researchers' choice of focus. Linguistic structures can be investigated primarily in terms of their internal characteristics, or on the basis of the functions they perform. This formal–functional divide can also bring with it important differences of opinion. Formally-oriented grammarians tend to account for shared features of languages—universals—in the belief that these reflect features of the language faculty in the human mind. Proponents of this view may postulate innate knowledge of what defines the range of possible grammars—so-called 'Universal Grammar' (UG)—on the grounds that we allegedly know things about our language for which the input provides inadequate evidence (the 'poverty of the stimulus' argument). A commonly used example concerns 'island constraints'. In an English complex sentence, a word like *who* or *what* can be used in a main clause to question an element in a dependent clause in some structures, but not others. For example:

You said that this nut goes on the wing mirror.
→ *What did you say that this nut goes on?*

John thinks this nut goes on the wing mirror.
→ *What does John think this nut goes on?*

You asked Paul whether this nut goes on the wing mirror.

→ *What did you ask Paul whether this nut goes on?

It is not a straightforward matter to establish a reliable innate rule which will account for the complex range of such constraints, generating correct structures like the first two examples above and disallowing incorrect structures, and which will work for the equivalent constraints in all languages (since UG, if it exists, is necessarily language-independent). Models which assume innate knowledge of grammar therefore tend to operate at a very high and, in the view of some critics, implausible level of abstraction and complexity. The difficulty of the enterprise is strikingly demonstrated by the remarkable changes of course of one prominent approach—Chomskyan generative grammar—over the last half century, with one key idea after another (e.g. transformations, government and binding, principles and parameters) being modified out of recognition or finally abandoned.

Functionally-oriented grammarians, in contrast, regard language universals primarily as reflecting the structural features that languages need to have in order to do what they do. Language acquisition and use, for many grammarians of this persuasion, can be accounted for on the basis of general principles of cognition rather than any wired-in knowledge unique to language. 'Usage-based associative learning' models attribute to the child learner a powerful unconscious capacity to detect regularities in the input, and to abstract patterns at increasing levels of generality (N. Ellis 2003 and this volume). Knowledge of constraints like those illustrated above, in this view, is perhaps explicable simply on the grounds that sentences like the incorrect ones have never occurred in the input, and have therefore never been registered as possible by the child's inbuilt monitor. While most grammatical models have little to say about how the proposed structures and operations might be instantiated in the brain, associative learning or 'connectionist' models incorporate hypotheses, in principle testable, concerning the possible functioning of neural networks.

Grammar and the world: models and applications

For a model of language to support investigation of a real-world problem, two things are necessary. The model must give reliable linguistic information, and it must do so in terms which can be applied effectively to the problem in question, as Crystal makes clear in relation to a case in clinical linguistics.

> In the field of grammar, it is easy to spot such morphological errors as *mouses* or *tooked*; far less easy to work out what is going on when there are problems with sentence structure. One six-year-old boy was able to say such sentences as *That car is red* and *My car is in the garage*, but could not be persuaded to say *That's a red car* or *My red car*. Asked "*Is that a red car or a yellow car?*" he would become non-fluent and produce such strings as *A car—a red*, losing control of the clause structure as a whole. The problem turned out to be a difficulty in simultaneously using

a developed noun phrase within a clause: as long as the noun phrase consisted solely of a determiner + noun, there was no problem. But asked to insert an adjective (or any other extra element), and the whole sentence structure broke down. To appreciate the nature of this difficulty requires the analyst not only to make an appropriate syntactic analysis but also to appreciate the implications of a syntactic hierarchy for mental processing. Both syntactic and psycholinguistic perspectives are essential.
(Crystal 2001: 675)

It is clear from Crystal's example that, while a reasonably fine-grained analysis is valuable for the clinical linguist, it needs to stay relatively close to the surface of the language. A more abstract analysis—perhaps of greater value to a generative grammarian—might be more difficult to apply and less directly illuminating. (For further discussion in the area of clinical linguistics, see Perkins and Howard, in this volume.) This is likely to be the case for many other applications of grammatical models to real-world problems, such as forensic linguistics (Rock, this volume), stylistics (Semino, this volume) or language teaching (see discussion below). Computational linguistics, in contrast, is an area where more complex models may be indispensable. Attempts to create analogues to the human language faculty, for such purposes as machine translation or machine reading, depend crucially on parsing algorithms, which can perhaps only operate successfully on the basis of relatively sophisticated grammatical analyses.

Grammar as a window on the world

Languages are used to convey messages about the world, so it seems reasonable to suppose that their structure must in one way or another reflect that of the world, at least as this is perceived by human beings. Given that we analyse our experience in terms of situations and events, and that we identify participants in these, it is not surprising that language structure distinguishes ways of referring to situations and events (prototypically verbs), from ways of identifying participants (prototypically nouns). Cognitive grammarians, indeed, (e.g. Langacker 2008) see language structure as reflecting in quite detailed respects, albeit at an abstracted and metaphorical level, our conceptual and perceptual engagement with the physical world.

For classical western philosophers like Aristotle and Plato, the relationship between language and the world was such that linguistic structure could in fact be taken as a key to the organization of reality: the categories into which Aristotle analysed the physical world coincided with the grammatical categories of the Greek language (Allan 2007: 44). Grammar was, so to speak, a window on the world. The structure of language and the structure of logic were also seen as being closely linked, so that a proper understanding of Greek and Latin grammar was taken to provide a basis for sound argument (Allan op. cit.: Ch. 3, 4). These ideas continued through later history. The 'speculative' grammarians of the late Middle Ages saw grammatical structure as mirroring the structure of God's creation—Latin *speculum* means 'mirror'—(Allan op. cit.: 155–7), while the rationalist philosophers of the 17th and 18th centuries saw grammar as reflecting the structure of the human mind, as do present-day generative grammarians. Leibniz believed that a tidied-up language, in which meanings could be expressed without ambiguity, would allow for precise and conclusive logical argument, a view echoed 300 years later by Bertrand Russell (2004: 540; 1919: 172).

A variant of the belief that language is a window on the world is found in the notion of linguistic relativity. In this view, any language gives us information not about an objective outside world, but about the subjective reality perceived by its speakers—indeed, it shapes that reality through the kinds of meaning encoded in its grammar. Indo-European languages, to take one example, typically use the verbal system to express certain kinds of time relation, whereas native American or Australian languages may not conceptualize time in the grammar at all. On the other hand, the choice of verb forms in some languages (e.g. Bulgarian, Turkish, some native American languages) may indicate evidentiality, showing, for instance, whether a speaker was an eyewitness to what he/she is reporting. The view that differences of this kind may entail different perspectives on external reality goes back to philosophers such as von Humboldt in the early 19th century, and was pursued energetically by American anthropological linguists, notably Sapir and Whorf (see for example Sapir 1921), 100 years later. For some recent discussions in this field, see Gentner and Goldin-Meadow (2003).

Grammar, the mind and the brain

Many grammarians claim that the characteristics of language structure must tell us something about the mental organ responsible for it. While there is considerable controversy in this area, it certainly seems highly possible that the organization of language can provide clues to the structure and operation of the mind and brain. A much-debated question concerns modularity: does the human mind have a special module, or modules, for handling language, distinct from the faculties involved in other aspects of cognition? There is evidence that language learning, storage and use are at least partly independent of other cognitive functions. For example, there seems to be a 'critical period' related specifically to language acquisition: after a certain age, most people do not achieve native-like command of all aspects of a new language. And in some recorded cases where young children have been deprived of linguistic input and only starting learning their mother tongue when older, their output has remained defective and ungrammatical. Confirmatory evidence for modularity comes from brain-damaged patients. Strokes or accidents sometimes cause people to lose some or all of their ability to use language, while leaving their other mental faculties apparently unimpaired. Conversely, it is possible for people with severe mental handicap to exhibit normal or even exceptional linguistic competence.

Knowledge of how language works can feed into investigations of the mind and brain, while information can also flow in the other direction, with the results of brain research confirming or extending our understanding of linguistic structure (Perkins and Howard, this volume). Studies of brain-damaged patients have long since demonstrated associations between specific parts of the brain and particular aspects of language behaviour, with lesions in one or other area being found to correlate with problems of comprehension, fluent production, control of syntactic and lexical categories, or handling of meaning. Our knowledge of such associations has been greatly extended and refined by modern functional neuro-imaging techniques, which make it possible to monitor changes in blood flow and electrical activity during language use, and thus to link patterns of excitation in specific areas with different categories of linguistic activity. However, the data that is being collected is complex and difficult to analyse, and while knowledge is growing very rapidly, much more work will be necessary before a clear picture emerges. For the moment, we still understand little about the physical correlates of our mental and linguistic representations of the world. (For detailed discussion, see Ahlsén, this volume.)

Grammar in society; standardization and education

For most people, perhaps, linguistics and everyday life intersect primarily in the area of education. Most societies have one language that is the principal vehicle of cultural transmission. This may be a high-status classical or foreign language (like Sumerian in ancient Mesopotamia, Latin in the European Middle Ages, Classical Arabic in the Islamic world, or the former colonial languages in some African countries); it may be one of several languages that are spoken in a country (like English in the United States); or it may be the single language of a mainly monolingual culture (like Icelandic or Hungarian). Whatever the situation, the study of that language necessarily features centrally in school curricula. Education and language study can indeed sometimes become almost synonymous. A large part of the mediaeval European educational syllabus, the 'trivium', was made up of grammar (correct language use), dialectic (language for valid argument) and rhetoric (language for effective public communication). Although the link between language, logic and the world later became less generally accepted, classical languages enjoyed continuing prestige in European education up to comparatively recently. Indeed, the study of their grammar is still often seen as having a special if ill-defined value as a training for the mind, and they may continue to feature in some educational curricula out of inertia long after outliving their original purpose, as Latin does in some British schools.

Even where a single local language is spoken and carries the culture of the community, different regional or social groups are likely to speak different varieties, and these differences may cause communication problems. This creates a need for language standardization, which is typically met by the emergence or designation of one variety as the national standard; this variety then becomes the main vehicle of administration, legislation, business, education and publishing. The favoured variety may simply be the dialect spoken by that section of the population which, through historical accident, has come to be socially and politically dominant, as in Britain and many other countries. Or it may be a deliberate creation, codified out of a need to facilitate communication in a country where no single standard has arisen, as happened for instance in Norway after it gained independence from Denmark (Foley 1997: 405). (See also Wee, this volume.)

The prestige and utility of a standard variety generates social and institutional pressure to master its conventions. Non-standard speakers must learn a new dialect in order to achieve literacy and operate effectively in society. Educational systems may use language as a social filter, putting such a premium on linguistic correctness that higher education and many career paths are effectively closed to those who fail to master the prestige variety, whatever their strengths in other areas. Grammar often has a starring role in this connection. Grammatical correctness, after all, has a powerful symbolic value: getting your language right implies that you can obey rules and respect authority. All of this can mean that a substantial part of an educational curriculum may be given up to study of the standard language. Even those who already speak this variety can have to work hard to master the written code: this is in a sense a foreign language for everyone, and may not be at all easy to learn. In French, to take a somewhat bizarre instance, the spelling of the written language preserves a number of grammatical distinctions which have long since disappeared from speech because of changes in pronunciation; so that French-speaking schoolchildren actually have to develop an explicit knowledge of older French grammar in order to be able to spell correctly. Without this knowledge, they cannot know whether to write, for instance, [aʃte] as *acheter, acheté, achetés, achetée, achetées, achetai, achetais, achetait* or *achetaient*—various forms of the verb for 'to buy' which are pronounced identically by most younger speakers of standard European French.

Unfortunately, elevating one variety of a language to standard status easily entails the devaluation of others, which may be stigmatized as 'incorrect' forms of speech, used by ignorant or uneducated people who have 'not learnt correct grammar', or who 'cannot be troubled to get things right'. This attitude is common in Britain, although all dialects of English have their own history, going back to the distinct forms of speech of the various early mediaeval Germanic and Scandinavian invaders, and although all well-preserved dialects have their own rich and systematic grammars, however much these may diverge from that of their standard counterpart. Interestingly, this is generally easier to accept for 'remote' dialects. Someone from Oxfordshire who says 'I wants them papers what I give you yesterday' may well be criticized for 'failing' to produce standard grammar. In contrast, a Scot who says 'He'll can tell us the morn' ('He'll be able to tell us tomorrow') is more easily seen as speaking an independent variety with its own rule system. In fact, though, the Oxfordshire speaker, just like the Scot, is using forms which are historically rooted and regular and correct in his or her dialect, however much they may upset the standard speaker next door.

Standard languages often acquire a body of prescriptive rules which are devised by individuals in the belief that their languages need regulating, tidying up or protecting against change, and which are frequently codified in 'usage guides'. Where one form is prescribed at the expense of another, the favoured alternative is often the more formal, written variant, or the older form: people in literate societies tend to give more prestige to the written language than to speech, and to regard language change as evidence of falling standards (Aitchison 2001). Many English prescriptive rules were laid down by eighteenth- and nineteenth-century grammarians, often because they believed that English grammar should imitate Latin, a language with higher prestige. Typical examples are the old condemnation of 'split infinitives' like *to boldly go* (a Latin infinitive is a single word, so cannot be split), or the lingering superstition that a preposition is a bad word to end a sentence with (Latin clauses do not end in prepositions, and anyway, it was felt, a *pre*position should logically precede). Logic is often invoked to condemn sentences like *It's me* or *John and me saw a good film* (both typical of informal standard British English): a nominative (subject) form is said to be 'logically' required in both cases. However, the choice between *I* and *me* depends in complex ways on syntactic environment and level of formality, and is not determined by a simple rule of the kind that works for pronouns in, say, Latin, Russian or German. Grammatical case systems actually vary considerably across languages, and many languages organize themselves in ways that cut right across typical European subject-object categories. To condemn *John and me saw* on the 'logical' grounds that 'subjects are nominative' is rather like insisting that penguins should get up in the air because 'birds fly'.

As Pinker points out (1994: 374), many prescriptive rules are so psychologically unnatural that only those with access to the right kind of education can learn to observe them. Once acquired they can serve as shibboleths, differentiating the elite from the rest ('I'm better than you because I get my pronouns right.'). To admit that these rules are mistaken or unimportant would mean abandoning such easy claims to superiority, as well as accepting that the effort expended on learning the rules was wasted. Not surprisingly, therefore, prescriptive rules have long lives.

It is unfortunate that a good deal of time is lost, in some educational systems, by insistence on a command of the standard variety at a level of correctness which goes far beyond any practical value that standardization may have. Uncertainty as to the effectiveness of explicit language instruction can also contribute to inefficiency, as educational philosophy swings from one extreme ('Kids today can't write a correct sentence—bring back grammar!') to the other ('This grammar teaching isn't doing a bit of good—kids today can't write a correct sentence!'). At the time of writing, it seems that the British National Literacy Strategy, brought in in 1998 to improve literacy through explicit grammar instruction, is about to be abandoned as we move into the second phase of the cycle.

However this may be, efficient grammar instruction, up to a point, is surely important in education. If knowledge of a standard language, spoken or written, is advantageous, it is clearly desirable that children be given accurate information at least about those more important aspects of its grammar which they find difficult to get right, in the hope that this may feed into more accurate linguistic performance. Well-informed grammar teaching can have other advantages. It can counteract the devaluation of non-standard dialects and their speakers by providing a more accurate view of language variation. It can perhaps help to illuminate the ways in which public attitudes can be deliberately manipulated by language (Cook 2003), as did the study of rhetoric in the Middle Ages. And, of course, the study of the workings of the mother tongue has general educational value in the same way as, for instance, the study of biology. Perhaps more so. After all, as Walter has put it (2008): while children are taught about photosynthesis, no child is called on to photosynthesize; but all children use language.

Grammar in foreign language teaching

Foreign languages have always had an important place in many educational systems, for both cultural and practical reasons. And with the steady growth in international communication, travel and emigration, more and more people now need to learn other languages—especially world languages such as English, Mandarin, Arabic or Spanish. However, foreign language study is time-consuming, expensive and difficult. Any language contains grammatical features which are hard to master after early childhood, whether because of their structural complexity, as with Russian noun morphology, or because they signal abstract meanings which are not easily grasped if the mother tongue does not encode equivalent concepts, as with article systems in western European languages. Teaching professionals are therefore faced with questions of principle to which there are no very clear answers. How much grammatical correctness should be expected of learners? How much is feasible: can foreign-language learners become as native-speaker-like as is considered desirable? What type of grammatical model is appropriate? What kinds of input and practice activity will enable learners to internalize the grammatical systems of the foreign language most effectively? Opinions in these areas have varied very widely, and continue to do so. The learning and teaching of grammar, in Larsen-Freeman's words, is 'the vortex around which many controversies in language teaching have swirled' (2003: 9).

The choice of a grammatical model is perhaps partly a non-question. Granted, theoretical perspectives on first-language acquisition may have some apparent relevance for foreign-language pedagogy. Views about whether 'Universal Grammar' remains available for the learning of new languages can impact on the question of what is, or is not, regarded as teachable and learnable (White 2003; Slabakova 2009). Usage-based models, which see grammatical knowledge as emerging by abstraction from patterns detected in the input (N. Ellis 2003 and this volume), can be invoked in support of 'lexical' approaches. In general, however, foreign language teaching does not seem to depend on specific theoretical models, and attempts to import, say, transformational grammar, cognitive grammar or construction grammar wholesale into the classroom have not been shown to work well. Theoretical grammarians seek relatively abstract generalizations which can be applied to languages and language as a whole. Day-to-day teaching, on the other hand, is directed at people who already have an implicit knowledge of how language works in general, and who are more concerned with language-specific details than with ways in which these details fit into higher-level abstractions.

The most useful kind of grammatical model as a starting-point for teaching, therefore, is arguably descriptive rather than theoretical—the close-to-the-surface picture offered for instance for English by Quirk et al (1985), Huddleston and Pullum (2002), or by the smaller grammars which teachers and students generally use. In this area, pedagogy owes a very considerable debt to linguistic research, past and present. Much of what we know about English grammar was established by early twentieth-century scholars from Jespersen (1909) onwards. More recent work in discourse analysis and related fields has greatly enriched our understanding of grammar above the sentence level. Although language corpora are not new—Jespersen and his contemporaries based their work on substantial written corpora, and even spoken corpora are over half a century old—their exploitation has been transformed out of recognition by our current ability to compile and analyse massive electronic databases of authentic language in use (see Adolphs and Lin, this volume). This makes it possible not only to verify and refine our traditional grammatical descriptions, but also to detect previously unobserved regularities and ongoing changes. Corpus analysis also allows us—in what amounts to a knowledge explosion—to investigate in detail the frontier between grammar and lexis, amassing far more complete and reliable information about the structural behaviour and external relations of individual words and word families than was previously available. In addition, technological developments have made it easier for structural descriptions to cover the whole range of spoken, written and signed language and to explore the significant ways in which these differ (see for example Biber et al 1999; Carter and McCarthy 2006; Woll and Sutton-Spence, this volume).

There are, however, crucial differences between descriptive and pedagogic grammars. Most importantly, a pedagogic grammatical description of a language is necessarily fragmentary. Time constraints do not allow language learners to learn, or their teachers to teach, anything approaching the whole of a language. The findings of descriptive grammarians, discourse analysts, corpus researchers or others cannot therefore be fed directly into teaching programmes: they only provide menus, from which course designers must select those high-priority elements that can be taught in the time available. While a descriptive grammar will aim at complete coverage, a pedagogic grammar will consequently miss out or simplify material of lesser practical importance. Further, a pedagogic grammar does not describe a language from a neutral standpoint. Ideally, it provides information which learners do not already possess, glossing over or leaving out what they already know by courtesy of their mother tongue. This may be a great deal. No learners need to be told that a new language has nouns and verbs. For Mandarin speakers, English SVO word order is unproblematic. French-speaking learners take it for granted that English relative clauses follow their nouns, and that they do not contain resumptive pronouns (whereas Japanese learners do need to be told where to put relative clauses, and Farsi-speaking learners do need to learn that, for instance, *That's the man that he sold me the bike* is not grammatical in English). German-speaking students of Italian (unlike Polish learners) need relatively little information about article usage. The very boundaries between grammar and vocabulary may be drawn differently for different learners. English *because*-clauses constitute a grammatical topic for students whose mother tongue does not handle clause structure on the European model; however, speakers of most European languages only need to learn that *because* corresponds to *perchè, parce que, weil, fordi, jer* or whatever. English prepositions are vocabulary for Swedish speakers, whose language also has prepositions; for Finnish speakers, whose language expresses the relevant notions mostly by noun-endings, prepositions are a difficult grammatical category. For these and other reasons (Swan 1994) a pedagogic grammar for a given group of learners may look very different indeed from an academic descriptive grammar.

Methodological questions in this area are especially intractable, and find few reliable answers. (For a detailed survey of past and present views on methodology, see Thornbury, this volume.) Does grammar teaching have any effect on learning? Most teachers probably think so, but how can we be sure? If students' grammar improves, is this because of the teaching, or would it have improved anyway as a result of unconscious acquisition processes acting on the input? If grammar teaching does work, how should it be approached? In particular—the key question—how useful is explicit instruction? When students learnt to read and write classical languages, this question was less crucial. In the time necessary to write a Latin sentence, a rule like 'use the subjunctive in indirect questions' could easily be recalled, and the appropriate form of the relevant verb retrieved from a memorized paradigm. Spontaneous speech is a very different matter: structures have to be chosen and forms retrieved far too quickly for conscious control to be exercised. This being so, is systematic explicit attention to structure a valuable starting-point none the less, on the basis that one can get from declarative to procedural knowledge of language 'by engaging in the target behaviour ... while temporarily leaning on declarative crutches' (DeKeyser 1998: 49), with a progressive reduction of conscious attention to form (Johnson 2001: 195)? Or is the grammar of a language best learnt incidentally in the context of communicative activity, as many current SLA theorists believe? Or is it pointless to pose the question in such general terms—does the answer depend mainly on the nature of the grammatical feature in question, the personality of the learner, the learning context, or other factors? While a great deal of valuable research has addressed this problem over the last half century or so, we are still a long way from a solution.

Successive approaches to language teaching are often described in terms of pendulum swings between one type of stance and its opposite. Although the metaphor is over-simple (especially in implying that there is no progress), it does have some validity. As a formal code, used to convey meaningful messages, a language necessarily has a dual character. Reflecting this, teaching philosophies oscillate between the two poles of form and meaning, control and freedom, imitation and expression, knowledge and skill, learning and using. At any one time, theorists and researchers claim that they have, at last, got the balance right, unlike the previous generation who, it is now clear, were excessively committed to a formal or functional view of the matter. The role of grammar in all of this—central, marginal or non-existent—depends largely on the current position of the pendulum.

At the time of writing there is a modest rehabilitation of grammar instruction in second language acquisition (SLA) theory, and a partial rejection of the earlier claim of Krashen (1981) and others that explicit grammatical teaching is irrelevant to the acquisition of linguistic competence. (See Norris and Ortega 2000; R. Ellis 2006.) Theoretically informed attitudes to language teaching are however still coloured by the heavily communicative bias of the last 30 years, and are situated well down towards the meaning–freedom–expression–skill–using end of the pendulum-swing. Language proficiency is often measured in 'can-do' terms (as in the specifications for the Council of Europe's *Common European Framework* 2001); with the danger that doing things with language may assume more importance than systematically learning the language needed to do the relevant things. Skills and strategies can receive more attention in teaching programmes than grammar, pronunciation and vocabulary. Grammar and pragmatics are often yoked together, to their mutual disadvantage (Swan 2007). Naturalistic 'real-world' activities are widely favoured, in the belief that classroom experience should approximate as closely as feasible to mother-tongue acquisition and use. 'Learner-centred', 'meaning-based', 'holistic', 'discourse', 'discovery', 'process', 'interaction', 'negotiation' and 'strategy' are good things to say. 'Teacher-dominated', 'form-based', 'discrete', 'sentence-level', 'transmission model', 'product', 'memorization', 'repetition' and 'drill' are not so good. The view that 'now, at last, we have got the balance right' surfaces in the common claim that language teaching has moved into a 'postmethod' era (e.g. Kumaravadivelu 2006). As Bell (2003) makes clear, however, postmethod thinking is not at all methodologically neutral. Kumaravadivelu's list of 'macrostrategies' (2006:

201) for language teaching has a powerful communicative orientation: while it refers to such things as negotiated interaction, learner autonomy, intuitive heuristics, social relevance and the raising of cultural consciousness, it has nothing whatever of substance to say about language and how to teach it.

Current orthodoxies, like earlier attitudes, are heavily dependent on hypotheses, often promoted with more assurance than they merit. To cite one among many: some researchers assert that linguistic regularities can only be effectively learnt during genuine communication while learners are carrying out 'real-world' tasks: interlanguage restructuring (it is claimed) is triggered by incidental 'focus on form' and conscious 'noticing' during communicative activity, for instance while resolving communication breakdowns (see for example contributions to Doughty and Williams 1998). For criticism of this and some other currently influential hypotheses, see Swan (2005).

Fashionable research interests can easily bias language-teaching content and methodology. This has sometimes been the case recently, for instance, with discourse grammar, pragmatics, the emergence of grammar from lexis, and formulaic language. Some specialists in corpus linguistics have stepped outside their territory to make powerful pedagogic recommendations regarding the use of corpora and 'real' corpus-attested language in teaching materials and practice. (For critical discussion see Carter 1998; Cook 1998; Widdowson 2003.) The specific research context can also create bias. Many scholars in the field have gained the bulk of their experience in 'English as a second language' (ESL) situations, working with university-level learners studying in English-speaking countries. Such learners typically have rich language input outside the classroom, and having studied English for many years at school, they may know far more than they can use effectively. This can naturally encourage a focus on language use, and away from systematic study of the linguistic basics. Unfortunately, theoretically-sanctioned approaches such as task-based teaching (R. Ellis 2003; Willis 1996), while suitable for students of this kind, may be far less suitable for many of the world's language learners, who are working under very much tighter time constraints in very different situations. The ESL bias also means that researchers work mostly with multilingual groups; this may explain a baffling feature of present-day mainstream SLA theory: the almost complete neglect of learners' mother tongues, as if these had no relevance to their learning of new languages (Butzkamm and Caldwell 2009; Cook 2010). It is also worth bearing in mind that experiential-learning models designed for teaching English (a language with few inflections) may not work well for languages which require beginning students to master parts of complex morphological systems.

Despite decades of research and theorizing, we still know little about the acquisition of second-language grammar, and pendulum swings will continue. One thing that could perhaps reduce their amplitude is a more realistic conception of what we are about. Teachers often seem to assume—consciously or unconsciously—that learners should aim at a close approximation to native-speaker competence. This is quite unrealistic: language learning and teaching are difficult, only a relatively small part of a language can be learnt in the time generally available, and limited success is all that can be hoped for. More general recognition of this fact might reduce the recurrent tendency to reject a viable language-teaching approach in the disillusioned belief that it has 'failed', only to replace it with something else that may work no better. In this connection the current interest in English as a lingua franca, and the associated questioning of native-speaker norms as an appropriate target for learners (see for example Kirkpatrick and Deterding, this volume), is an extremely constructive development.

Summary and conclusion

Grammatical analysis may not, as classical philosophers believed, give us information about the world. Nor, probably, does it give us a direct insight into the nature of cognition. None the less, the cluster of mechanisms that we call 'grammar' is central to language, and it is language that enables us to conceptualize and theorize about our world, to progressively expand our knowledge, and to consolidate and pass on our discoveries through cultural transmission. This being so, the better we understand grammar—what it is, how it operates in language and languages, how it is acquired, how it is instantiated in the brain—the better our grasp is likely to be of the many human activities and concerns in which language is implicated: from foreign-language teaching at the most practical extreme, through the many other matters that engage the attention of applied linguists, to the very nature of consciousness itself.

Note

1 In this article, all references to 'this volume' are to *The Routledge Handbook of Applied Linguistics*, 2011.

PART TWO
Satirical pieces

Introduction to Part two

The following pieces, and others that I have written in the same spirit, were meant principally to make people laugh. Ours is generally a serious business, and a little light relief does no harm. The late great Humphrey Lyttelton once said:

> As we journey through life, discarding baggage along the way, we should keep an iron grip, to the very end, on the capacity for silliness. It preserves the soul from dessication.

Some of the pieces, however, also have a more serious aim. There is a fair amount of nonsense around in our profession, as in all the social sciences, and one way of showing it up is by reductio ad absurdum—*the kind of satire which agrees warmly with its object, helping it on its way until it goes right over the cliff. Although this approach can easily be unfair and destructive, it can sometimes highlight the weaknesses of a ridiculous line of thought more effectively than rational confrontation.*

19
The use of sensory deprivation in foreign language teaching

(Written with Catherine Walter and originally published in *ELT Journal* Volume 36/3 April 1982.)

This is, I believe, the only spoof article ever to have graced the august pages of ELT Journal. *It was written during the heyday of fringe methods, when experimentation ran wild. Our purpose was partly just to satirize the sort of thing that was going on at the time. The article was, however, also partly a stylistic exercise—an attempt to write the kind of parody of a learned article that keeps the reader wondering, for as long as possible, whether it is serious or not. John Swales, in his book on genre analysis (1990), commented favourably on our success in doing this. One or two readers, astonishingly, got right through to the end without realizing what they were reading. We had a serious request for more information about the method; and references to the article turned up from time to time in the literature.*

The term 'sensory deprivation' is probably familiar to most of us from recent reports of interrogation procedures, but it may seem strange to find the expression used in a discussion of language teaching, especially since, at first sight, it is difficult to imagine how deprivation of sensory input could contribute to learning. However, recent experiments in this field (carried out principally by the Chilton Research Association at Didcot, near Oxford) have suggested that sensory deprivation (SD) could well become a powerful pedagogic tool in the not too distant future. The purpose of this article is simply to provide a résumé of current research in SD; readers who would like more complete information are referred to the very detailed account by Groboshenko and Rubashov (1980).

Background

Interest in the use of SD in language teaching arose initially as a natural extension of the work of such researchers as Gattegno, Rand Morton, Lozanov, and Watanabe. Gattegno's refusal (in the 'Silent Way') to allow learners more than minimum access to the second language (L2) model; Rand Morton's insistence on eliminating meaning entirely from the early 'phonetic programming' stages of language learning; Lozanov's concern to purge the student of his former identity and to build a new, autonomous L2 personality through 'Suggestopaedia'; and finally Watanabe's controversial but impressive use of 'hostile environment' as a conditioning factor—all these elements are clearly recognizable in current SD practice. But SD goes a great deal further.

The experiment

Perhaps the simplest way to understand SD is to look at what happens in a 'lesson' (more correctly, 'conditioning module'). Recent work by the Chilton Research Association has focused on the validation and comparison of a variety of module types; the best results to date have been obtained from a five-stage sequence.

Stage 1: Disorientation

Students, or 'subjects', are placed in a bare room cooled to a temperature of 5°C. They are told to sit in rows facing the front, with a round-shouldered posture, and to refrain from talking. (For the effect of body posture on learning readiness, see the paper by Kaama, Zing, and Vidmi (1979).) During this time, they are treated with coldness or outright hostility by the training staff, or 'deprivers', as they are generally known. The hostility has several purposes: in particular the facilitation of disorientation and the discouragement of positive child-parent affective attitudes towards the deprivers. After subjects have settled down, they are left to sit in silence for a considerable time. Any attempt to talk or move around is suppressed.

Stage 2: Exposure

When the appropriate moment is judged to have arrived, the subjects are exposed to a tape-recording of great length in the L2. No clues are provided as to the meaning, but from time to time slides are briefly flashed on to a screen. These slides have no relation to the text.

Stage 3: Sensory deprivation

Subjects are then taken to their individual SD chambers. These are soundproof and lightproof cells, each containing a bath in which the water is kept at a constant temperature of 37°C—blood heat. Subjects are undressed and immersed in the baths, which are designed so as to force subjects to adopt a foetal position. Once the SD chambers are closed, subjects suffer almost total deprivation of sensory input.

Stage 4: Creative hallucination

This is the point at which SD becomes interesting from a language-teaching point of view, and indeed makes necessary a radical reassessment of conventional models of language acquisition. After a certain period (between three and five hours in most cases), subjects begin to hallucinate. Although the nature and content of hallucinations vary enormously, it has been established by Brindle, Halloran and their colleagues (1980) that sensory input experienced in the last half hour before the onset of SD is invariably incorporated, in particularly vivid form, into SD-induced hallucinations. To put this in simple terms, the subject's hallucination will contain material from the tape-recording which he heard in Stage 2, and he will attach meaning to this material.

Stage 5: Babel; negotiation; resocialization

Now begins the process of resocialization, using the student's newly acquired L2 material as the vehicle. Subjects are removed from their SD chambers, dried off and dressed. They are then allowed to meet each other, but are instructed to communicate only in the L2. (The use of the mother tongue is severely discouraged.) At first, of course, no effective communication is possible, because each subject has attached his own private hallucination-generated meanings ('H-meanings') to the L2 elements that he has internalized. (Suppose, for example, that one subject uses a particular expression—say, 'Commission agricole'—as a greeting. His interlocutor is certain to have attached a completely different H-meaning to it—he could for instance regard it as a threat and run away in terror.) However, as the encounter proceeds, common meanings begin to be negotiated. Just as a child learns to realize that it is of little value to go on saying 'Bligb' if other people express the same idea by saying 'Biscuit', so SD subjects, under the pressure of their need to communicate, begin to modify their H-idiolects in the direction of an H-sociolect. This process continues until students are able to communicate effectively within the limitations of their restricted sample of the L2. They are then free to rest until the following day, when the cycle begins again at Stage 1.

According to data so far available, an acceptable level of L2 performance is achieved with the majority of subjects in a matter of weeks. It is, however, evident that there are a number of problems still to be solved. For one thing, there is a worryingly high drop-out rate, and follow-up studies have revealed the existence of disquieting symptoms among some unsuccessful subjects. More seriously, no way has yet been found of bridging the gap between the L2 sociolect established by the group and the way in which the L2 is used by the community at large. In other words, although SD subjects learn to communicate among themselves in the L2 with great efficiency, they are totally unable to make sense of the utterances of native speakers, and no-one else can understand a word they say. However, research currently going on in the field of intensive hostility conditioning offers some promise of a breakthrough in this area.

So much for the experimental scene. What are the implications for our classroom teaching? Obviously few establishments will be prepared, at this stage, to invest in a full SD lab. However, quite good results can be obtained in an ordinary classroom by using surprisingly simple techniques. Here is a suggested procedure:

1 Go into the classroom, sit down and remain totally silent. Refuse to give any information about the language (or indeed to say anything at all) until the students have worked themselves up into a frenzy.
2 Tell the students, in a cold patronizing tone of voice, that they are extremely fortunate in having been selected to take part in a language teaching experiment. Give them brief (and preferably misleading) information about the nature and purpose of SD conditioning.
3 Issue blindfolds and ask students to curl up on the floor in a foetal position. Play the tape which you have prepared. (The topic is unimportant, provided the text cannot be understood by the students.) When the tape has finished, issue the class with earplugs. Wait until hallucinations are well under way, and then proceed as above.

References

Brindle, Halloran, Wells, Farrago, and **Donnerkasten.** 1980. Einige noch nicht ausgewertete Ergebnisse einer ersten Versuchsreihe mit psychisch behinderten Kaninchen. Sprachwissenschaftliche Mitteilungen des Otto von Henkersdorf-Instituts, Iserlohn. Vol. 6 No.1, February 1980.

Chilton Research Association for Psychological and Pedagogical Orientation (CRAPPO). 1979. *The effects of sensory deprivation on the mating call of the male song thrush* (see especially Appendix B). Didcot Academic Press.

Groboshenko, Z. and **K. Rubashov.** 1980. 'La déprivation sensorielle, les fantasmes et l'apprentissage des langues'. *Helsinki Journal of Behavioural Linguistics* Vol. 3/2, July 1980.

Hotchkiss, Gale. 1965. *Fluctuations in the market price of iron ore 1956–58.* New York: OUP.

Juul Kaama, Walt Zing, Matilda Vidmi and collaborators. 1979. *Concave body posture and learning rate parameters: some tentative correlations.* Chicago South Side Institute of Anthropometrics Occasional paper No. 2.

20

Brief abstracts (supplied by the BAAL abstract-abstracting service)

(Originally published in *BAAL Newsletter* 1991.)

This and the following five pieces are among a number that were written for the newsletter of the British Association for Applied Linguistics. Readers who like this sort of thing can find others on my website: www.mikeswan.co.uk.

Aligote, Carlos and **Colophon, Eulalia.** 1990. 'Interlanguage in MA students.' *South Shields Journal of Prophylactic Linguistics* 22/3.
Utterances of Applied Linguistics students can be sited along a continuum running from pure L1 forms (e.g. *We have to teach them to understand English*) to pure TL forms (e.g. *Our prime pedagogic task is to foster strategies which will enhance learners' capacity to attend to the pragmatic communicative semiotic macro-content*). The paper offers a choice of five models to account for non-systematic variability in the data, treating L1, IL and TL as hierarchically independent semipermeable systems in each case.

Smith, Mohammed K., Jones, Jeff and **Bangalore-Torpedo, Lieut-Col Alison C.** 1990. 'A taxonomy of bibliographies.' *Zeitschrift für Grundsatzfragen* (Munich) 111/1.
Bibliographies can be classified into *epistemic* (designed to show what the writer has read) and *deontic* (aimed at telling the reader what to read). These categories correlate to some extent with *defensive* and *aggressive* approaches to bibliography. Special cases studied include the *cannibal bibliography*, which swallows up smaller bibliographies, the *onanistic bibliography*, which lists only works by the authors of the article to which it is appended, and the *autonomous bibliography*, whose accompanying paper has atrophied or completely disappeared. The paper is accompanied by a comprehensive bibliography.

Carruthers, Norbert St-C. Foulkes. 1989. 'Phonetician's palate.' *Colorado Review of Articulatory Phonetics* 12/2.
Phonetician's palate has attracted some attention in medical circles recently, since the much-publicised case of Professor Solomon Andrex of Knokke, who suffered a spectacular breakdown while researching into nasal plosion. It is now becoming clear that PP is a widespread condition, analogous to the degeneration of the meniscus in 'Runner's Knee'. The palate, weakened by years of cushioning tiny but repeated percussive strikes, loses its resilience and begins to transmit shocks directly to the brain, with the unfortunate results that we see all around us.

Brisket, Gladys P. 1990. 'Coming clean on cohesion.' *Reading Research as a Cottage Industry* (South Molton) 432/12.
If you refer more than once to a person, thing or event, the second mention can be made either by using the same words as before (iteration), other content words (synonymy), grammatical substitutes (anaphora) or no words at all (ellipsis). All of these are cohesive devices. This has led some critics of the theory to ask what would not count as a cohesive device. The answer is: nothing. Everything is cohesive. Life itself is a cohesive device.

Sackbottle, Caliban Q. 1990. 'Does instruction work? An in-depth study.' *Occasional Papers from the Seville Colloquium* 16.
A group of four Spanish-speaking nuns from Tierra del Fuego was exposed to comprehensible input containing numerous instances of English quantifiers over a period of six hours. At the same time, they were given explicit instruction in the semantics of English attitudinal disjuncts. A test to determine whether their command of quantifiers had improved more or less than their command of disjuncts was inconclusive: $t = 1.476$, $df = 14$, $p > .05$.

Dzhugashvili, J. V. 1991 'An ice-breaker for that first session.' *The Humane Practitioner* (Jackson Hole) 1/1.
Get all the students to write out name badges for themselves. Then collect up the name badges, shuffle them and redistribute. Tell students that they have to find and interview 'themselves'; they must elicit three new pieces of information about 'themselves' that they didn't know before. Having done this, they must find someone in the class who doesn't like repairing bicycles, and tell him/her how they feel about what they have just experienced. Identity-transfer of this kind helps students bridge the gap between autocentric and allocentric modes of communication, and prepares the ground for classroom parameter-setting activities.

21

Module 2: Critical text study. Paper 1: Cross-examining the text

(Originally published in *BAAL News* Autumn 2006.)

Read the following text and answer the questions

Our cognitive processes are ultimately embodied in our physical nature; hence our most basic linguistic tokens are derived from and expressive of our awareness of ourselves as individuals located and moving in three-dimensional physical space. At the same time, however, language and thought are not the property of individuals, but are distributed among the members of a community. They are therefore defined by and in turn define the underlying discursive formations of that community: the social group's self-constructed reality and the power relations, both intra- and inter-community, in which the group's members are enmeshed. All uses of language are thus doubly metaphorical (and what is conventionally called 'metaphor' would be more appropriately labelled 'meta-metaphor'). A text has meaning not because of its inherent objective linguistic make-up, but because it is a product of these multi-metaphorical awarenesses and multi-level discursive formations. Every text is therefore a political and ideological statement, since every discursive formation is political and ideological in nature. Analysing a text is essentially a matter of identifying, analysing and accounting for the operative discursive formations and their ways of assigning power. No text—indeed, no word—is innocent.

(From Katzenjammer and Sauwetter: *Putting the Text on Trial*. Didcot Academic Press 2005.)

1 Analyse the political and ideological content of the following texts:
   A The square on the hypotenuse is equal to the sum of the squares on the other two sides.
   B Sunrise is at 5.26 tomorrow morning.
   C Your next service is due at 20,000 miles.
   D English has ten central modal verbs.
   E Read the following text and answer the questions.
   F Bullshit Rules, OK?

2 Do you feel the inherent objective linguistic features make a small contribution to the meaning of any of texts A–F, or can they be ignored entirely?

3 Since no text is innocent, what sentence would you recommend for each of texts A–F after identifying and rounding up the discursive formations lurking in the shadows behind it, stripping the text of its power, putting it on trial and finding it guilty?

4 Does the text by Katzenjammer and Sauwetter quoted above have any inherent objective meaning, or can it only be understood as an expression of a certain ideology and its ways of assigning power?

5 Would a description of this ideology have any objective meaning, or would it only be an expression of a certain meta-ideology and its meta-ways of assigning power?

6 What are the meta-metaphorical implications of:
Montezuma
Met a puma
Coming through the rye?

7 How much do you care?

22

Notes from the broom cupboard

(Originally published in *BAAL News* Autumn 2008.)

Dear Julie

Thanks for your letter—lovely to hear from you. I'm glad things are going well at Lower Heyford. You never know with these new places, do you? Did LH keep on the old Dance Academy when they got university college status? I have this vision of you tangoing over the Cotswolds …

Not much has happened since you left. The main news, I guess, is that we've been restructured again. The original system where we had three departments with six schools in each wasn't felt to be 'fit for purpose', so now we have six departments with three schools in each. Richard and I have been promoted, we think, but we appear to have ended up on a lower salary scale, so it's not all that clear just where we stand. Paul is the only one who understands exactly what's happening, but he's off sick having a nervous realignment, so for the moment it's all a muddle—i.e. business as usual.

We had one of our subgroup meetings in the broom cupboard yesterday. (I know, it's silly to keep calling it that, it's been the Coffee Recess for two years now, but old habits die hard. Though I mustn't let Peter the Chomskyan hear me saying that, must I?) We talked a lot about the status of models in these ELF days, and about the notion of a Fully Competent and Knowledgeable Speaker of English as a Lingua Franca—a cumbersome label, but nobody's yet come up with a universally acceptable acronym. Ramona insisted that the model–target dichotomy can be resolved by applying insights from modern physics, in particular current views on quantum uncertainty and the collapse of the wave function, but we weren't totally convinced. She's always going on about that kind of thing; it's just a question of what book she's picked up off the popular science shelf this week. Last time it was the big bang and inflation as a metaphor for acquisition, and UG was the cosmic microwave background. Next time, the relevance of string theory to the negotiation of meaning? Who knows?

Plagiarism is getting everybody worked up. It's even worse than in your day. They used to put in spelling mistakes to make it look as if they'd written the stuff themselves, but now they don't even bother. Mary got an assignment last week that simply consisted of the entire text of one of her own papers, unattributed. I try to give them the benefit of the doubt, but when you get 3000 words of high-level argument in elegant flawless English on the scope of Applied Linguistics, concluding '© H Widdowson 1998', you do begin to wonder.

The thing that really got us all going, though, was Maggie's notes from a seminar she went to at UCL on Tuesday. This was given by a chap called Krszysztof Grgorczch, from one of those Eastern European places with Acute Vowel Deficiency Syndrome. Vowel trouble or not, it seems this guy was red hot. To summarise Maggie's account: Grgorczch and his colleagues have been working within a sociocognitive framework developed by Anopheles Fairfax and his team at Reykjavik, but they've taken the paradigm a whole lot further. Broadly speaking, they see all of human communication as falling into four categories: natural, transgressive, reversative and accommodatory. SLA, in this view, involves the acquisition of the target language's rhetorical perspectives and associated rhetorical macro-, meso- and microstrategies up to a point where an adequate level of interdiscursivity is achieved. An absolute prerequisite for an appropriate pedagogy is therefore a prior analysis of the relevant socio-political contexts, and in particular of the role of hegemonic positioning in determining speakers' and hearers' appraisal systems and the reflection of these in discourse commodification. Well, of course, once it's put in those terms the logic is pretty well inescapable. When Maggie had finished we were all wildly excited, and in no doubt at all about what direction we need to take. (Apart from Richard, who kept saying 'What about grammar?' He's a lovely guy, but that sort of thing mustn't be encouraged.) So the big question in all our minds now is: how can we best put all this across to the 45 Mexican secondary-school teachers who are coming for a two-week intensive on methodology next Monday? An interesting challenge! I'll keep you posted.

Love, and happy tangoing.
Pauline

23
Trajectories of identity construction

It has long been realised that conceptualisations of SLA are highly metaphorical in character: language students and their teachers may see the learning process in terms of play, work, discovery, travel, consumption, construction, interaction, negotiation or many other things (apWilliams 1984). It is also a matter of common experience that instruction works best where learners' and teachers' metaphors are in harmony (Anderssen 2001): gamelike practice activities are frequently resisted by students who conceptualise language learning as a matter of hard work, while conversely, students who feel that a language is learnt mainly through conversational interaction tend not to take kindly to the systematic study of language forms.

A recent study in this area (Carruthers et al. 2008) has looked at three different conceptual frameworks (CFs) which are prevalent in current theorising about instructed SLA, with a view to comparing their possible impact on learners' achievement. While such comparisons are notoriously resistant to quantitative treatment, they can none the less throw up interesting results which may suggest profitable directions for more rigorous further enquiry. The following is an informal outline account of the study; readers who would like detailed information are referred to Carruthers et al.'s paper.

Forty-eight lower-intermediate learners of English were divided into three groups on the basis of a preliminary questionnaire and interview, whose purpose was to ascertain whether their thinking about language learning tended to favour a dynamic–topological conceptual framework, a narrative–identity framework, or an integrated–constructional framework (see below). Each group was assigned to a team of teachers whose conceptualisation of language learning corresponded, broadly speaking, to that prevalent in the group. Groups were each given three two-hour orientation sessions whose purpose was to explore and elaborate the key ideas of the relevant CF, and to consolidate the group's positive stance vis-à-vis the framework. Students then received 24 hours of appropriately designed CF-congruent instruction, spread over six weeks. A control group was given 30 hours of conventional language lessons. Pre- and post-tests were administered; these were identical for all four groups.

CF1: dynamic–topological

In this framework, learning is conceived of primarily as a dynamic progress along a constantly evolving complex of ecological trajectories (Brik and Tajin 2005). The context and process of learning (and indeed of all communication) are seen as being in a continual state of flux, analogous to the circulation of liquids or gases in the physical world, but more appropriately modelled in an abstract phase space using concepts from sociological telemetry, topology, four-dimensional fluid dynamics, ballistics and other relevant disciplines (Wasserspeier and Gargolla 2007a, b). Learners in the CF1 group were encouraged throughout the study to conceptualise their 'journeys' through the semiotic fluid in visual terms, constructing maps of their trajectories first in two or three dimensions, and then later with the aid of möbius strips, klein bottles, nesting toroids and other dimensionally indeterminate matrices. Several students produced impressive work; one indeed gained a prize from a major art foundation for an Escher-like wallpaper pattern showing herself and her fellow-students trapped in an eddy under a morphosyntactic waterfall.

CF2: narrative–identity

Scholars who espouse this framework concur in seeing the modern self as a conglomeration of mutually permeating and reinforcing narratives, in which centrifugal and centripetal discursive dynamics contribute to the formation of shifting multiple identities (Lametta, Spekulatius and Glühwein 2006). The language-learning context necessarily requires the learner to confront, negotiate, situate and integrate further multiple identities which may be in conflict both with each other and with those rooted in earlier narratives (Carbonara 2008). Students in the CF2 group took part in a series of game-like activities in which they were given multiple ID cards (one or more for each sociolinguistic macrocontext) and required to act out scenarios designed to foster an ethnographic exploration of their individual and social language learning, seen primarily in terms of narrative-identity construction, deconstruction and reconstruction. The insights gained from this work are well exemplified in a comment made by one of the students towards the end of the study: "In the pub I am Chiquita and I can say 'bugger'. In Mr Gallbone's office I am Miss Carambo and I cannot say 'bugger'." Problems were few, though the researchers report one case of identity theft which deprived the student in question of all but two of his personae, leaving him as 1) an Inuit shaman and 2) a shoplifter named Agnes, about whom little information could be gleaned beyond the fact that she had a pet crocodile.

CF3: integrated–constructional

The powerful analytical tools developed in connection with recent work on Construction Grammar are increasingly being extended beyond the lexico-syntactic domain to handle discursive-rhetorical dimensions of communication, enabling researchers for the first time to bring under one conceptual roof the structural features of both the linguistic and the non-linguistic constituents of interactive discourse. It was the ground-breaking realisation by von Muesli (2005) that a remark about the weather, a conversation about the weather, and the act of talking about the weather are all examples of constructions, and can be handled jointly by an integrated system of analytical categories, that effectively set the stage for current work in this area. The framework, though complex, is intuitively compelling, and corresponds well to the naive instinct of many learners and teachers that, as FitzRabitt (1974) put it many years ago, 'Actually, everything is pretty much the same'. Students in this group followed a programme in which they 1) interacted in simple communicative tasks, 2) worked in groups to reconstitute and transcribe their interactions, 3) identified and analysed the constructions used, and finally 4) examined the roles that these constructions play in a multi-dimensional functional–cognitive space, establishing how individual linguistic features can be construed as micro-systems embedded in larger discoursal and interactive edifices in whose architecture the speakers themselves, and their ongoing interactions as they repeatedly co-construct their reciprocal positioning, are constitutive structural elements.

Results

Perhaps unsurprisingly, the post-test results were consistent with Kant's characterisation of the nature of scholarly activity in *Prolegomena* VI–2: 'Was man dreinsteckt, das zieht man natürlich wieder raus' (roughly: 'You get out what you put in'). The CF1 group did somewhat better than the others at diagramming information-flow and making origami representations of aspect- and time-relations. CF2 subjects scored particularly well on measures relating to story-telling and lying. The CF3 students showed impressive progress in social integration, which the researchers attribute to the fact that they spent a great deal of time in discussion trying to decide what a construction was. Overall, however, no significant difference was observed in the total scores of the three experimental groups. The control group, for reasons which are unclear, did substantially better on those components of the test which measured improvement in language knowledge and skills.

References

Anderssen, Jeroboam. 2001. 'Are we on the same hymn sheet?' *Utah Metapedagogic Quarterly* 16/3.
apWilliams III, Goliath. 1984. 'Metaphors we learn by—or not.' *University of Roscommon Occasional Papers* No 13.
Brik, Lancelot and **Nick Tajin.** 2005. 'Learners' trajectories: it's all ballistics.' *Applications of Tensor Calculus* 98/1.
Carbonara, Farfalle. 2008. 'Bill, Willi and Guillaume: the sad story of a ménage à trois.' *TELFELF* 1/1.
Carruthers, Dwane, Peter Pringle, Julian Babayaga, Hanako Ushiyama and **Selena van Dango.** 2008. 'Inside the Frame.' *Studies in Classroom Ecology* 14/2.
FitzRabitt, Wanda. 1974. *Can the Sayable Be Said to Be What Can Be Said? Essays in the Restatement of the Obvious.* Penrith: The Peatbog Press.
Lametta, Jake, Oliver Spekulatius and **Hans-Peter Glühwein.** 2006. 'Who was that lady? Identity shift in a group of retired Shakespearean actresses.' *Journal of Previously Rejected Papers* 19/4.
Mortensen, Caradoc. Forthcoming. 'Annual and seasonal variations in the death rate of dormice.' *Nature* 2375.
von Muesli, Erika. 2005. 'Constructing constructions, and vice versa.' *Interlaken Philosophical Almanac* 16/2.
Wasserspeier, Kurt and **Sven Gargolla.** 2007a. 'Physical schemata for the modelling of information flow.' *Hydraulics Monthly* 1246.
Wasserspeier, Kurt and **Sven Gargolla.** 2007b. 'The academic journal as catheter.' *Hydraulics Monthly* 1247.

24
PIGTESOL 2007

(Originally published in *BAAL News* Summer 2007.)

This year's one-day conference of the Pitcairn Islands Group of Teachers of English to Speakers of Other Languages was, if anything, an even greater success than last year's. There were some logistical difficulties arising from the committee's decision to hold the sessions in the new West Cliff Conference and Leisure Centre, which is only accessible by boat and rope ladder, but these were overcome in typical PIGTESOL can-do style, and the occasional drenching was generally taken in good part.

The dominant theme of the 2007 conference was 'Strategies'. In his thought-provoking opening plenary, Professor Humbert Mähdrescher, Disney Professor of Experimental Morphology at the University of Deadman's Rock, Montana, addressed the topic of 'What strategies are relevant to teaching learning strategies and learning teaching strategies?' This was followed by a panel discussion, chaired by Dr Grommit Pucklechurch of Hereward the Wake Agricultural Polytechnic, Bicester North. Panellists exchanged views on a number of interesting strategy-related questions raised by members of the audience, including:

> 'The more language you learn, the more language input you can access for further learning. So is language learning a language learning strategy?'

> 'Choosing appropriate metacognitive strategies is itself a strategy. Do we therefore need to establish a category of hypermetacognitive strategies, and if so, what would be other instances?'

> 'Is guessing unknown words from context a strategy, given that it doesn't work? If so, should we add 'ineffective strategies' to the standard taxonomies?'

> 'How can you train students to be autonomous if they won't follow your instructions?'

After a traditional PI 'Catch it yourself' lunch, the afternoon was devoted to parallel sessions. Participants were able to choose among no less than 40 papers, on a wide range of topics more or less closely related to the theme of the conference. These were:

- Using Fourier analysis in teaching pronunciation.
- Put that empty bottle to communicative use!
- The future perfect progressive: a multi-disciplinary approach.
- A simple mime game for mastering the apostrophe.

- Subvocalisation and the relationship between articulatory setting and academic writing skills.
- Task-based work with driftwood.
- Bringing free radicals into the classroom.
- Is English really a crypto-tone language?
- Let's all dress up! A new route to mastery of conditionals.
- Developing reading skills through rugby songs.
- Pope Gregory VII—a methodological innovator?
- Exploiting the wastebasket.
- The assault course as a motivational aid.
- Why don't my students understand me? A cry for help.
- 'I am a parking meter': role play in the elementary class.
- Explaining tense use with paper aeroplanes.
- Word poker.
- Learning inflectional morphology through internet chat groups.
- Physio-linguistic programming: safety rules for attaching electrodes.
- Developing pragmatic competence by working with a gang of muggers: a student's diary.
- A good icebreaker: talking about body hair.
- Learning to mutter in English: the effectiveness of task rehearsal as against task repetition.
- New ways with seashells.
- Parasitic gaps and *wh*-extraction—do learners need the whole truth?
- Using the mid-brain: the legacy of our reptilian ancestors.
- English for outrigger-building.
- Whole-body learning of phrasal verbs.
- Intonation through acupuncture.
- ZZZ—pros and cons.
- Promoting fluency through Boolean logic.
- How can subcutaneous implants help the advanced learner?
- Language as clothing, clothing as language.
- Madrigals: a note of caution.
- Group activities for developing register-specific grammars.
- Exploiting unintelligibility.
- Syntactic development through the casting of tantric horoscopes.
- Glove puppets: a neglected resource?
- A humanistic approach to teaching irregular verbs.
- Never mind materials—all you need is yourself and one coconut.
- The converse of multiple intelligence: a failed attempt to teach present tenses to a group of civil servants.

Planning for next year's PIGTESOL conference is already underway. The theme will be 'Altered states and the language classroom'. For registration details, membership information and other enquiries, go to the website or contact Lorraine in the Lagoon Bar in the usual way.

25

Learning the piano in Fantasia

(Originally published in *Peer Perspectives*, Kanda University, Japan, 2010.)

Under its satirical camouflage, this is a perfectly serious piece. No one educational system is the target; readers who have worked in a number of countries will recognize the situation described.

I'm just back from a visit to Fantasia. (Fantasia, as some of you may know, is a small country on the planet Largon, which orbits Star 446193B in the Lion's Head Galaxy. Don't ask me how I got there and back—it's classified.) Fantasia has a problem.

The problem is this. Countries on the planet Largon have different means of communication, and over the last century or so a planetary lingua franca has grown up. Largonians from different countries communicate with each other by playing the piano. Fantasians, who have no musical tradition, find this difficult. However, Fantasia needs to take its place in the modern world, where international communication is becoming increasingly important, and the Fantasian government therefore decreed some time ago that all young Fantasians must take piano lessons for two or three hours a week. Unfortunately this program has had little success: Fantasians regularly leave school, after seven or eight years of musical study, unable to play a note.

Musical education in Fantasia proceeds on somewhat traditional lines. The majority of piano teachers are in fact unable to play the piano. In their music lessons, pupils learn the names of the black and white notes, memorize the names of the different major and minor keys, study musical notation, and take turns to translate lines of sheet music into Fantasian. Most pupils find these lessons boring and pointless. The syllabus is quite demanding, especially at higher levels. In order to pass the examinations which will enable the more musically oriented young Fantasians to enter university and train as piano teachers, candidates must give correct answers to a large number of questions testing knowledge of musical theory and the ability to translate long passages of sheet music. Ability to play the piano is not tested. It is widely recognized in Fantasia that the present system is unsuccessful, and a number of younger teachers who have travelled abroad have suggested changes to the approach. These involve pupils actually practising the piano, the use of recordings of piano music in the classroom, and the engagement of teaching assistants from piano-playing countries to support the local teachers. While some progress has been made in these areas, there is little overall difference; young Fantasians still leave school, after seven or eight years' study, unable to play the piano.

Knowing my interest in education, some of my friends in the Fantasian government asked me if I had any suggestions about what could be done. I told them that I did not feel competent to comment in detail on a situation about which I knew little. However, for what it was worth, my view was as follows. First of all, Fantasia is spending a great deal of money on giving children piano lessons and getting nothing for it. This is clearly pointless: one does not go into a shop, put a large sum of money on the counter, and walk out empty-handed. In these circumstances the country is faced with a perfectly simple choice. It can stop paying for piano lessons and spend the money on something else: roads, hospitals, sports facilities or whatever. Or it can spend the money differently and get something for it. If Fantasia wishes to go down the second route, I suggested, radical action is needed, and it should consider the following seven-point plan.

1 **Immediate action.** Since there is no point at all in having piano lessons given by teachers who cannot play the piano, compulsory music teaching should be abolished for the time being, and these teachers should be given something else to do. Where there are teachers who can play the piano, these should offer voluntary music lessons only to those pupils who wish to learn and are prepared to work at their music.
2 **Teacher education.** The training of piano teachers should be completely reorganized under the direction of suitably qualified specialists, home-grown or imported, who are capable of establishing a program which will bring future teacher-trainers and teachers up to an appropriate level of practical competence in both piano-playing and pedagogy. The purpose is not to produce either academic theorists or concert pianists at native-playing level. What is needed is trainers and teachers who can play well enough and confidently enough to pass on their knowledge and skills, and who have been trained in appropriate practical methods of doing this. As many as possible of the existing non-piano-playing teachers should be sent on intensive courses for long enough to achieve a minimum acceptable standard. As the stock of competent teacher trainers grows, increasing numbers of adequate teachers will emerge from the system, and nation-wide piano teaching can gradually be reintroduced. Bear in mind that this is likely to take several years.
3 **Methods.** In teaching methodology, to a great extent you get out what you put in. If what you put in is translating musical notation into Fantasian, that is what you will get out: the ability to translate musical notation into Fantasian. If you want to get out piano playing, you must provide appropriate input. Effective piano playing requires both knowledge and skills, and teachers must therefore be trained in methods which achieve a balance between these two elements: in particular, methods which do not prioritize theory over practice. Most importantly, teaching should aim to produce, and encourage, modest success, not perfection. Perfectionism in musical education is disastrous—learners never achieve the standards required,

are continually corrected for small mistakes, and end up discouraged, unmotivated, and unwilling to try. (Many of the teachers who 'can't play the piano' actually can play—but their education has convinced them that they cannot.)

4 **Materials.** This is not a serious problem. There are excellent materials available for practical piano-teaching, published in many countries all over Largon. The important thing is to make sure that, as musical education is restructured, these are adopted in preference to the over-theoretical materials traditionally used in many Fantasian schools.

5 **Syllabus.** The traditional Fantasian approach is to put a great deal into the syllabus. This looks good to outsiders ('See how much we teach in our schools'), but it is totally counter-productive. There is far too much to learn, and in their efforts to tick all the boxes, teachers cannot actually teach anything properly. In learning a musical instrument, where confidence is crucial, the key is to do more with less. The syllabus should contain just enough essential material for pupils to be able to work at it at a reasonable pace, master it, and establish a core repertoire of music that they can play easily and with confidence. This will give them a solid basis on which they can build in the future, and which will provide most of what they will need for practical purposes. (International communication on Largon takes place almost entirely in the key of C major in 4/4 time.)

6 **Time.** If Fantasia wants its young people to learn the piano, it must allocate the time necessary. Only the most gifted and motivated pupils can learn the piano in two hours a week. Five hours a week is probably reasonable for most learners. Anything less, and the money spent on musical education will continue to be wasted.

7 **Examinations.** Fantasians who urge reform are regularly told 'Well, yes, of course, we'd like to teach children to actually play the piano, but we have to get them through the exams, so that they can get into university.' The examination system has a stranglehold on music education in Fantasia. As long as the examinations require a knowledge of theory and no command of practical skills, this will necessarily be reflected in the classroom. So this part of the system must be radically overhauled along with everything else.

'But this will mean finding more money,' my friends objected, 'out of the overstretched education budget'. 'Yes, very probably,' I said. 'But that doesn't mean it will cost more, in real terms, because you will get something for it. Which is more expensive: a bicycle for 1000 Fantasian Grotniks, or half a bicycle for FG200? The half-bicycle is more expensive, of course, because you get nothing useful for your money. At the moment you're spending billions of Grotniks on half a bicycle.'

Is all this feasible? Yes, I think so. I believe that if Fantasia took these steps, it would have large numbers of reasonably competent piano players coming out of its schools in ten years or so. Will it happen? It's hard to say. There are considerable obstacles in the way. Change on this scale requires the political will to invest for the long term, with little visible short-term benefit. Attempts to replace existing structures typically run up against institutional opposition: those in charge may be comfortable with the status quo, which gives them power and prestige, and may be very unwilling to accept major upheavals which could threaten their position. And in education in particular, unsatisfactory structures tend to be very stable: those who succeed in learning by bad methods are the ones who get to the top; once in authority, they are likely to feel well-disposed to the methods by which they learnt, and see little reason to change them. We will have to wait and see. I'm off to Fantasia again in 2020. I'll let you know.

Bibliography

Abbs, B., A. Ayton, and I. Freebairn. 1975. *Strategies*. Harlow: Longman.
Aitchison, J. 1994. *Words in the Mind*. Oxford: Blackwell.
Aitchison. J. 2001. *Language Change: Progress or Decay?* Cambridge: Cambridge University Press.
Albert, M. and L. K. Obler. 1978. *The Bilingual Brain*. New York: Academic Press.
Alexander, L. G. 1967. *First Things First*. Harlow: Longman.
Alexander, L. G. 1977. Handout for seminar at the British Council, Paris.
Alexander, L. G. 1988a. *Longman English Grammar*. Harlow: Longman.
Alexander, L. G. 1988b. 'The three best kept secrets about grammar.' *Practical English Teaching* 9/2.
Allan, K. 2007. *The Western Classical Tradition in Linguistics*. London: Equinox.
Allwright, R. 1981. 'What do we want teaching materials for?' *ELT Journal* 36/1.
Anthony. E. M. 1963. 'Approach, method and technique.' *English Language Teaching* 17/2.
Arabski, J. 1979. *Errors as Indicators of the Development of Interlanguage*. Katowice: Universytet Slaski.
Arcaini, E. 1968. 'L'Interférence au niveau du lexique.' *Audio-Visual Language Journal* 5.3.
Backus, A. 1996. *Two in One: Bilingual Speech of Turkish Immigrants in the Netherlands*. Tilburg: Tilburg University Press.
Bartelt, G. 1992. 'Rhetorical transfer in Apachean English' in S. Gass and L. Selinker (eds.): *Language Transfer in Language Learning*. Amsterdam/Philadelphia: John Benjamins.
Batstone, R. 1994. *Grammar*. Oxford: Oxford University Press.
Bell, D. M. 2003. 'Method and postmethod: are they really so incompatible?' *TESOL Quarterly* 37/2.
Bell, D. M. 2007. 'Do teachers think that methods are dead?' *ELT Journal* 61/2.
Bialystok, E. 1994. 'Analysis and control in the development of second language proficiency.' *Studies in Second Language Acquisition* 16.2.
Bialystok, E. and M. Sharwood Smith. 1985. 'Interlanguage is not a state of mind: an evaluation of the construct for second language acquisition.' *Applied Linguistics* 6.3.
Biber, D., S. Conrad, and G. Leech. 2002. *Longman Student Grammar of Spoken and Written English*. Harlow: Longman.
Billows, F. L. 1961. *The Techniques of Language Teaching*. London: Longman.
Block, D. 2001. 'An exploration of the art and science debate in language education' in M. Bax and J-W. Zwart, (eds.): *Reflections on Language and Language Learning: In Honour of Arthur van Essen*. Amsterdam: John Benjamins.
Blum-Kulka, S. and E. Levenston. 1983. 'Universals of lexical simplification' in *Strategies in Interlanguage Communication*. London: Longman.
Blum-Kulka, S. and E. Levenston. 1987. 'Lexical-grammatical pragmatic indicators.' *Studies in Second Language Acquisition* 9.2.
Blundell, L. and J. Stokes. 1981. *Task Listening*. Cambridge: Cambridge University Press.
Bongaerts, T., E. Kellerman, and A. Bentlage. 1987. 'Perspective and proficiency in L2 referential communication.' *Studies in Second Language Acquisition* 9.2.
Bowen, J. and R. Stockwell. 1965. *The Sounds of English and Spanish*. Chicago: University of Chicago Press.

Bowler, B. and S. Parminter. 2002. 'Mixed-level teaching: tiered tasks and bias tasks' in J. Richards and W. Renandya (eds.): *Methodology in Language Teaching: An Anthology of Current Practice*. Cambridge: Cambridge University Press.

Brown, H. D. 2002. 'English language teaching in the "postmethod" era: towards better diagnosis, treatment and assessment' in J. Richards and W. Renandya (eds.): *Methodology in Language Teaching: An Anthology of Current Practice*. Cambridge: Cambridge University Press.

Brumfit, C. J. 1978. Review of D. A. Wilkins's *Notional Syllabuses*. *ELT Journal* 33/1: 79–82.

Brumfit, C. J. 1981. 'Accuracy and fluency.' *Practical English Teaching* 1/3.

Bruton, A. 2000. 'Focus on form: a useless term?' in *IATEFL 2000: Dublin Conference Selections*. Whitstable: IATEFL.

Bruton, A. 2002a. 'How can TBI not contribute to language development?' *IATEFL Issues* 170: 6–7.

Bruton, A. 2002b. 'From tasking purposes to purposing tasks.' *ELT Journal* 56/3: 280–8.

Bruton, A. 2002c. 'When and how the language development in TBI?' *ELT Journal* 56/3: 296–297.

Butzkamm, W. and J. Caldwell. 2009. *The Bilingual Reform*. Tübingen: Gunter Narr Verlag.

Bygate, M. 2001. 'Effects of task repetition on the structure and control of oral language' in M. Bygate, P. Skehan, and M. Swain (eds.).

Bygate, M., P. Skehan, and M. Swain (eds.). 2001. *Researching Pedagogic Tasks: Second Language Learning, Teaching and Testing*. Harlow: Longman.

Cambridge International Dictionary of English. 1995. Cambridge: Cambridge University Press.

Candlin, C. (ed.). 1981. *The Communicative Teaching of English*. London: Longman.

Candlin, E. F. 1968. *Present Day English for Foreign Students* (4th edn.). London: University of London Press.

Carey, S. 1978. 'The child as word learner' in M. Halle, J. Bresnan, and B. Miller (eds.): *Linguistic Theory and Psychological Reality*. Cambridge, MA: MIT Press.

Carter, R. 1998. 'Orders of reality: CANCODE, communication and culture.' *ELT Journal* 52/1.

Carter, R. and M. McCarthy (eds.). 1988. *Vocabulary and Language Teaching*. London: Longman.

Carter, R. and M. McCarthy. 2006. *Cambridge Grammar of English*. Cambridge: Cambridge University Press.

Celce-Murcia, M. 2007. 'Towards more context and discourse in grammar instruction.' *TESL-EJ* 11/2.

Celce-Murcia, M. and D. Larsen-Freeman with H. Williams, 1999. *The Grammar Book*. Boston, MA: Heinle & Heinle.

Chang, J. 1987. 'Chinese speakers' in Swan and Smith (eds.).

Channell, J. 1988. 'Psycholinguistic considerations in the study of L2 vocabulary acquisition' in Carter and McCarthy (eds.).

Charlot, M., G., Hocmard, and J. Morgan. 1977. *Let's Go On! Classe de Seconde*. Paris: Armand Colin/Longman.

Clark, E. 1993. *The Lexicon in Acquisition*. Cambridge: Cambridge University Press.

Coe, N. 1987. 'Speakers of Spanish and Catalan' in Swan and Smith (eds.).

Cook, G. 1998. 'The uses of reality: a reply to Ronald Carter.' *ELT Journal* 52/1.

Cook, G. 2000. *Language Play, Language Learning*. Oxford: Oxford University Press.

Cook, G. 2001. 'The authenticity of theory, translation and play: perspectives on past and future ELT'. *International House Journal* April 2001.

Cook, G. 2003. *Applied Linguistics*. Oxford: Oxford University Press.

Cook, G. 2010. *Translation*. Oxford: Oxford University Press.

Cook, V. 1993. *Linguistics and Second Language Acquisition*. London: Macmillan.

Cook, V. 2008. *Second Language Learning and Language Teaching* (2nd edn.). London: Hodder Arnold.

Corder, S. P. 1967. 'The significance of learners' errors.' *IRAL* 5.4. Reprinted in *Error Analysis and Interlanguage.* 1981. Oxford: Oxford University Press.
Council of Europe. 2001. *Common European Framework of Reference for Languages: Learning, Teaching, Assessment.* Cambridge: Cambridge University Press.
Cowie, A. 1992. 'Multiword lexical units and communicative language teaching' in P. Arnaud and H. Béjoint (eds.): *Vocabulary and Applied Linguistics.* London: Macmillan.
Crawford, J. 2002. 'The role of materials in the language classroom: finding the balance' in J. Richards and W. Renandya (eds.): *Methodology in Language Teaching: An Anthology of Current Practice.* Cambridge: Cambridge University Press.
Cross, J. 2002. 'Noticing in SLA: Is it a valid concept?' *TESL-EJ* 6/3.
Crystal, D. 2001. 'Clinical linguistics' in M. Aronoff and J. Rees-Miller (eds.): *The Handbook of Linguistics.* Oxford: Blackwell.
Dąbrowska, E. 2004. *Language, Mind and Brain.* Edinburgh: Edinburgh University Press.
Dagut, M. B. and B. Laufer. 1985. 'Avoidance of phrasal verbs by English learners, speakers of Hebrew—a case for contrastive analysis.' *Studies in Second Language Acquisition* 7.
Day, R. and J. Bamford. 1998. *Extensive Reading in the Second Language Classroom.* Cambridge: Cambridge University Press.
de Bot, K. and R. Schreuder. 1993. 'Word production and the bilingual lexicon' in R. Schreuder and B. Weltens. (eds.) 1993. *The Bilingual Lexicon.* Amsterdam/Philadelphia: John Benjamins.
DeKeyser, R. 1998. 'Beyond focus on form: cognitive perspectives on learning and practicing second language grammar' in J. Doughty and J. Williams (eds.).
DeKeyser, R. 2001. 'Automaticity and automatization' in P. Robinson (ed.).
Dickinson, L. 1987. *Self-instruction in Language Learning.* Cambridge: Cambridge University Press.
Doughty, C. 2001. 'Cognitive underpinnings of focus on form' in P. Robinson (ed.).
Doughty, C. and J. Williams (eds.). 1998. *Focus on Form in Classroom Second Language Acquisition.* Cambridge: Cambridge University Press.
Dulay, H., M. Burt, and S. Krashen. 1982. *Language Two.* Oxford: Oxford University Press.
Dušková, L. 1969. 'On sources of error in foreign language learning.' *IRAL* 7.1.
Ellis, N. 2002. 'Frequency effects in language acquisition: a review with implications for theories of implicit and explicit language acquisition.' *Studies in Second Language Acquisition* 24: 143–188.
Ellis, N. 2003. 'Constructions, chunking and connectionism: the emergence of second language structure' in C. Doughty and M. Long (eds.): *The Handbook of Second Language Acquisition.* Oxford: Blackwell.
Ellis, N. and A. Beaton. 1993. 'Psycholinguistic determinants of foreign language vocabulary learning.' *Language Learning* 43.4.
Ellis, R. 1985. 'Sources of variability in interlanguage.' *Applied Linguistics* 6.2.
Ellis, R. 1994. *The Study of Second Language Acquisition.* Oxford: Oxford University Press.
Ellis, R. 2001. 'Non-reciprocal tasks, comprehension and second language acquisition' in M. Bygate, P. Skehan, and M. Swain (eds.).
Ellis, R. 2002. 'The place of grammar instruction in the second/foreign language curriculum' in E. Hinkel and S. Fotos (eds.): *New Perspectives on Grammar Teaching in Second Language Classrooms.* Mahwah, NJ: Lawrence Erlbaum.
Ellis, R. 2003. *Task-based Language Teaching and Learning.* Oxford: Oxford University Press.
Ellis, R. 2005. 'Principles of instructed language learning.' *System* 33/2.
Ellis, R. 2006. 'Current issues in the teaching of grammar: an SLA perspective.' *TESOL Quarterly* 40.
Færch, C. and G. Kasper. 1986. 'Cognitive dimensions of language transfer' in Kellerman and Sharwood Smith (eds.).
Field, J. 1998. 'Skills and strategies: towards a new methodology for listening.' *ELT Journal* 52/2.

Finney, D. 2002. 'The ELT curriculum: a flexible model for a changing world' in J. Richards and W. Renandya (eds.): *Methodology in Language Teaching: An Anthology of Current Practice.* Cambridge: Cambridge University Press.

Foley, W. 1997. *Anthropological Linguistics.* Oxford: Blackwell.

Folse, K. 2004. *Vocabulary Myths.* Ann Arbor: University of Michigan Press.

Foster, P. 1998. 'A classroom perspective on the negotiation of meaning.' *Applied Linguistics* 19/1: 1–23.

Fotos, S. 1998. 'Shifting the focus from forms to form in the EFL classroom.' *ELT Journal* 52/4: 301–7.

Fotos, S. 2002. 'Structure-based interactive tasks for the EFL grammar learner' in E. Hinkel and S. Fotos (eds.): *New Perspectives on Grammar Teaching in Second Language Classrooms.* Mahwah, NJ: Lawrence Erlbaum.

Garioch, R. 1980. *Collected Poems.* Manchester: Carcanet.

Gentner, D. and S. Goldin-Meadow (eds.). 2003. *Language in Mind.* Cambridge, MA: MIT.

Gimson, A. C. 1962. *An Introduction to the Pronunciation of English.* London: Edward Arnold.

Gnutzmann, C. 1973. 'Zur Analyse lexikalischer Fehler' in Nickel (ed.): *Fehlerkunde.* Berlin: Cornelsen-Velhagen & Klasing.

Goldberg, A. E. 1995. *Constructions: a Construction Grammar Approach to Argument Structure.* Chicago: University of Chicago Press.

Grabe, W. and F. L. Stoller. 2002. *Teaching and Researching Reading.* Harlow: Pearson Education Ltd.

Granger S. 1998. 'Prefabricated patterns in advanced EFL writing; collocations and formulae' in A. Cowie (ed.): *Phraseology: Theory, Analysis, and Applications.* Oxford: Oxford University Press.

Grauberg, W. 1971. 'An error analysis in German of first-year university students' in G. Perren and J. Trim (eds.): *Applications of Linguistics.* Cambridge: Cambridge University Press.

Green, G. M. 2004. 'Some interactions of pragmatics and grammar' in Horn and Ward (eds.).

Greenbaum, S. and R. Quirk. 1990. *A Student's Grammar of the English Language.* Harlow: Longman.

Gregg, K. 1995. Review of Cook 1993. *Second Language Research* 11.1.

Griffiths, C. 2007. 'Language learning strategies: students' and teachers' perceptions.' *ELT Journal* 61(2).

Gurrey, P. 1955. *Teaching English as a Foreign Language.* London: Longmans, Green and Co. Ltd.

Halliday, M. A. K, A. McIntosh, and P. Strevens. 1964. *The Linguistic Sciences and Language Teaching.* London: Longman.

Harley, B. and M. Swain. 1984. 'The interlanguage of immersion students and its implications for second language teaching' in A. Davies, C. Criper, and A. Howatt (eds.): *Interlanguage.* Edinburgh: Edinburgh University Press.

Harmer, J. 2001. *The Practice of English Language Teaching.* Harlow: Longman.

Hawkins, J. 2004. *Efficiency and Complexity in Grammars.* Oxford: Oxford University Press.

Hill, R. 1982. *A Dictionary of False Friends.* London: Macmillan.

Horn, L. and G. Ward (eds.). 2004. *The Handbook of Pragmatics.* Oxford: Blackwell.

Hornby, A. S. 1954. *Guide to Patterns and Usage in English.* London: Oxford University Press.

Howarth, P. 1998a. 'Phraseology and second language proficiency.' *Applied Linguistics* 19/1.

Howarth, P. 1998b. 'The phraseology of learners' academic writing' in A. P. Cowie. (ed.): *Phraseology: Theory, Analysis, and Applications.* Oxford: Oxford University Press.

Howatt, A. P. R. with H. G. Widdowson. 2004. *A History of English Language Teaching.* Oxford: Oxford University Press.

Huddleston, R. and G. Pullum. 2002. *The Cambridge Grammar of the English Language.* Cambridge: Cambridge University Press.

Hulstijn, J. 1995. 'Not all grammar rules are equal: giving grammar instruction its proper place in foreign language teaching' in R. Schmidt (ed.): *Attention and Awareness in Foreign Language Learning*. Honolulu: University of Hawaii Press.

Hulstijn, J. 2002. 'Towards a unified account of the representation, processing and acquisition of second language knowledge.' *Second Language Research* 18/3: 193–223.

Hymes, D. H. 1971. 'On communicative competence' in Pride and Holmes (eds.).

Irún-Chavarria, M. 2005. 'Doing, reflecting, learning.' *English Teaching Professional* 40.

Jain, M. 1974. 'Error analysis: source, cause and significance' in J. Richards (ed.): *Error Analysis*. London: Longman.

James, C. 1983. 'The exculpation of contrastive linguistics' in B. Robinett and J. Schachter (eds.): *Second Language Learning*. Ann Arbor: University of Michigan Press.

James, C. 1990. 'Learner language.' *Language Teaching* 23/4. Cambridge: Cambridge University Press.

Jerome, J. K. 1900. *Three Men on the Bummel*. Leipzig: B. Tauchnitz Verlag.

Jespersen, O. 1909. *A Modern English Grammar on Historical Principles*. Heidelberg: Winter.

Johansen, L. 1993. 'Code copying in immigrant Turkish' in G. Extra and L Verhoeven (eds.): *Immigrant Languages in Europe*. Clevedon: Multilingual Matters.

Johnson, K. 1981. Introduction to Johnson and Morrow (eds.).

Johnson, K. 1996. *Language Teaching & Skill Learning*. Oxford: Blackwell.

Johnson, K. 2001. *An Introduction to Foreign Language Learning and Teaching*. Harlow: Longman.

Johnson, K. 2008. *An Introduction to Foreign Language Learning and Teaching* (2nd edn.). Harlow: Pearson Longman.

Johnson, K. and H. Johnson. 1998. *Encyclopaedic Dictionary of Applied Linguistics*. Oxford: Blackwell.

Johnson, K. and K. Morrow (eds.). 1981. *Communication in the Classroom*. London: Longman.

Jones, M. and S. Haywood. 2004 'Facilitating the acquisition of formulaic sequences' in N. Schmitt (ed.): *Formulaic Sequences*. Amsterdam: John Benjamins.

Kasper, G. 1992. 'Pragmatic transfer.' *Second Language Research* 8/3.

Kay, P. 2004. 'Pragmatic aspects of grammatical constructions' in Horn and Ward (eds.).

Kellerman, E. 1978. 'Giving learners a break: native language intuitions as a source of predictions about transferability.' *Working Papers on Bilingualism* 15.

Kellerman, E. 1984. 'The empirical evidence for the influence of the L1 in interlanguage' in A. Davies, C. Criper, and A. P. R. Howatt (eds.): *Interlanguage*. Edinburgh: Edinburgh University Press.

Kellerman, E. 1986. 'An eye for an eye: crosslinguistic constraints on the development of the L2 lexicon' in Kellerman and Sharwood Smith (eds.).

Kellerman, E. 1987. Aspects of Transferability in Second Language Acquisition. Unpublished manuscript, University of Nijmegen.

Kellerman, E., and M. Sharwood Smith (eds.). 1986: *Crosslinguistic Influence in Second Language Acquisition*. Oxford: Pergamon Press.

Klapper, J. and J. Rees. 2003. 'Reviewing the case for explicit grammar instruction in the university foreign language learning context.' *Language Teaching Research* 7/3: 285–314.

Kohn, K. 1986. 'The analysis of transfer' in Kellerman and Sharwood Smith (eds.).

Kramsch, C. 2007. 'Re-reading Robert Lado 1957, *Linguistics across Cultures: Applied Linguistics for Language Teachers*.' *International Journal of Applied Linguistics* 17.

Krashen, S. 1981. *Second Language Acquisition and Second Language Learning*. Oxford: Pergamon.

Kroll, J. 1993. 'Assessing conceptual representations' in R. Schreuder and B. Weltens (eds.): *The Bilingual Lexicon*. Amsterdam/Philadelphia: John Benjamins.

Kruisinga, A. 1932. *A Handbook of Present-day English*. Groningen: Noordhoff.

Kumaravadivelu, B. 2006. *Understanding Language Teaching: From Method to Postmethod*. Cambridge: Cambridge University Press.

Lado, R. 1957. *Linguistics across Cultures: Applied Linguistics for Language Teachers.* Ann Arbor: University of Michigan Press.

Langacker, R. 2008. *Cognitive Grammar: A Basic Introduction.* New York: Oxford University Press.

Larsen-Freeman, D. 2003. *Teaching Language: from Grammar to Grammaring.* Boston, MA: Thomson Heinle.

Laufer, B. 1990. 'Why are some words more difficult than others?' *IRAL* 28/4.

Leech, G. and J. Svartvik. 1975. *A Communicative Grammar of English.* Harlow: Longman.

Levelt, W. 1989. *Speaking: from Intention to Articulation.* Cambridge, MA: Bradford Books/MIT Press.

Levinson, S. 1983. *Pragmatics.* Cambridge: Cambridge University Press.

Lewis, M. 1993. *The Lexical Approach.* Hove: Language Teaching Publications.

Lightbown, P. 1998. 'The importance of timing in focus on form' in J. Doughty and J. Williams (eds.).

Lightbown, P. 2000. 'Classroom SLA research and second language teaching.' *Applied Linguistics* 21/4: 431–62.

Lightbown, P. and N. Spada. 1999. *How Languages are Learned* (2nd edn.). Oxford: Oxford University Press.

Long, B. and J. Kurzweil. 2002. 'PPP under the microscope.' *English Teaching Professional* 25: 18–20.

Long, M. 1988. 'Instructed interlanguage development' in L. Beebe (ed.): *Issues in Second Language Acquisition: Multiple Perspectives.* Rowley, MA: Newbury House.

Long, M. 1991. 'Focus on form: a design feature in language teaching methodology' in K. de Bot, R. Ginsberg, and C. Kramsch (eds.): *Foreign Language Research in Cross-cultural Perspective.* Amsterdam: John Benjamins.

Long, M. and G. Crookes. 1992. 'Three approaches to task-based syllabus design.' *TESOL Quarterly* 26: 27–55.

Long, M. and P. Robinson. 1998. 'Focus on form: theory, research and practice' in C. Doughty and J. Williams.

Macaro, E. 2001. *Learning Strategies in Foreign and Second Language Classrooms.* London: Continuum.

Macaro, E. 2006. 'Strategies for language learning and for language use: revising the theoretical framework.' *The Modern Language Journal* 90 (3).

McWhorter, J. 2001. *The Power of Babel: A Natural History of Language.* London: Heinemann.

Meara, P. 1982. 'Vocabulary acquisition, a neglected aspect of language learning' in V. Kinsella (ed.): *Surveys 1.* Cambridge: Cambridge University Press.

Meara, P. 1984. 'The study of lexis in interlanguage' in A. Davies, C. Criper, and A. Howatt (eds.): *Interlanguage.* Edinburgh: Edinburgh University Press.

Meara, P. 1993. 'The bilingual lexicon and the teaching of vocabulary' in R. Schreuder and B. Weltens, B. (eds.): *The Bilingual Lexicon.* Amsterdam/Philadelphia: John Benjamins.

Moravcsik, E. 2006. *An Introduction to Syntactic Theory.* London: Continuum.

Munby, J. 1978. *Communicative Syllabus Design.* Cambridge: Cambridge University Press.

Naiman, N., M. Fröhlich, H. H. Stern, and A. Todesco. 1978. 'The good language learner.' *Research in Education Series 7.* Ontario: Ontario Institute for Studies in Education.

Norris, J. and L. Ortega. 2000. 'Effectiveness of L2 instruction: a research synthesis and quantitative meta-analysis.' *Language Learning* 50/3: 417–528.

Nunan, D. 1988. *The Learner-centered Curriculum.* Cambridge: Cambridge University Press.

Nunan, D. 1989. *Designing Tasks for the Communicative Classroom.* Cambridge: Cambridge University Press.

Nunan, D. 1991. 'Communicative tasks and the language curriculum.' *TESOL Quarterly* 25/2: 279–95.

Nunan, D. 1998. 'Teaching grammar in context.' *ELT Journal* 52/2.

O'Malley, J. and **A. Chamot**. 1990. *Learning Strategies in Second Language Acquisition.* Cambridge: Cambridge University Press.

O'Neill, R. 1977. 'The limits of functional/notional—or "My guinea pig died with its legs crossed" ' in S. Holden (ed.): *English for Specific Purposes.* London: Modern English Publications.

Odlin, T. 1989. *Language Transfer.* Cambridge: Cambridge University Press.

Oxford, R. 1990. *Language Learning Strategies: What Every Teacher Should Know.* Boston: Heinle & Heinle.

Palmer, H. E. and **D. Palmer** 1925. *English through Actions.* Tokyo: IRET.

Parry, K. 1991. 'Building a vocabulary through academic reading.' *TESOL Quarterly* 25.

Pawley, A. and **F. Syder**. 1983. 'Two puzzles for linguistic theory' in J. Richards and R. Schmidt (eds.): *Language and Communication.* London: Longman.

Perdue, C. (ed.). 1993. *Adult Language Acquisition: Cross-linguistic Perspectives.* Cambridge: Cambridge University Press.

Pienemann, M. 1998. *Language Processing and Second Language Development: Processability Theory.* Amsterdam: John Benjamins.

Pinker, S. 1994. *The Language Instinct.* London: Allan Lane, The Penguin Press.

Poulisse, N. 1993. 'A theoretical account of lexical communication strategies' in R. Schreuder and B. Weltens (eds.): *The Bilingual Lexicon.* Amsterdam/Philadelphia: John Benjamins.

Poulisse, N. and **T. Bongaerts**. 1994. 'First language use in second language production.' *Applied Linguistics* 15.1.

Prabhu, N. 1987. *Second Language Pedagogy: A Perspective.* Oxford: Oxford University Press.

Pride, J. and **J. Holmes** (eds.). 1971. *Sociolinguistics.* London: Penguin.

Pullum, G. K. 1991. *The Great Eskimo Vocabulary Hoax.* Chicago: University of Chicago Press.

Quirk, R. 1968. *The Use of English.* London: Longman.

Quirk, R., **S. Greenbaum, J. Leech,** and **J. Svartvik**. 1985. *A Comprehensive Grammar of the English Language.* Harlow: Longman.

Ramachandran, S. and **H. Rahim**. 2004. 'Meaning recall and retention: the impact of the translation method on elementary level learners' vocabulary learning.' *RELC Journal* 35/2.

Rees-Miller, J. 1993. 'A critical appraisal of learner training: theoretical bases and teaching implications.' *TESOL Quarterly* 27.

Richards, J. 2002. 'Theories of teaching in language teaching' in J. Richards and W. Renandya (eds.): *Methodology in Language Teaching: An Anthology of Current Practice.* Cambridge: Cambridge University Press.

Richards, J. and **T. Rodgers**. 2001. *Approaches and Methods in Language Teaching.* Cambridge: Cambridge University Press.

Ridley, J. and **D. Singleton**. 1995. 'Strategic L2 lexical innovation: case study of a university-level ab initio learner of German.' *Second Language Research* 11.2.

Ringbom, H. 1978. 'The influence of the mother tongue on the translation of lexical items.' *Interlanguage Studies Bulletin* 3/1: 80–101.

Ringbom, H. 1986. 'Crosslinguistic influence and the foreign language learning process' in Kellerman and Sharwood Smith (eds.).

Ringbom, H. 1987. *The Role of the First Language in Foreign Language Learning.* Clevedon, Philadelphia: Multilingual Matters Ltd.

Robinson, P. (ed.). 2001. *Cognition and Second Language Instruction.* Cambridge: Cambridge University Press.

Robinson, P. 2001. 'Task complexity, cognitive resources, and syllabus design: a triadic framework for examining task influences on SLA' in P. Robinson (ed.).

Russell, B. 1919. *Introduction to Mathematical Philosophy.* London: Allen and Unwin.

Russell, B. 2004. *History of Western Philosophy* (first published 1946). London: Routledge.

Samuda, V. 2001. 'Guiding relationships between form and meaning during task performance: the role of the teacher' in M. Bygate, P. Skehan, and M. Swain (eds.).

Sapir, E. 1921. *Language: An Introduction to the Study of Speech.* New York: Harcourt, Brace.

Schmidt. R. 1983. 'Interaction, acculturation and the acquisition of communicative competence' in N. Wolfson and E. Judd (eds.): *Sociolinguistics and Second Language Acquisition*. Rowley, MA: Newbury House.

Schmidt, R. 1990. 'The role of consciousness in second language learning.' *Applied Linguistics* 11/2: 129–58.

Schmidt, R. 1994. 'Implicit learning and the cognitive unconscious: of artificial grammars and SLA' in N. Ellis (ed.): *Implicit and Explicit Learning of Languages*. London: Academic Press.

Schmidt, R. 2001. 'Attention' in P. Robinson (ed.).

Schmidt, R. and S. Frota. 1986. 'Developing basic conversational ability in a second language: a case study of an adult learner of Portuguese' in R. Day (ed.): *Talking to Learn: Conversation in Second Language Acquisition*. Rowley, MA: Newbury House.

Scott, R. 1981. 'Speaking' in Johnson and Morrow. (eds.).

Seedhouse. P. 1999. 'Task-based interaction.' *ELT Journal* 53/3: 149–55.

Segalowitz, N. 2003. 'Automaticity and second languages' in C. Doughty and M. Long (eds.): *The Handbook of Second Language Acquisition*. Oxford: Blackwell.

Sharwood Smith, M. 1983. 'On explaining language loss' in S. Felix and H. Wode, (eds.): *Language Development at the Crossroads*. Tübingen: Gunter Narr Verlag.

Sheen, R. 1993. 'Double standards in research selection and evaluation: the case of comparison of methods, instruction and task-work.' *RELC Journal* 24.

Sheen, R. 1994. 'A critical analysis of the advocacy of the task-based syllabus.' *TESOL Quarterly* 28/1: 127–151.

Sheen, R. 2002. 'A response to Lightbown's (2000) "Anniversary article: classroom SLA research and second language teaching".' *Applied Linguistics* 23/4.

Sheen, R. 2003. 'Focus on form—a myth in the making?' *ELT Journal* 57/3: 225–33.

Sinclair, J. (ed.). 1990. *Collins Cobuild English Grammar*. London: Collins.

Skehan, P. 1989. *Individual Differences in Second-Language Learning*. London: Edward Arnold.

Skehan, P. 1994. 'Second language acquisition strategies, interlanguage development and task-based learning' in M. Bygate, A. Tonkyn, and E. Williams (eds.): *Grammar and the Language Teacher*. Hemel Hempstead: Prentice Hall.

Skehan, P. 1998. *A Cognitive Approach to Language Learning*. Oxford: Oxford University Press.

Skehan, P. and P. Foster. 2001. 'Cognition and tasks' in P. Robinson (ed.).

Slabakova, R. 2009. 'L2 fundamentals' in R. Slabakova (ed.): *The Fundamental Difference Hypothesis Twenty Years Later*. *Studies in Second Language Acquisition*, 31/2 (special issue).

Soars, L. and J. Soars. 1993. *Headway*. Oxford: Oxford University Press.

Sowden, C. 2007. 'Culture and the "good teacher" in the English language classroom.' *ELT Journal* 61/4.

Stewart, I. 1995. 'Juggling by numbers.' *New Scientist* 20 May 1995.

Storch, N. 2002. 'Patterns of interaction in ESL pair work. *Language Learning* 52/1: 119–58.

Swain. M. 1998. 'Focus on form through conscious reflection' in J. Doughty and J. Williams (eds.).

Swain, M. 2002. 'Peer-peer dialogue as a means of second language learning.' *Annual Review of Applied Linguistics* 22: 171–85.

Swales, J. 1990. *Genre Analysis: English in Academic and Research Settings*. Cambridge: Cambridge University Press.

Swan M. 2005b. 'Legislation by hypothesis: the case of task-based instruction.' *Applied Linguistics* 26/3.

Swan M. 2006. 'Two out of three ain't enough: the essential ingredients of a language course' in *IATEFL Conference Selections* 2006.

Swan, M. 1984. *Basic English Usage* (1st edn.). Oxford: Oxford University Press.

Swan, M. 1985a. 'A critical look at the communicative approach (1).' *ELT Journal* 39/1: 2–12.

Swan, M. 1985b. 'A critical look at the communicative approach (2).' *ELT Journal* 39/2: 76–87.

Swan, M. 1987. 'Non-systematic variability: a self-inflicted conundrum?' in R. Ellis, (ed.): *Second Language Acquisition in Context*. London: Prentice-Hall.

Swan, M. 1994. 'Design criteria for pedagogic language rules' in M. Bygate, A. Tonkyn, and E. Williams (eds.): *Grammar and the Language Teacher*. Hemel Hempstead: Prentice Hall.

Swan, M. 1996. *Language Teaching is Teaching Language*: Hornby Lecture given at IATEFL Conference, Keele 1996, reprinted in *IATEFL 1996 Annual Conference Report*.

Swan, M. 2005a. *Grammar*. Oxford: Oxford University Press.

Swan, M. 2007. 'Grammar, meaning and pragmatics: sorting out the muddle.' *TESL-EJ* 11/2.

Swan, M. and B. Smith (eds.) 1987. *Learner English*. Cambridge: Cambridge University Press.

Swan, M. and C. Walter. 1984. *The Cambridge English Course*. Cambridge: Cambridge University Press.

Swan, M. and C. Walter. 1990. *The New Cambridge English Course, Teacher's Book Level 1*. Cambridge: Cambridge University Press.

Swan, M. and C. Walter. 1990, 1992. *The New Cambridge English Course, Student's Book 2, Student's Book 3*. Cambridge: Cambridge University Press.

Tarone, E. 1983. 'On the variability of interlanguage systems.' *Applied Linguistics* 4.2.

Tarone, E. 1988. *Variation in Interlanguage*. London: Edward Arnold.

Tarone, E. and G.-Q. Liu. 1995. 'Situational context, variation and second language acquisition theory' in G. Cook and B. Seidlhofer (eds.): *Principle and Practice in Applied Linguistics*. Oxford: Oxford University Press.

Taylor, J. R. 1989. *Linguistic Categorization*. Oxford: Clarendon Press.

Thomson, A. J. and A. V. Martinet. 1980. *A Practical English Grammar* (3rd edn.). Oxford: Oxford University Press.

Thornbury, S. 1998. 'Comments on Marianne Celce-Murcia, Zoltán Dörnyei, and Sarah Thurrell's "*Direct Approaches in L2 Instruction: A Turning Point in Communicative Language Teaching?*".' *TESOL Quarterly* 32/1.

Thornbury, S. 1999. *How to Teach Grammar*. Harlow: Longman.

Todd, L. and I. Hancock. 1986. *International English Usage*. Andover: Croom Helm.

Tomasello, M. 2003. *Constructing a Language*. Cambridge, MA: Harvard University Press.

Tomlin, R. S. and V. Villa. 1994. 'Attention in cognitive science and second language acquisition.' *Studies in Second Language Acquisition* 16/2: 183–203.

Tomlinson, B. (ed.). 2003. *Developing Materials for Language Teaching*. London: Continuum.

Tops, G., X. DeKeyser, B. Devriendt, and S. Geukens. 1987. 'Dutch speakers' in Swan and Smith (eds.).

Truscott, J. 1998. 'Noticing in second language acquisition: a critical review.' *Second Language Research* 14/2: 104–35.

Ur, P. 1984. *Teaching Listening Comprehension*. Cambridge: Cambridge University Press.

Van Patten, B. and T. Cadierno. 1993. 'Explicit instruction and input-processing.' *Studies in Second Language Acquisition* 15/2: 225–43.

Vildomec, V. 1963. *Multilingualism*. Leyden: Sythoff.

Walter, C. 2007. 'First- to second-language reading comprehension: not transfer, but access.' *International Journal of Applied Linguistics* 17 (1).

Walter, C. 2008. Conference presentation, IATEFL Poland, Łódź.

Walter, C. and M. Swan. 2008. 'Teaching reading skills: mostly a waste of time?' in *IATEFL 2008: Exeter Conference Selections*.

Weinreich, U. 1963. *Languages in Contact: Findings and Problems*. The Hague: Mouton.

Weir, R. H. 1970. *Language in the Crib*. The Hague: Mouton.

Wesche, M. and P. Skehan. 2002. 'Communicative, task-based and content-based instruction' in R. Kaplan (ed.): *The Oxford Handbook of Applied Linguistics*. Oxford: Oxford University Press.

White, L. 2003. 'On the nature of interlanguage representation: universal grammar in the second language' in C. Doughty and M. Long (eds.): *The Handbook of Second Language Acquisition*. Oxford: Blackwell.

Widdowson, H. G. 1978. *Teaching Language as Communication*. Oxford: Oxford University Press.

Widdowson, H. G. 2003. *Defining Issues in English Language Teaching*. Oxford: Oxford University Press.

Wilkins, D. 1976. *Notional Syllabuses*. Oxford: Oxford University Press.

Wilkins, D. 1983. 'Some issues in communicative language teaching and their relevance to the teaching of languages in secondary schools' in K. Johnson and D. Porter (eds.): *Perspectives in Communicative Language Teaching*. London: Academic Press.

Williams, E. 1983. 'Communicative reading' in K. Johnson and D. Porter (eds.): *Communicative Language Teaching*. London: Academic Press.

Willis, D. 1990. *The Lexical Syllabus*. London: Collins ELT.

Willis, D. 1993. 'Syllabus, corpus and data-driven learning' in C. Kennedy (ed.): *Plenaries from the 1993 IATEFL Conference*. Swansea, Wales.

Willis, D. 2003. *Rules, Patterns and Words*. Cambridge: Cambridge University Press.

Willis, D. and J. Willis. 1988. *The Collins Cobuild English Course*. London: Collins ELT.

Willis, D. and J. Willis. 2001. 'Task-based language learning' in R. Carter and D. Nunan (eds.): *The Cambridge Guide to Teaching English to Speakers of Other Languages*. Cambridge: Cambridge University Press.

Willis, J. 1996. *A Framework for Task-Based Learning*. Harlow: Longman.

Wilson, L. and M. Wilson. 1987. 'Farsi speakers' in Swan and Smith (eds.).

Wong, S. 1993. 'Overproduction, under-lexicalisation and unidiomatic usage in the 'make' causatives of Chinese speakers: a case for flexibility in interlanguage analysis.' *Language Learning and Communication* 2.

Wray, A. 2000. 'Formulaic sequences in second language teaching: principle and practice.' *Applied Linguistics* 21/4: 463–89.

Wray, A. 2002. *Formulaic Language and the Lexicon*. Cambridge: Cambridge University Press.

Yule, G. 1996. *Pragmatics*. Oxford: Oxford University Press.

Zandvoort, R. W. 1957. *A Handbook of English Grammar* (1st edn.). London: Longmans, Green & Co.